CONTEMPORARY SOCIAL RESEARCH SERIES
General Editor: Martin Bulmer

8

In the Field

CONTEMPORARY SOCIAL RESEARCH SERIES

In the Field

An Introduction to Field Research

ROBERT G. BURGESS

London
GEORGE ALLEN & UNWIN
Boston   Sydney

George Allen & Unwin (Publishers) Ltd,
40 Museum Street, London WC1A 1LU, UK

George Allen & Unwin (Publishers) Ltd,
Park Lane, Hemel Hempstead, Herts HP2 4TE, UK

Allen & Unwin, Inc.,
9 Winchester Terrace, Winchester, Mass 01890, USA

George Allen & Unwin Australia Pty Ltd,
8 Napier Street, North Sydney, NSW 2060, Australia

First published in 1984

British Library Cataloguing in Publication Data

Burgess, Robert G.
   In the field. – (Contemporary social research series)
1. Social sciences – Field work
2. Social sciences – Methodology
I. Title   II. Series
300'.723   H61
ISBN 0-04-312017-2
ISBN 0-04-312018-0 Pbk

Library of Congress Cataloging in Publication Data

Burgess, Robert G.
   In the field.
Includes bibliographical references and index.
1. Sociology – Research – Addresses, essays, lectures.
2. Ethnology – Field work – Addresses, essays, lectures.
3. Social sciences – Field work – Addresses, essays, lectures.
I. Title.
HM48.B87 1984   300'.723   83-25694
ISBN 0-04-312017-2
ISBN 0-04-312018-0 (pbk)

Set in 10 on 11 point Times by Fotographics (Bedford) Ltd.
and printed in Great Britain by Biddles Ltd, Guildford, Surrey

Contents

For Hilary

Series Editor's Preface

The structure of the social sciences combines two separate elements, theory and empirical evidence. Both are necessary for successful social understanding; one without the other is barren. The *Contemporary Social Research* series is concerned with the means by which this structure is maintained and kept standing solid and upright, a job performed by the methodology of social research.

The series is intended to provide concise introductions to significant methodological topics. Broadly conceived, research methodology deals with the general grounds for the validity of social scientific propositions. How do we know what we do know about the social world? More narrowly, it deals with the questions: how do we actually acquire new knowledge about the world in which we live? What are the strategies and techniques by means of which social science data are collected and analysed? The series will seek to answer such questions through the examination of specific areas of methodology.

Why is such a series necessary? There exist many solid, indeed massive, methodology textbooks, which most undergraduates in sociology, psychology and the social sciences acquire familiarity with in the course of their studies. The aim of this series is different. It focuses upon specific topics, procedures, methods of analysis and methodological problems to provide a readable introduction to its subject. Each book contains annotated suggestions for further reading. The intended audience includes the advanced undergraduate, the graduate student, working social researchers seeking to familiarise themselves with new areas, and non-specialists who wish to enlarge their knowledge of social research. Research methodology need not be remote and inaccessible. Some prior knowledge of statistics will be useful, but only certain titles in the series will make strong statistical demands upon the reader. The series is concerned above all to demonstrate the general importance and centrality of research methodology to social science.

In the Field, by Robert Burgess, complements the author's earlier anthology in this series, *Field Research: a Sourcebook and Field Manual* (1982), which has been well received. *In the Field* provides a more detailed and focused treatment of the central topics of field research, drawing extensively upon the author's own experience of doing research in a secondary school. He provides a comprehensive overview of this style of research, together with numerous suggestions for further reading, both methodological and substantive.

MARTIN BULMER
London School of Economics and Political Science

Sociological research was, at one time, closely identified with survey methods, while anthropological research was based upon intensive studies using field methods including participant observation. Such a sharp dichotomy between the research practice and research procedures of these two disciplines no longer exists, for sociologists are as likely to use field methods as anthropologists are to engage in survey work. Furthermore, members of both disciplines now increasingly focus attention on the study of their own culture using a range of research strategies and methods. Accordingly, intensive studies using field methods are now conducted in urban–industrial settings such as factories, hospitals, prisons, schools and classrooms.

Alongside these developments in research, more courses and seminars are devoted to field research, drawing on vast bodies of American literature and utilising American textbooks. For there is relatively little British material that brings together a discussion of the literature with practical examples drawn from the study of British society. This book is, therefore, an attempt to begin to fill this gap. However, it is not intended to be an encyclopaedic coverage of the literature on field methods. Instead, like its companion volume *Field Research: a Sourcebook and Field Manual* (Burgess, 1982a) it covers some of the main issues and problems involved in field research. The aim is to provide insights on the research process while raising critical issues on field methods to which any researcher needs sensitising. In turn, this leads into a consideration of the relationship between the principles and practice of field research together with a discussion of the conduct and evaluation of field studies. There is also a guide to some of the literature on field research through the annotated reading lists at the end of each chapter and the complete list of references at the end of the book.

I have written this book with a number of audiences in mind. First, undergraduates, postgraduates and researchers in sociology and social anthropology who are coming to field research for the first time. Secondly, students who are conducting field studies in their own society. Thirdly, students who are required to evaluate field studies and who seek to understand the conduct of field research. I hope they will all find material here which will go some way towards promoting discussion and dialogue about the conduct of field research in urban–industrial settings.

In writing this book I have drawn on a range of empirical examples including my own field experiences while conducting research in an urban comprehensive school. I would, therefore, like to thank once more the teachers and pupils in 'my school' who not only co-operated with my study but also helped to advance my understanding of the problems and processes involved in doing field research.

I am indebted to a number of friends and colleagues who have provided me with much assistance. In particular, I would like to thank Martin Bulmer, Marjorie Lodge, Virginia Olesen and Marten Shipman who were kind enough to read and offer advice on the complete manuscript, while Alison Andrew, Eileen Fairhurst, Janet Finch and Wyn Lewis commented on particular chapters. My wife, Hilary, gave me much encouragement and provided very helpful comments on the conduct of research in school settings. She has also spent countless hours discussing my school study for which I am very grateful. While writing this book I have also been very fortunate to have the secretarial services of Diana Lea who produced accurate drafts at high speed, while Valerie Campling patiently prepared the final manuscript with her usual efficiency. However, none of these people should be blamed for the deficiencies of this book which are, of course, my own.

ROBERT BURGESS
University of Warwick

Introduction

Imagine yourself suddenly set down surrounded by all your gear, alone on a tropical beach close to a native village, while the launch or dinghy which has brought you sails away out of sight. Since you take up your abode in the compound of some neighbouring white man, trader or missionary, you have nothing to do, but to start at once on your ethnographic work. Imagine further that you are a beginner, without previous experience, with nothing to guide you and no one to help you. For the white man is temporarily absent, or else unable or unwilling to waste any of his time on you. This exactly describes my first initiation into field work on the south coast of New Guinea. (Malinowski, 1922, p. 4)

Imagine a large, stately Edwardian building set in pleasant grounds on a hill top in an expensive residential suburb. Go through the green double doors into a panelled hall, and up the spiral staircase to the first floor. Follow the panelled corridor to the north-east corner of the building, and enter the room situated there. It is cold. The central heating must either be faulty, or someone has turned it down very low. There are four large windows facing north and east, so the room is light but not sunny. The walls are pale yellow, with a photographic reproduction of the Parthenon frieze round near the ceiling. One wall is lined with locked cupboards, and the glass-fronted bookcases are also locked. Two notice-boards display information about forthcoming events to raise charitable funds and instructions in case of fire, power cuts or illness. It is very quiet. No one in the room moves or speaks, though occasional shouts can be heard from outside. Three teenage girls are sitting bent over their books, while an elderly spinster sits facing them, intent on her work. (Delamont, 1976, p. 9)

These two statements are separated by almost sixty years and the locations are thousands of miles apart. The first scenario is a tropical beach on the Trobriand Islands, off the eastern tip of New Guinea, while the second situation is a girls' public school in Scotland. Both scenes are 'fields'; that is circumscribed areas of study which have been the subject of social research. In both cases, the style of research that has been used relies on an observational approach involving a relationship between the researcher and those who are researched. This type of research has been principally conducted by social anthropologists and sociologists and is known as *fieldwork, ethnography, case study, qualitative research, interpretative procedures* and *field research*. Each of these terms results in this kind of research being conceptualised slightly differently as a different emphasis is given to the work which is done by particular people. Among social anthropologists *fieldwork* is synonymous with the collection of data using observational methods. However, for sociologists the term is also used to refer to the collection of data using a social survey (cf. Srinivas, 1966, p. 156; Moser and Kalton, 1971). *Ethnography* has been defined by Conklin (1968) as the data of cultural anthropology that are derived from the direct observation of behaviour in a particular society. The making, reporting and evaluation of these observations is the task of ethnographers. For he adds that if these tasks are to be successful they should be related to interpretations derived from social and cultural anthropology. However, Wolcott (1975, 1982) has argued that there has been much confusion around the term 'ethnography' as it has become equated with the techniques of doing research. Instead, he argues that it is the cultural perspective not the research technique that distinguishes ethnography from other work. Nevertheless, many British researchers, especially those engaged in the study of schools and classrooms, have used the term 'ethnography' to describe their style of work (cf. Woods, 1977; Hammersley, 1980; 1982). However, Stenhouse (1984) has argued against using this term as he considers ethnographers to be aggressive to their subjects through a link that he perceives between ethnography and colonialism (cf. Asad, 1973). Furthermore, for Stenhouse, ethnographers are strangers to the situations they research, a position, he argues, which cannot be adopted by most researchers who study schools and classrooms. Accordingly, he refers to his own research as *case study* based on condensed field experience involving observation (rather than the classic participant observer strategy), tape-recorded interviews and the collection of documents (cf. Stenhouse, 1982).

A similar range of methods is encompassed by the term *qualitative research* but with a different emphasis. This term has been used by sociologists such as Filstead (1970), Bogdan and Taylor (1975) and Bogdan and Biklen (1982) to refer to a series of research strategies: participant observation, and in-depth, unstructured or semi-structured interviews. Here again the focus is upon research strategies that allow the researcher to learn about the social world at first hand. Qualitative methods, it is argued, allow researchers 'to get close to the data' and provide opportunities for them to derive their concepts from the data that are gathered (cf. Glaser and Strauss, 1967). While this term has the virtue of highlighting particular dimensions of the research process it often does so at the expense of other methods. Filstead (1970), for example, has remarked:

> The assets of qualitative methodology in sociology need to be stressed and the shortcomings of quantitative methodology need to be exposed in their boldest relief. (Filstead, 1970, p. 8)

The result, as Halfpenny (1979) has clearly shown, is some polarity between qualitative and quantitative methods where the former is considered to be soft, subjective and speculative, while the latter is described as hard, objective and rigorous. Yet in reality researchers have shown how these approaches may complement each other (Zelditch, 1962) and may be integrated in the practice of social research (Sieber, 1973).

Many sociologists utilise participant observation, in-depth or unstructured interviews and documentary evidence in the course of their research in order to elucidate the meaning of social situations. Essentially their focus of interest is the way in which different people experience, interpret and structure their lives. Accordingly, the methods of investigation that are used have been developed in relation to those theoretical perspectives or theoretical orientations that are concerned with the way in which the social world is structured by the participants. Bogdan and Biklen (1982) indicate that much research of this kind involves a phenomenological perspective whereby researchers attempt to understand the meaning of events for people in particular situations. The focus is upon the way in which participants interpret their experience and construct reality (Berger and Luckmann, 1967). The ultimate aim is to study situations from the participants' point of view. Williams (1981) has shown how these methods that are often termed *interpretative procedures* owe much to the theoretical tradition known loosely as 'interactionism' which is represented in the work of sociologists such as Becker (1963, 1970a), Blumer (1969) and Hughes (1971). For it is this theoretical perspective that has been the major influence on field research in sociology. The perspective adopted by symbolic interactionists is clearly articulated in the papers edited by Rose (1962) and Manis and Meltzer (1967). Basically, interactionists provide an interpretative view of sociology which puts emphasis on understanding the actions of participants on the basis of their active experience of the world and the ways in which their actions arise from and reflect back on experience (cf. Williams, 1981).

This emphasis upon meanings that individuals construct and modify during the process of interaction holds implications for the research process. For as Blumer remarks, the study of action has to be conducted from the position of the actor in order to see the way in which actors perceive situations.

> In short, one would have to take the role of the actor and see his world from his standpoint. This methodological approach stands in contrast to the so-called objective approach so dominant today, namely that of viewing the actor and his action from the perspective of an outside, detached observer ... the actor acts toward his world on the basis of how he sees it and not on the basis of how that world appears to the outside observer. (Blumer, 1966, p. 542)

Using this theoretical perspective it therefore becomes essential to gather statements made by participants with a view to examining the various dimensions of the situation that they construct. It is also important to focus upon ongoing patterns of interaction.

While this approach to sociological research is rooted in the symbolic interactionist tradition, it does overlook other theoretical positions that have been used to orientate field research. For example, classic anthropological studies by Malinowski (1929, 1935a) utilised a structural functionalist perspective, while more recently field researchers in social anthropology (cf. Middleton, 1978) and in sociology (cf. Sharp and Green, 1975; Sharp, 1981) have demonstrated how Marxism can influence the collection and analysis of field data. Nevertheless, no matter which of these approaches are used they are not simply neat-fitting theoretical models that can be imposed on field situations and on data. Instead, they provide an orientation to field research that can be moulded and remoulded by the researcher in the course of collecting and analysing data.

The terminology that is, therefore, used to discuss our mode of research is very broad. Some of these terms have much in common and cover a broadly similar approach, while others lead towards restrictive usage and a particular emphasis. In an introductory text of this nature the aim is to provide a broad survey of the area of study in order to display the widest range of conceptual and methodological tools that can be used by the researcher while conducting investigations in the empirical world. Accordingly, the term *field research* will be used within this book to include material that is drawn from anthropology and sociology, to incorporate different theoretical perspectives and to explore the relationships between a variety of different methods. It covers what is colloquially known as participant observation, unstructured interviews and documentary methods; although depending on the problem at hand other approaches can be used. As in Burgess (1982a) this term will be used to draw together a wide range of ideas and materials that can be utilised by the researcher while doing research. In this sense, my view of the field researcher is close to the position adopted by Schatzman and Strauss who maintain that:

> The field researcher is a methodological pragmatist. He sees any method of inquiry as a system of strategies and operations designed – at any time – for getting answers to certain questions about events which interest him. (Schatzman and Strauss, 1973, p. 7)

The researcher is, therefore, engaged in a variety of tasks. A central feature of this work involves monitoring the research process and the research design. For the design will be continually modified and developed by the researcher throughout the project. Alongside observational work, formal and informal interviews may be conducted and life histories and personal documents may be collected. In addition, techniques will need to be developed for gathering, storing, retrieving and analysing data as well as checking the reliability and validity of that data. However, basic to the conduct of field research is the development of relationships between the researcher and those who are researched. Field researchers have, therefore, to take roles, handle relationships, and enter into the commerce and conflict of everyday life. The daily routine of field research is captured by Gravel when he remarks:

> The substantive part of fieldwork has no glamour. It is made up of routine matters about which it is difficult to be expansive. Fieldwork is really made up of the same little administrative tasks we try to get away from. It is made up of trying to make ends meet. It is made up of wiping dishes, of sweeping floors, of book-keeping, of keeping things and equipment in shape, of filing away notes, letters and photographs or writing endlessly and eternally trying to remember more. It is made up of attempts at disentangling the red tape of local bureaucracies and at reviving moribund requests and permissions. It is made up of constantly trying to reschedule timeless time and to fathom bottomless pits. It is made up of supervision of assistants, of correcting errors, covering faux-pas, and of re-instilling a sense of purpose in your crew. It is made up of the tedium of daily life with suddenly no one to share it with. (Gravel, 1976, p. 121)

While this account comes from an anthropologist commenting on the study of another culture, it is equally applicable to researchers who study their own society. As a consequence, field research cannot be neatly fitted into a linear model of steps or stages, for the field researcher has to cope with a variety of social situations, perspectives and problems. Doing field research is, therefore, not merely the use of a set of uniform techniques but depends on a complex interaction between the research problem, the researcher and those who are researched. It is on this basis that the researcher is an active decision-maker who decides on the most appropriate conceptual and methodological tools that can be used to collect and analyse data. Field research is concerned with research processes as well as research methods. Field research methodologists have therefore focused on issues involved in starting research, gaining access, selecting informants, and handling ethical problems as well as collecting, analysing and reporting data (cf. Bogdan, 1972; Lofland, 1971; Wax, 1971; Schatzman and Strauss, 1973; Bogdan and Taylor, 1975; Johnson, 1975; Agar, 1981; Bogdan and Biklen, 1982; Burgess, 1982a, 1982b). Some of these issues will be discussed in this book drawing on examples from studies conducted in urban industrial society.

The Organisation of the Book

This book has three specific aims. First, to provide a link between the abstract principles of research and the *actual* practice of doing field research. Secondly, to provide a commentary on issues involved in contemporary field research practice; and finally to provide an account of how some field problems have been resolved by researchers in particular settings. Taking note of Becker's injunction that 'methodology is too important to be left to methodologists' (Becker, 1970b, p. 3) the focus will be upon the problems that confront the researcher in the field. Accordingly, methodological problems will be discussed in relation to empirical studies that have been conducted by sociologists and social anthropologists especially in Britain and the USA. In particular, examples will be drawn from substantive areas such as education, work, deviancy and health and illness, for field research and field researchers have now come home from Pacific islands and Indian reservations to study people who live and work within a few miles of the university and research institute. It is this theme that is focused upon in the first chapter.

In *Chapter 1* we examine the traditional approach to field research within anthropology, its translation to similar fields of study within sociology, and the problems which sociologists have encountered in studying their own culture. These problems are centrally placed in the opening chapter as examples of work that has been done within the researcher's own society are used in subsequent chapters. *Chapter 2* looks at the problems involved in starting research: preparations for the field including a discussion of grants and sponsorship and the gaining of research access. *Chapter 3* turns to problems of selection and sampling including the use of key informants, while *Chapter 4* explores the relationship between researcher and researched drawing on the range of relationships that researchers have participated in and the implications that their roles have for the collection and analysis of data.

It is to the relationship between data collection and data analysis that we also turn in the subsequent two chapters. *Chapter 5* focuses on unstructured interviews while *Chapter 6* looks at the ways in which field researchers can use documentary evidence. In *Chapter 7* the focus is upon the use of different research strategies alongside one another. Here, special emphasis is given to the range of methods that are employed by field researchers, the ways they have been used and in particular the potential for integrating different kinds of methods within field projects. Meanwhile, *Chapter 8* turns to questions concerning the recording and analysis of data and to the relationships between theorising and field research. All of these processes are considered central to work that is conducted in the field. Finally, *Chapter 9* brings us back to looking at the whole of the research process by focusing upon the ethical and political problems that all researchers encounter to a greater or lesser degree. A brief concluding chapter discusses some of the criteria that can be used to evaluate field studies.

The emphasis of this book is, therefore, upon the processes and problems involved in the conduct of field research. It does not seek to codify procedure nor does it imply that 'all it needs is (occasionally a suitable disguise, but always) just a notebook, a pencil, and a lot of stamina and free time' (Ditton and Williams, 1981, p. 46). While it is not denied that these are essential tools and resources of the field researcher, they are no substitute for research skill, creativity, imagination, and theoretical flair. Together they constitute the experience of the field researcher whose analysis of methodological issues will deepen our understanding of the ways in which research problems can be handled.

Research Experience: Sources and Resources

There are now many examples of field research experience in the literature from social anthropologists (cf. Golde, 1970; Spindler, 1970) and from sociologists (cf. Hammond, 1964; Shipman, 1976; Bell and Newby, 1977; Shaffir, Stebbins and Turowetz, 1980; Roberts, 1981; Burgess, 1984a). In addition many empirical studies, especially in the area of deviancy, have utilised field research methods (cf. Humphreys, 1970; Young, 1971; Plant, 1975) so much so that many examples from the study of deviancy are used and quoted by field researchers (cf. Douglas, 1976; Rock, 1979, pp.. 178–216). However, there are also many British studies where field research methods have been used to examine everyday settings in industrial society: hospitals (Atkinson, 1981), factories (Cavendish, 1982; Pollert, 1981), schools (Ball, 1981; Burgess, 1983) and localities (Cohen, A. P., 1982). Accordingly, this book will focus on examples of field experience that have been drawn from a range of British and American studies.

The study which I will use in all the chapters to illustrate some of the problems and processes involved in doing field research will be my own research in a purpose-built co-educational Roman Catholic comprehensive school which I called Bishop McGregor (Burgess, 1983). This school had a House system for pastoral care and a departmental system for academic, non-academic and practical subjects. These Houses and departments were located in separate blocks that were situated on a 34-acre site.

In this study I was concerned with the way in which a comprehensive school worked in practice; how the House system was used by teachers and pupils and how pupils who were regarded as the 'less willing' and 'less able' fared within a comprehensive school. Such a focus involved looking at the way in which situations were defined and redefined and as Stebbins (1967) has indicated, required the observation of events, situations and groups. Detailed observations needed to be made if I was to acquire the definitions and meanings that were attributed to social situations in the school.

To conduct this study I established myself as a permanent part-time teacher in the school's Newsom Department, a department that provided courses for pupils for whom the maximum expectation of success in public examinations seemed likely to be three Certificate of Secondary Education (CSE) grade fives or less. I took this role as it allowed me to become a member of the school, of a House and of a department, all of which were bases from which I could conduct research. Secondly, it allowed me to utilise my previous professional experience as a secondary school teacher and finally, it gave me sufficient time to observe situations, conduct interviews, collect documents and write field notes (cf. Lacey, 1976). The study of this school is available in Burgess (1983) and examines from an inter-actionist perspective the ways in which teachers, pupils and teachers and pupils defined and redefined the rules and routines in the everyday life of the school. All the names of people, situations and events used in this book and elsewhere have been disguised by means of pseudonyms in order to offer some anonymity to those who generously gave of their time. The material that is taken from this study is used to consider major issues in the conduct of research that occurs in the field.

Suggestions for Further Reading

Methodology

The following references refer to the different styles of field research that have been briefly discussed in this introduction.

Agar, M. (1981), *The Professional Stranger: An Informal Introduction to Ethnography* (New York: Academic Press); gives an anthropological perspective on the conduct of field research.

Burgess, R. G. (1982) (ed.), *Field Research: a Sourcebook and Field Manual* (London: Allen & Unwin). A companion volume to this book which reviews the main issues and problems in field research. It includes writings from experienced field researchers in sociology and social anthropology and a discussion of the use of historical sources in field research.

Conklin, H. C. (1968), 'Ethnography' in D. L. Sills (ed.), *International Encyclopaedia of the Social Sciences* (New York: Macmillan and The Free Press); provides a brief discussion of the meaning of the term 'ethnography' and its current usage.

Filstead, W. J. (1970) (ed.), *Qualitative Methodology: Firsthand Involvement with the Social World* (New York: Markham). A collection of papers that are principally American. The introduction includes a discussion by the editor of the term 'qualitative methodology'.

Rock, P. (1979), *The Making of Symbolic Interactionism* (London: Macmillan). A useful review of the main literature on interactionism. Chapter 6 examines the relationship between symbolic interactionism and participant observation.

Schatzman, L. and Strauss, A. L. (1973), *Field Research: Strategies for a Natural Sociology* (Englewood Cliffs, NJ: Prentice Hall). A highly readable review of American material on strategies of field research. The general approach is similar to that adopted here.

Stenhouse, L. (1982), 'The conduct, analysis and reporting of case study in educational research and evaluation', in R. McCormick (ed.), *Calling Education to Account* (London: Heinemann), pp. 261–73. A paper in which Lawrence Stenhouse discusses the problems involved in conducting, analysing and reporting research using a case study approach. He examines the parallels with historical research and suggests ways in which case study work can be conducted.

Williams, R. (1981), 'Learning to do field research', *Sociology*, vol. 15, no. 4, pp. 557–64 contains a useful review of issues relating to field research and interpretative methods.

Empirical Studies

The following studies reflect some of the different perspectives used in field research. These studies can be examined to see the way in which the perspectives used influence the researcher's questions and analyses.

Atkinson, P. (1981), *The Clinical Experience: The Construction and Reconstruction of Medical Reality* (Aldershot: Gower).

Ball, S. J. (1981), *Beachside Comprehensive: a Case Study of Secondary Schooling* (Cambridge: CUP).

Cavendish, R. (1982), *Women on the Line* (London: Routledge & Kegan Paul).

Corrigan, P. (1979), *Schooling the Smash Street Kids* (London: Macmillan).

Ditton, J. (1977), *Part-Time Crime: An Ethnography of Fiddling and Pilferage* (London: Macmillan).

Pollert, A. (1981), *Girls, Wives, Factory Lives* (London: Macmillan).

Sharp, R. and Green, A. (1975), *Education and Social Control* (London: Routledge & Kegan Paul).

Spradley, J. and Mann, B. (1975), *The Cocktail Waitress* (New York: Wiley).

Stenhouse, L., Verma, G. K., Wild, R. D. and Nixon, J. (1982), *Teaching about Race Relations* (London: Routledge & Kegan Paul).

Willis, P. (1977), *Learning to Labour* (Farnborough: Saxon House).

Wolcott, H. (1973), *The Man in the Principal's Office* (New York: Holt, Rinehart & Winston).

1

From Coral Garden to City Street: Field Research 'Comes Home'

For social anthropologists, the conduct of field research in another culture and preferably in another country is an essential *rite de passage* (Van Gennep, 1960). Originally this research in some other society was seen as an ordeal; a test in which anthropologists had to engage. This style of anthropological work is well summarised by Fried who writes:

> Fieldwork remains central in cultural anthropology. Basic data come not from laboratories but from living cultures. An anthropologist goes to live in another culture. He settles down amidst unfamiliar surroundings and, if he is successful, his status slowly changes from clumsy alien to friendly stranger. Ideally, he speaks or will learn to speak the local language but inevitably he will rely on certain people more than others as teachers, interpreters, or informants. To some extent the anthropologist lives like his hosts, as well as among them. This is quite variable depending on the culture, the personality of the fieldworker and the situation itself. In any event, the fieldworker participates in activities as well as he is able and as far as he is permitted. He observes whatever he can of the endless series of events and the tangle of relationships which surround him. He maps, questions, records, photographs, jokes, mourns, and gets drunk at local blowouts. Sometimes he gets sick because he may be exposed to hazardous sanitary conditions. (Fried, 1968, p. 136)

In such situations, the anthropologist becomes socialised by the people who are studied and produces a monograph about 'their' culture. In these circumstances, a relationship is established which results in 'a gulf, a social chasm between those who study and those who are studied' (Cassell, 1977a, p. 412). Indeed, the social distance between the anthropologist and those who are studied is revealed in the subsequent books which bear titles such as *Other Cultures* (Beattie, 1964). However, as Srinivas (1966) and Firth (1981) have shown, anthropologists are as likely to engage in field research within their own societies as in other cultures. In these circumstances, questions have been raised about the applicability of anthropological methods to the study of industrial society. After a brief review of early developments in field research, the debate about applicability will be discussed.

Early Anthropological Models of Field Research

As Urry (1972) among many commentators has shown, field research in the way in which we know it today was a twentieth-century development in social anthropology where Malinowski's work was particularly influential. Before the 1920s many anthropologists relied on explorers, traders, missionaries and government officials for accounts of the peoples they studied. However, each of these groups had vested interests to 'change' the peoples amongst whom they worked, which in turn resulted in some bias in the accounts provided for anthropological work (Kaplan and Manners, 1971).

By the beginning of the twentieth century anthropologists were engaging in field trips to foreign parts but their work was still conducted at some distance from the villages in which the people lived and worked. In 1910 Radcliffe-Brown went to Australia with an expedition to conduct research among the Aborigines. After a police raid interrupted their work, Radcliffe-Brown took his party to Bermer Island which was the site of a lock-up hospital for Aborigines who were infected with venereal disease. Here, the Aborigines were not only 'captive' in the hospital but also in relation to the researchers who treated the inhabitants as informants, questioning them about the Aboriginal marriage system. From here, Radcliffe-Brown went on to study Aboriginal communities that were settled around mission stations. As a result of working in this way, it has been argued that Radcliffe-Brown misunderstood the ways in which the Aborigines lived and drew several false conclusions in his work (cf. Kuper, 1973). This approach to field study, which was used by several anthropologists, involved working from the veranda of the missionary and government official. Often the researchers viewed their informants with considerable contempt. The people researched were regarded as 'primitive savages' who were seen as simple, childish and primeval, and socially inferior to the researcher. In these circumstances, researchers summoned individuals to the veranda where they were treated as specimens to be measured, photographed and questioned for several hours about their language and customs. The result was that the day-to-day lives of the people were largely ignored and few if any first-hand observations were made. Such an approach to field research is referred to by Wax and Cassell (1979) as the veranda model; an approach that was vigorously attacked by

Malinowski who argued that the anthropologist must relinquish the relative comforts of the chair on the veranda where it was customary to collect statements, write down stories and 'savage' texts. Instead Malinowski exhorted his colleagues to go into the villages to see the natives at work, to sail with them on their trading ventures with other tribes and to observe them fishing, trading and working. The data that would be obtained would then be based on first-hand observations rather than second-hand accounts that had been squeezed out of reluctant informants.

It was this style of field research that Malinowski practised throughout his work in the Trobriand Islands (Malinowski, 1922, 1935a, 1935b, 1948). These islands which lie 120 miles north from the eastern tip of New Guinea were the location for studies of economic exchange reported in *Argonauts of the Western Pacific* (1922), of social control in a society lacking formal legal institutions in *Crime and Custom in Savage Society* (1926), of domestic organisation in *The Sexual Life of Savages* (1929) and systems of native gardening in *Coral Gardens and their Magic* (1935a, 1935b). In conducting field research Malinowski attempted 'to grasp the native's point of view, his relation to life, to realize *his* vision of *his* world' (Malinowski, 1922, p. 25, emphasis in original). In these terms, Malinowski has been credited with advocating first-hand observation using the technique of participant observation. For Malinowski field research involved a field trip of one or two years, working in the native language, 'cut off' from contacts with Europeans in order to live as a member of the community under study. However, when Malinowski's diary was published (Malinowski, 1967) it was evident that the great anthropologist found it impossible to live up to the lofty heights that he had set for himself and others. Indeed, in *Coral Gardens*, Malinowski indicates that he was aware of some of his own shortcomings when he evaluates his 'blunders in fieldwork' (1935a, pp. 324–30) and provides an appendix which he entitled 'Confessions of ignorance and failure' that includes a discussion of his errors in the field (1935b, pp. 452–82). Nevertheless, he provided an ideal that others attempted to follow (Leach, 1966; Powdermaker, 1966; Xiaotong, 1980).

Malinowski's approach to field research has been referred to by Wax and Cassell (1979) as the *noblesse oblige* model. They see the researcher as a wealthy patron in the society under study with the result that two cultures come to co-exist within the same locality. This traditional mode of anthropological field research has come in for much criticism as it has been argued that the field anthropologist was linked officially or unofficially with a Western power with the result that anthropologists became tools of the exploiting interest group as they ignored the exploitation to which the peoples were subjected (Asad, 1973). However, some anthropological work took place before colonial expansion (Stocking, 1971) and as Firth (1981) has indicated, some anthropologists working in the colonial period were critical of the colonial use of land and labour and over any policy which disregarded the customary norms of the people studied.

This debate applies to much of the anthropological field research that was conducted in the 1930s and 1940s. Indeed, Evans-Pritchard's classic work on the Nuer (1940) which was based upon the field research tradition of Malinowski was financed by the Sudan government. Meanwhile, with the development of British colonial policy in Central Africa, the Rhodes-Livingstone Institute for Social Research in Northern Rhodesia (later Zambia) was established; a research institute on which others were later modelled. Here, studies developed under the directorship of Godfrey Wilson (briefly) and then Max Gluckman that focused upon urban as well as rural societies. It was these developments that were later mirrored in the work of the Department of Social Anthropology at the University of Manchester where it was Gluckman's idea to apply the field methods of social anthropology to the study of complex society. The Manchester School of Social Anthropology, which extended into sociology, therefore involved work that included the study of British communities, factories and later schools (cf. Gluckman, 1964; Frankenberg, 1982). It is studies such as these that illustrate the use of field methods in research on industrial society.

Anthropology and the Study of Complex Society

Anthropology has now 'come home'. It is as likely that social anthropologists will be found conducting field research in their own societies as in other cultures. Several reasons have been advanced to account for this development. First, it is maintained that funding of work overseas is now in rapid decline especially given the high costs involved (cf. Boissevain, 1975, p. 11). Secondly, that newly independent countries and former colonies no longer want anthropologists conducting field studies among their people and have developed exclusionary tactics. The anthropologist is no longer free to study 'natives' in a decolonialised world (cf. Hayano, 1979). Thirdly, social anthropologists in Britain and North America are now finding that they do not hold the monopoly and that there is much interest among indigenous anthropologists to study their own people (Kuper, 1973; Messerschmidt, 1981). Finally, increasing specialisation in areas such as urban anthropology, medical anthropology, educational studies, women's studies and law has meant that the focus of work has shifted from overseas to the local neighbourhood. Anthropologists are now to be found working in towns and cities in industrial society as well as in Africa, Oceania or the highlands of New Guinea. An article in *Time* magazine entitled 'Studying the American tribe' reported:

> When two well-dressed strangers turned up at a sleek apartment building on Chicago's Gold Coast the doorman called the cops. The men explained they were anthropologists from the University of Chicago anxious to study rich families. 'The policeman couldn't believe it,' said one of the men. 'He looked first for my *Encyclopaedia Britannica,* then for my vacuum cleaner and then asked what was the gimmick.' (*Time,* 1974, p. 49)

The policeman's 'gimmick' is the researcher's methodology based on an observational approach that has not been easy to describe. When some social anthropologists have been asked to explain their work they have likened it to the study of small tribes. Hence, when Wolcott was asked about his study of an elementary school principal (Wolcott, 1973) he remarked that he was viewing the principal as if he were the chief of a small tribe and was accompanying him everywhere to gain an understanding of what it was like to be a chief. At this his listeners indicated that they understood his analogy by replying 'Oh sorta like Margaret Mead' (Wolcott, 1982).

However, explaining the nature of anthropological study is but one problem. All social anthropologists studying 'at home' have to consider how to apply those techniques that are central to the anthropological perspective when studying urban life. In particular, they have had to consider how the methodological concerns of participant observation and holism can be reconciled with the study of life in towns and cities. The scale and diversity of urban life means that it is only possible either to study people superficially or to study a small number of informants in depth. This leaves the researcher with the problem of extrapolation from a small-scale study to the whole of a city or segment of a city. To overcome this problem anthropologists have shifted away from holistic studies towards the detailed treatment of particular topics and themes. Basham and De Groot (1977) have identified three ways in which this has been achieved. First, holism has been sacrificed for a micro level ethnography of a segmented population. Among these studies are Liebow's research on negro street corner men (1967), Agar's study of drug takers (1973), and Spradley and Mann's study of cocktail waitresses (1975). Secondly, urban interactional networks have been traced through field studies. A classic British example is Elizabeth Bott's study of families (Bott, 1957, 1971). Finally, macro level ethnographies of entire cities have brought together survey material, historical data, and ethnographic evidence. This combination of different research strategies is evident in Pons's study of *Stanleyville* (now Kisangani) (Pons, 1961, 1969).

The traditional anthropological field research model has, therefore, not been static but has been applied to the new circumstances in which social anthropologists have chosen to conduct their work. Accordingly, field research in urban areas has retained several features associated with the traditional model: residence *in situ*, participant observation, unstructured interviews and the use of key informants. However, it has also involved modification of research designs to meet the demands of new settings using different methods and different theories. Anthropologists have, therefore, borrowed concepts and methods from other social science disciplines, especially sociology, where researchers have had some experience of working within their own society.

Social Researchers, Sociologists and the Study of their Own Society

Just as social anthropologists had studied the native peoples in the societies in which they lived (Firth in New Zealand and Gluckman in South Africa) so the early social researchers worked similarly among the 'native' peoples in their own society. The early English social researchers such as Charles Booth and Sidney and Beatrice Webb all used observational methods alongside other approaches to study individuals who were not of their class (Burgess, 1982a, pp. 4–6). In these terms their work has much in common with the social anthropologists as they were outsiders to the individuals and groups with whom they worked.

In America the work of the Chicago School of Sociologists (whom Hannerz (1980) has referred to as the 'Chicago ethnographers') used observational methods to study diverse groups: homeless men, street gangs, delinquents, and dance hall girls among many others. In short, the focus was mainly upon groups with whom the researcher shared little or no experience; the only exception to this was Nels Anderson who did have a family connection with homeless men (cf. Anderson, 1923). However, many of the researchers were 'outsiders' to the groups studied. Like the social anthropologists they were strangers in their own society. However, there were further parallels with anthropology here. Robert Park, the joint founder with W. I. Thomas of the Chicago School of Sociology, indicated in a paper that was to be a blueprint for the Chicago School studies that anthropological methods which had been used to study North American Indians should be employed in the study of inhabitants in the city of Chicago (Park, 1952, originally published in 1916). There was, therefore, some interchange between social anthropology and sociology both in terms of the methods used and the perspectives employed.

A further strand to this approach comes from the 'community' studies or locality studies tradition in sociology in Britain and the USA which has consistently used field methods (Burgess, 1982a, pp. 7–9). Among the earliest studies were those conducted by the Lynds whose investigations of *Middletown* (Lynd and Lynd, 1929) and *Middletown in Transition* (Lynd and Lynd, 1937) involved living in the town, the use of key informants, observational methods and unstructured interviews alongside the collection of statistical and documentary evidence. One group of studies which are indebted to social anthropology and the use of field methods is the Yankee City series conducted by Lloyd Warner and his associates in Newburyport in the 1930s. Warner had recently returned from studying Australian Aborigines where he had used field methods. In Newburyport he used similar methods to examine the culture of this American community. Furthermore, his work was also connected to the Chicago School tradition of social research (Warner and Lunt, 1941, 1942; Warner and Srole, 1945; Warner and Low, 1947; Warner, 1959). Many of these approaches were used in subsequent studies of urban areas as in James West's (Carl Withers) study of *Plainville* (West, 1945). However, the term 'community' is a slippery concept (Stacey, 1969b; Bell and Newby, 1972) with the result that many studies have been incorporated within this approach. For example, Vidich, Bensman and Stein (1964) take the term 'community' to embrace studies of street gangs in an urban slum (Whyte, 1955, 1964, 1981) and a mental hospital (Schwartz, 1964) as well as geographical localities in urban America.

In Britain field research methods were used by sociologists engaged in studies of geographical localities. Stacey and her co-workers researching in Banbury between 1948 and 1951 used a combination of methods based on observation, interviews and the social survey (Stacey, 1960); an approach that was also used by Williams in his study of Gosforth (Williams, 1956), by Frankenberg in his study of Pentredaiwaith (Frankenberg, 1957), by Littlejohn in his study of *Westrigg* (Littlejohn, 1963) and by Stacey and her research team when restudying Banbury in 1966 (Stacey *et al.*, 1975).

Nevertheless, the major site for the discovery of American ethnography by British sociologists was the sociology of deviance where sociologists have used observational methods to study drug takers (Becker, 1963), pool room players (Polsky, 1969) and homosexuals (Humphreys, 1970) among many others (cf. Rubington and Weinberg, 1968). This approach was embraced by British sociologists of deviance (Young, 1971; Cohen, 1972). Yet as Payne *et al.* (1981) argue, this resulted in some distance between British sociologists engaged in ethnographic work and social anthropologists, even though it did lead to the consolidation of links between field research and symbolic interactionism (cf. Rock, 1979; Cohen, 1980, pp. i–xxxiv). One thing that this approach still held in common with social anthropology was the study of 'natives'; individuals with whom sociologists were not familiar in their own society.

Field research methods have also been deployed by sociologists in several other substantive fields including: the sociology of labour and industry, the sociology of health and illness, and the sociology of education. In the area of industrial studies Gluckman had encouraged Manchester sociologists to engage in workshop studies (Lupton, 1963; Cunnison, 1966); a trend that was continued in Manchester in the work of Morgan (1969) and Purcell (1982). As Emmett and Morgan (1982) indicate, these studies employed a methodological approach that was common to British social anthropology. Here, researchers were required to learn about a field of study from those who lived within it. This involved collecting data in order to understand the situation and to make behaviour comprehensible to those outside and inside the system studied. Accordingly, those Manchester sociologists who have studied factories have not only observed the situations in which factory workers have been located but have taken jobs within factories in order to share in the work experiences of those whom they have studied. In these circumstances, the sociologists began as outsiders who although familiar with the location of the factories had none the less had little detailed knowledge or understanding of the workers' situation until they engaged in their research. Further studies in the same area but with a radical political approach have also used a similar range of field methods in studying workers' experiences (Beynon, 1973; Nichols and Beynon, 1977; Pollert, 1981; Cavendish, 1982) and on the transition between school and work (Willis, 1977). However, even here the researchers were outsiders. The latest contributor (Cavendish, 1982) in this line of radical field research remarks that left-wing intellectuals come from middle-class backgrounds, and hold professional jobs with sufficient incomes and spare time to cushion them from the harsh realities of life experienced by workers. The result is that considerable difficulties are experienced by those sociologists with middle-class life styles who attempt to understand the life of working-class factory workers (Cavendish, 1982, p. 2). Indeed, she goes on to discuss the absence of neat categories around which experiences can be organised. For Cavendish reports:

My experience of the work was the same as that of all the other women in the factory and it affected my outside life in much the same way; it was a means of livelihood for me as for them but I was also observing what went on while they had no pressing need to do so. My account of the factory and the work is therefore that of an outsider. (Cavendish, 1982, p. 6)

The sociologist as outsider is also apparent within studies on the sociology of health and illness. Observational work has been done within doctors' surgeries (Fletcher, 1974; Stimpson and Webb, 1975); within teaching hospitals (Atkinson, 1981); among students engaged in health visitor training (Dingwall, 1977) and patients (Roth, 1963). While in the case of Fletcher, Atkinson and Dingwall they came as outsiders to the situation, Roth's position was very different. Roth had a history of tuberculosis and after completing his Ph.D was admitted to a tuberculosis hospital. On the basis of his interest in the sociology of institutions and occupations he decided that a period of hospitalisation would provide a research opportunity for him to record observations from a hospital bed. As a hospital patient he kept detailed field notes on staff, room mates, conversations, routines, rules and procedures. After being discharged, he obtained a research grant and studied several other hospitals as a sociological observer. Such work indicates that field researchers can be insiders as well as outsiders; an approach that has also been adopted in a slightly different form by sociologists engaged in the study of schools and classrooms.

Over the last decade changing theoretical and substantive concerns in the sociology of education have resulted in sociologists engaging in the study of schools and classrooms from an interactionist perspective using field methods (Hargreaves, 1972; Delamont, 1976; Burgess, 1982b). Among the earliest British studies within this tradition were those that were started under the direction of Max Gluckman and were conducted by Hargreaves (1967) in a secondary modern school for boys, by Lacey (1966, 1970, 1974) in a boys' grammar school and by Lambart (1970, 1976, 1982) in an unstreamed girls' grammar school. This work, which was supervised by Ronald Frankenberg and Valdo Pons, extended the Manchester School's interest in social processes and the perspectives of actors (Lacey, 1981) and forms part of the second generation of Manchester studies. Lacey cites Stephen Ball's *Beachside Comprehensive* (Ball, 1981) as part of the third generation of studies to which I would also add my own study (Burgess, 1983). My study was initially supervised by Valdo Pons who encouraged me to work within a broad inter- actionist tradition using the anthropological methods that had been developed by Gluckman (1964, 1967), Turner (1957, 1964, 1974), Epstein (1967), Mitchell (1956) and Van Velsen (1967) to collect and analyse data.

A common thread that runs through all these educational studies besides their links with the anthropological concerns of the Manchester School is the fact that all the researchers taught classes while doing their research. Indeed, Lacey, Hargreaves and I acknowledge that we utilised our former teacher status as a base from which to conduct the research. In this respect, while we were outsiders to the particular schools that we joined we were nevertheless familiar with schools, teachers, the teaching profession and the ways in which schools operated; we were not strangers in schools and classrooms (cf. Stenhouse, 1984). In my own study I acknowledge this position and indicate that the situation in which the researcher is familiar with the social setting can be turned to advantage (cf. Roth, 1974) with the result that my study is written from a teacher's point of view. However, Birksted (1976) and Corrigan (1979) have argued that those studies that are written from a teacher perspective are problematic, at least as far as pupil accounts of schooling are concerned. It is their view that other roles should be taken in schools.

Researchers who have been engaged in detailed studies of their own societies have worked within different traditions and written from different perspectives. Some sociologists have remained 'outsiders', some have been insiders, often through force of circumstance, while others have simultaneously been outsiders and insiders within the same study. This has resulted in different models of field research being used by social anthropologists and sociologists engaged in contemporary field research (cf. Wax and Cassell, 1979). First and most common is a *'going native' model* in which the researcher learns to behave like a 'native' in the setting under study. In this respect, the anthropologists Spradley and Mann (1975) learned how to behave as customer and waitress respectively while studying male–female relations in an urban bar. Meanwhile, Joan Cassell (1977b) became another recruit to the American feminist movement whose consciousness was being raised and who learned how to behave as a feminist. Such roles of 'native' in a familiar setting have also been taken by sociologists acting as patients, student doctors and teachers. A second model is that of *'undercover agent'* where the researcher attempts to expose behaviour that is traditionally hidden from view. This style of research although conducted in familiar settings often involves covert participation (cf. Bulmer, 1982) and is discussed below in Chapter 9. Among the work that has been conducted in this way are studies of homosexual activity (Humphreys, 1970; Delph, 1978) and of sectarian groups (Festinger *et al.*, 1956; Homan, 1978) and of the police (Holdaway, 1982). Thirdly, there is an *advocate research model* where researchers intervene in social situations to help improve the position of those individuals who are studied. In this situation the advocate may be someone who hardly knows those who are studied or someone who is deeply committed to them (cf. Cavendish, 1982). Regardless of the model that is adopted by contemporary field researchers working in their own culture, they all share one thing in common in that they are familiar with the societies that are studied. This raises particular problems that have to be handled in the course of an investigation, and to these we now turn.

Problems of Studying a Familiar Setting

Writing in the mid-1960s the Indian sociologist M. N. Srinivas reflected on some reviews of his work on Indian society (Srinivas, 1952, 1962) and noted that reviewers had focused upon the fact that he was an Indian sociologist who was engaged in the study of his own society. In particular, he identifies three views: first, that as a sociologist studying his own society he was at a distinct advantage (Radcliffe-Brown, 1952). Secondly, that his description and interpretation were better when he no longer wrote in the language of his discipline but allowed himself 'the cultured Indian townsman, to describe and interpret the life of some of the peasantry of his own country' (*Times Literary Supplement*, 1952). Thirdly, that there were several methodological points which Edmund Leach identified when he wrote:

> For Professor Srinivas there are aspects of Hinduism in general and Brahminism in particular was he *knows* from the inside but which even the most erudite European can never learn. But is this an advantage or a disadvantage from the view point of sociological analysis?
> One of Professor Srinivas' most notable contributions to Indian sociology has been his development of the concept of 'sanskritization', the basic theme of which is that there is a long term tendency for caste groups which are low in the social hierarchy to initiate a certain fluidity into the total hierarchy of castes. That such fluidity exists has been clearly demonstrated, but that it should be seen as arising from an emulation of the Brahmins seems to me odd – a specifically 'Brahminocentric' point of view! If Professor Srinivas had been of Shudra origin would this have coloured his interpretation? (Leach, 1963, pp. 377–8, emphasis in original)

Here, Leach has raised the key question: how far can sociologists understand their own society? Furthermore, he poses questions about Srinivas's perspective which stems from being a member of the society under study. Indeed, Leach considers how being a Brahmin influenced the social scientific concepts that Srinivas deployed within his study.

Some of these points have also been made by American anthropologists (Aguilar, 1981; Messerschmidt, 1981; Stephenson and Greer, 1981) who have raised similar questions concerning the perspectives used by social scientists engaged in the study of their own society. The key issue is whether field researchers working within their own society experience advantages and disadvantages that are less likely to be encountered by researchers working in societies and cultural settings other than their own. Stephenson and Greer point to five sets of issues. First, the extent to which familiarity with the culture is of assistance when translating observations into data as they ask: will researchers recognise patterns in a society in which they are thoroughly acculturated? Are there problems in selecting what to study? Will researchers give full coverage to situations with which they are already familiar? Is the researcher who is a 'native' in a better position to elucidate meanings in events? Secondly, they discuss some of the problems concerning the relationship between researchers and informants: are the experiences of the native researcher different from the 'outsider' when identifying and relating to informants? Are informants sought out who are most like the researcher? Will the native researcher cover the full range of informants who can provide different sources of information? Thirdly, they consider the roles of the researcher and ask: to what extent does knowing a locale assist in gaining and establishing entrée and gaining rapport? What are the problems and advantages of occupying a familiar role in a particular social setting? Fourthly, they identify personal, political, ethical and value questions: what is the potential for role conflict and value conflict when a researcher studies a familiar setting? Is the sensitivity of a researcher heightened when the ethical and political issues in a society are known? Finally, they discuss the relationships between the researcher and the researched and ask: are there special problems relating to those who are researched after the research is completed? In short, Stephenson and Greer consider that the main problems for researchers working within their own societies are recognising culture patterns in familiar situations, and interpreting meanings attached to events and problems relating to participation, observation and field relations. However, they conclude that many of the principles underlying these problems are themselves familiar to field researchers and include: bias, oversimplification, prior judgement and the inability to separate observation from feeling.

In the classic field settings, researchers have reported how they were confronted with some of these problems. Nash (1963) indicates that the researcher in the field has to adapt to a role and that the objectivity of the field report will reflect the degree of adaptation. Yet as Nadel (1951) indicated, total objectivity is impossible, as the researcher may begin work in another culture as a stranger but has to become familiar with the surroundings. In these circumstances, it has been argued that being a stranger, an outsider in the social setting, gives the researcher scope to stand back and abstract material from the research experience. Indeed, it is maintained that the outsider's experience is more conducive to social science research. The outsider as far as Beattie (1964) is concerned, has 'stranger value'. This idea of the researcher as a stranger rests on Simmel's notion of the individual who is free of commitments to those who are studied and therefore more likely to be objective, for Simmel considered that the stranger will survey conditions with less prejudice having few links with those who are studied (cf. Simmel, 1950, pp. 404–5). This position is supported by Merton (1972) who maintains that 'it is the stranger . . . who finds what is familiar to the group significantly unfamiliar and so is prompted to raise questions for inquiry less apt to be raised at all by Insiders' (Merton, 1972, p. 33).

This position can be adopted by sociologists working within their own society, for if a situation they encounter is strange, questions can be raised about the way the members of the host community see it. There may also be situations where researchers conduct investigations in a geographical area with which they are familiar but where the people studied live in a different socio-cultural world and hold different perspectives from those adopted by the researchers. In these terms sociologists who study deviants – drug addicts, delinquents, pick pockets, prostitutes and thieves – will be outsiders to the settings that they encounter.

Nevertheless, there are some situations where researchers are insiders who are familiar with the cultural setting. Here, they may blend into the situation and meet the demands made upon them by the participants with whom they share similar frames of reference. In such situations, interaction is considered 'natural', for the researcher has rapport with those who are researched, sharing the same language and the same socio-political context. The African anthropologist Nukunya who has conducted research among his own people, the Anlo Ewe, supports this line of argument as he reports:

Because I was one of them and not a 'foreign intruder', the fear and suspicion which always lurk in the minds of subjects and informants during social research in general were almost absent. They had confidence in me because they knew I could not 'sell them'. Many a time informants were met who admitted 'this is a thing we normally don't divulge to outsiders, but since it is you we shall give you all the necessary help'. (Nukunya, 1969, p. 19)

In this setting, the experiences of the insider would appear to outweigh the experiences of the outsider. However, there are difficulties that have to be overcome in this situation; additional effort is required to ensure that the insider researcher does not take things for granted or overlook situations that at first sight appear all too familiar. Stephenson and Greer (1981) suggest that researchers working within their own culture should adopt an artificial naiveté by recording as much detail as possible about the people present and topics of conversation regardless of their relevance. In these terms, they maintain that familiar topics should be given 'stranger value' and seen through the eyes of the stranger.

Within the study of educational settings this movement between the strange and the familiar is apparent in anthropological and sociological work. Spindler and Spindler (1982) indicate that for the field researcher working in societies and in cultures which appear different, unusual and exotic it is the task of the researcher to make the strange familiar and understandable by translating the data that are gathered. However, they indicate that making the strange familiar was not the task that confronted George Spindler while doing research in an elementary school which while strange was also a mirror of his own strangeness. George Spindler summarises his problem as follows:

I sat in classes for days wondering what there was to 'observe'. Teachers taught, reprimanded, rewarded, while pupils sat at desks, squirming, whispering, reading, writing, staring into space as they had in my own grade-school experience, in my practice teaching in a teacher training program, and in the two years of public school teaching I had done before World War II. (Spindler and Spindler, 1982, p. 24)

In this location it was essential for the researcher to make the familiar strange by considering patterns of interaction, patterns of role play, cultural conflict, ritual exercises, classroom strategies and negotiations which in turn could be translated back into the familiar again.

This kind of problem in the study of educational settings has also been identified by Howard Becker who comments:

We may have understated a little the difficulty of observing contemporary classrooms. It is not just the survey method of educational testing or any of those things that keeps people from seeing what is going on. I think instead that it is first and foremost a matter of it all being so familiar that it becomes impossible to single out events that occur in the classroom as things that have occurred, even when they happen right in front of you ... it takes a tremendous effort of will and imagination to stop seeing only the things that are conventionally there to be seen. (Becker, 1971, p. 10)

Indeed, Becker has identified the familiarity of schools in terms of their routines which are problematic for the researcher who may see 'nothing' beyond the everyday patterns and processes with which everyone is familiar. In this respect, researchers need to move away from abstract descriptions in their fieldnotes. Studies of classrooms should not merely report that teachers were 'teaching' and pupils were 'learning' but provide specific details about what was being said and done (cf. Bogdan and Biklen, 1982).

In order that researchers might deal with the problem of working in their own culture, Delamont (1981) has put forward four strategies that can be used when dealing with familiar situations. First, she suggests studying unusual, 'bizarre' or different classrooms. She argues that researchers might focus on classrooms for adults rather than children, for the deaf, blind and physically handicapped rather than the able bodied, and might examine subjects such as physical education and art rather than English and Mathematics. By focusing on unfamiliar territories, it will give some highlight to the familiar. Secondly, she considers that studies should be done by sociologists working in other cultures, as comparative material would provide further thought on familiar settings. Thirdly, she maintains that the study of non-educational settings could be used to give a novel perspective to the work on schools and classrooms. Finally, she suggests that researchers could develop self conscious strategies to make the familiar problematic by either questioning a taken-for-granted aspect of schooling such as gender, which has been successfully done by Serbin (1978) and by Delamont (1980). To these approaches can be added the study of aspects of education that are usually neglected by sociologists of education such as postgraduate education (Porter and Scott, 1981) and aspects of medical education (Dingwall, 1977; Atkinson, 1981) which are often treated as part of the sociology of health and illness rather than the sociology of education.

Handling the Familiar and the Strange

The debate concerning the degree of familiarity or strangeness which the sociologist may encounter in a cultural setting appears to have been polarised in some of the literature. The assumption seems to be made that situations are either totally familiar or totally strange, yet my research experience points towards a series of situations within the same social setting which were both familiar and strange.

Of all social institutions, schools are highly familiar settings. Everyone has been to school and at least knows these institutions from a pupil's perspective. For some people, schools are also known from a number of other perspectives: as teachers, as parents, as governors, as advisers, as inspectors and so on. In all cases the result is familiarity. When I began my research at Bishop McGregor Comprehensive School there was a degree of familiarity mixed with some strangeness. I had been a pupil in a number of schools including two secondary schools but I had not attended a comprehensive school. Secondly, I had trained as a secondary school teacher and held a full-time teaching post in a secondary school which was organised on comprehensive lines in anticipation of comprehensive reorganisation, but I had never taught in a comprehensive school. Thirdly, McGregor was a co-educational secondary school and I was familiar with this situation having been a pupil in a co-educational school and having taught in mixed schools. Finally, McGregor was a Roman Catholic school. The school in which I had held a full-time post was a Church school (of Church of England foundation) and so I was familiar with this element but I was unfamiliar with Roman Catholic schools as I had not been a member of a Catholic school nor was I a Roman Catholic. In these circumstances, the situation was simultaneously familiar yet strange.

The familiar elements of schooling were further reinforced. I was familiar with the routine of marking registers, morning assembly, lesson bells, double periods, dinner queues and staff rooms. However, at McGregor there was a new language to learn with form tutors rather than form teachers, the staff common room where no work was taken and working staff rooms where books could be marked and work prepared. Simple items of vocabulary, essential in getting around the site, helped me to come to terms with carefully observing what occurred within particular parts of the school.

Assembly is a familiar routine to everyone. Yet the researcher has to pose questions about the situations which are observed and to keep a set of notes on the observations that are made. It is easy to note that assembly is where pupils listen to one or more teachers, sing hymns, say prayers, and listen to notices before going to their first lesson. Such a description tells us very little and emphasises what *should* happen rather than what *actually* happens. At McGregor a distinction was made between school assembly and House assembly. School assembly involved two House groups on one day each week and was taken by either the Headmaster, Deputy Head or Senior Mistress, while House assembly was with one House alone, was taken by the Head of House and was held on three days each week.

In observing a school assembly the researcher can pose a number of questions. Do the pupils stand or sit? Are they assembled in particular groups? Are all the pupils present? Are teachers present? What do pupils do? What do teachers do? What is said? What is not said? How do the activities relate to other activities in the school? In short, researchers have constantly to pose questions about the settings in which they find themselves. Woods (1977, p. 11) has indicated that the perspective which is taken by the researcher will influence the kind of questions that are posed. A researcher who is interested in 'improving' school assembly might ask: is the Headmaster effectively communicating with the teachers and the pupils? What other approaches could be used? A functionalist might ask: how does school assembly function to maintain social order? A conflict theorist might consider: in whose interest is the assembly organised? Meanwhile, a neo-Marxist might look at school assembly as part of the pupils' training and indoctrination in a capitalist society. In my study, I was concerned with the meanings, definitions and redefinitions of situations that were established by the Headmaster and by House Heads in their assemblies. My questions were, therefore, informed by an interactionist perspective and included: how does the Headmaster use religion to define school rules? How do House Heads redefine school rules within their House assemblies? In conducting research in such situations the researcher may begin with naive questions in order that detailed field notes can be written on the situation under study. However, further questions are also required in order that some focus is given to the data that are collected and the observations that are made. In my research, I kept detailed notes on each assembly that I attended. I drew diagrams to summarise the situation: who had attended assembly, where they had been standing, with whom they had spoken and where possible what they had said. My notes also contained a detailed description of what had been said by the teacher who had taken the assembly (cf. Burgess, 1983, pp. 41–8, and pp. 100–14).

When I reviewed my field notes I found that patterns began to emerge in terms of the similarities and differences between school assembly taken by the Headmaster and House assembly which was taken by other teachers. Themes that arose could be cross-referenced to other events and activities that I had witnessed in the school. For example, I worked upon the data that I had gathered on school assembly and the way in which the Headmaster's talks were related to the aims and objectives that he had for the school. The result was that school assembly was seen as a reality-defining situation where the Headmaster presented his version of the school. Meanwhile, House assembly involved some reinforcement of the situation that had been defined but also a redefinition of the situation when in some cases, in the same week, Heads of Houses reinterpreted what the Headmaster had said in order to apply it to their Houses (see Burgess, 1983, pp. 41–72).

A further theme that could be developed using data that were gathered in the assembly was the influence of Catholicism on the school. Here, links could be developed between the liturgical cycle throughout the year, the transmission of norms and values and links with the school curriculum. In particular, I examined the kind of activities that were associated with Lent. Here, I found that the Headmaster suggested a series of activities centring on House masses and charity collections when the focus would be a celebration of the Passion and death of Christ. The Head indicated that he intended these activities to be used to generate Christian values. Meanwhile, in the House Heads' assemblies I found pupils were encouraged, harangued and berated to collect more money than other Houses. The result was conflict between House Heads and pupils and anger and cynicism from many staff who were also encouraged to participate in the charity collections. A situation that had been intended to generate consensus resulted in conflict and competition among the participants. In the course of examining House assembly I also observed how teachers made direct links in their assembly talks between Catholicism and school work. Pupils were asked to pray about working hard, obeying school rules, handing in good work and passing examinations. Indeed, they were told that if they worked hard in school it would allow them to give account of themselves to God. In these circumstances I could establish how religion was used to reinforce school rules, school routines, orderliness and hard work.

Here, I have selected data that were collected on assemblies to illustrate the ways in which a familiar setting could be studied and themes developed from the observations that were made. On the basis of my experience in working in a familiar setting I would recommend several strategies that can be used. First, researchers should continually pose questions about the settings within which they are located. Secondly, researchers should write down in as much detail as possible what they have observed. Thirdly, observations should be regularly reviewed and cross-referenced to other activities and events that have been observed so that themes can be developed and in turn linked with the theoretical perspective that is deployed within the research project. At first sight, there would appear to be some distance between school assembly and the aims and objectives of a comprehensive school. Yet to understand the ways in which the aims and objectives of Bishop McGregor School were defined, redefined and transmitted to teachers and to pupils, assemblies were used as the source material out of which these accounts were constructed.

Conclusion

This chapter has addressed some of the issues and problems involved in using field research methods in familiar social situations. The historical trends and approaches used in field research (reviewed in Burgess, 1982a, pp. 1–11) are briefly discussed in order to indicate the shifting emphasis that has occurred in fields of study. Field research is no longer confined to the coral gardens of the Trobriand Islands but is also used to study urban settings. Field research has now 'come home' and with it has come a set of social problems that researchers have to try and resolve during the course of their research. A key problem is how to study situations which are familiar to you. In the subsequent chapters of this book central issues involved in field research and methods used to study situations in the researcher's own society will be discussed.

Suggestions for Further Reading

Methodology

A set of references that focus on the debate concerning the application of field research methods to familiar social settings:

Basham, R. and De Groot, D. (1977), 'Current approaches to the anthropology of urban and complex societies', *American Anthropologist*, vol. 79, no. 2, pp. 414–40; provides a review of the application of field methods to urban anthropological study. The article contains a useful and extensive bibliography.

Delamont, S. (1981), 'All too familiar? A decade of classroom research', *Educational Analysis*, vol. 3, no. 1, pp. 69–84; provides a review of the familiar–strange debate in relation to the study of schools and classrooms.

Frankenberg, R. (1982) (ed.), *Custom and Conflict in British Society* (Manchester: Manchester University Press); is a set of essays on the way in which Max Gluckman's approach to field study has been applied to social situations in British society.

Messerschmidt, D. A. (1981) (ed.), *Anthropologists at Home in North America: Methods and Issues in the Study of One's Own Society* (Cambridge: CUP). A collection of papers that deal with substantive and theoretical themes relating to the study of familiar cultures.

Spindler, G. D., and Spindler, L. (1982), 'Roger Harker and Schönhausen: From the Familiar to the Strange and Back Again' in G. D. Spindler (ed.), *Doing the Ethnography of Schooling* (New York: Holt, Rinehart & Winston), pp. 20–46; reviews the familiar–strange debate in relation to the authors' own research on schools and schooling in different cultures over three decades.

Srinivas, M. N. (1966), 'Some thoughts on the study of one's own society', in M. N. Srinivas (ed.) *Social Change in Modern India* (Berkeley, Calif.: University of California Press), pp. 147–63. A classic statement in which the issues and problems of studying a familiar culture are raised.

Stephenson, J. B. and Greer, L. S. (1981), 'Ethnographers in their own cultures: two Appalachian cases', *Human Organization*, vol. 40, no. 2, pp. 123–30; consists of a discussion of the authors' own experiences in conducting research in two different locations in the Appalachian region of the USA.

Empirical Studies

These studies were all conducted in the respective researchers' own society. Some include familiar settings while others deal with the unfamiliar. Examine the ways in which the researchers handle this issue.

Ball, S. J. (1981), *Beachside Comprehensive: a Case Study of Secondary Schooling* (Cambridge: CUP).

Cavendish, R. (1982), *Women on the Line* (London: Routledge & Kegan Paul).

Coffield, F., Robinson, P. and Sarsby, J. (1980), *A Cycle of Deprivation? A Case Study of Four Families* (London: Heinemann).

Cohen, A. P. (1982) (ed.), *Belonging: Identity and Social Organisation in British Rural Cultures* (Manchester: Manchester University Press).

Humphreys, L. (1970), *Tearoom Trade* (London: Duckworth).

Mars, G. (1982), *Cheats at Work* (London: Allen & Unwin).

Patrick, J. (1973), *A Glasgow Gang Observed* (London: Eyre-Methuen).

Plant, M. (1975), *Drugtakers in an English Town* (London: Tavistock).

Roth, J. A. (1963), *Timetables* (New York: Bobbs-Merrill).

2

Starting Research and Gaining Access

It is customary for methodologists to begin discussions of research by considering the relationships between different phases of a research project. Accordingly these discussions are presented in terms of research design which, it is argued, should precede *all* social research, research practice involving work in the field when data collection takes place and finally data analysis. While such presentations provide neat, tidy accounts of the conduct of research they are nothing short of misleading, for in this context, research is presented as a linear model with a beginning, a middle, and an end. Yet the reality is very different and infinitely more complex. Accounts by researchers have revealed that social research is not just a question of neat procedures but a social process whereby interaction between researcher and researched will directly influence the course which a research programme takes (see the accounts in Hammond (1964), Shipman (1976), Bell and Newby (1977), Bell and Encel (1978), Shaffir, Stebbins and Turowetz (1980), Roberts (1981) and Burgess (1984a). Accordingly the project, and the methodology, is continually defined and redefined by the researcher and in some cases by those researched. In these terms, researchers have constantly to monitor the activities in which they are engaged.

Nowhere is this more essential than in the conduct of field research, which is characterised by flexibility. Here, there are no set rules, rigid procedures and fixed roles. For field research predominantly involves the use of observation, participant observation, unstructured interviews and documentary evidence, all of which have to be applied to a specific social setting. Much will depend upon the researcher, those who are researched and the setting in which the researcher works. This is clearly demonstrated by Evans-Pritchard in his remarks about his anthropological work among the Azande and the Nuer when he states:

> Because I had to live in such close contact with the Nuer I knew them more intimately than the Azande, about whom I am able to write a much more detailed account. Azande would not allow me

to live as one of themselves; Nuer would not allow me to live otherwise. Among Azande I was compelled to live outside the community; among Nuer I was compelled to be a member of it. (Evans-Pritchard, 1940, p. 15)

In this context, Evans-Pritchard indicates that field research is not merely the translation of a set of techniques from one social situation to another. The anthropological methods that have been used in the study of small-scale societies cannot be simply translated over to studies of industrial societies (cf. Messerschmidt, 1981). Indeed, researchers need to consider the conditions in their fields of study if they are to conduct effective research in a particular social setting.

Yet how do field researchers begin to prepare to do research? How do they select problems? How do they design a study? How do they gain access to their field of study? How do they select informants, observe situations, collect and analyse data? It is these questions that we shall concentrate upon. The focus will, therefore, be upon key phases and key methods used in the research process.

The most difficult question to address is: when does research begin? Certainly with all projects there is a formal starting date, but this will no doubt have been preceded by wide reading and an initial research design. It is usual for research reports to indicate that the literature review constitutes the *real* start of research. For it is the reading that has been done by the researcher, it is argued, that helps to generate a research problem. However, these accounts overlook the relationship between the sociological training of researchers and their personal experiences in a social setting that may help to generate a research problem and a programme of research. For sociologists studying their own societies may have experience of particular roles and social settings that can be utilised in their own research.

This interaction of sociological expertise together with experience of a social situation is clearly illustrated by Stacey (1982) in her account of how she became involved in studying the sociology of health and illness. She indicates that she was a mother of young children when the Platt report (Ministry of Health, 1959) on the welfare of children in hospitals was published, which suggested that mothers should go into hospitals with their children. As a mother who was also a sociologist she followed the progress of the report and examined it to see what sociological implications were involved. On the basis of her reflections and experiences she identified gaps in our knowledge about the division of labour in the hospital ward which resulted in a programme of research in health and illness (cf. Stacey *et al.*, 1970; Hall and Stacey, 1979).

Similarly, my own research activities within the sociology of education are based on a combination of personal experience and sociological expertise. Before conducting research in schools I had trained as a teacher, taken a degree in sociology and worked as a teacher in a secondary modern school. On the basis of this experience I was aware that teachers were continually confronted with problems about the ways in which schools worked and with particular groups of pupils within schools. In addition, I knew that relatively little sociological work had been done on schools by the beginning of the 1970s. It was, therefore, clear to me that there were gaps in our knowledge about schools and schooling particularly with regard to comprehensive education. My intention was, therefore, to conduct a field study in a comprehensive school.

When I began my research in October 1972 the only British ethnographic studies of schools that were easily available were those by Lacey (1970) in a grammar school and Hargreaves (1967) in a secondary modern school, both having conducted their work from the Manchester University Department of Social Anthropology and Sociology. Their studies were influenced by the social anthropological training provided by Max Gluckman (cf. Gluckman, 1964; Frankenberg, 1982) and were supervised by Ronald Frankenberg and Valdo Pons both of whom had worked within the 'community studies' tradition (cf. Frankenberg, 1957; Pons, 1969). Indeed, Lacey (1970) comments that:

> In launching its first project in the sociology of education the Manchester department was concerned to harness some of the skills and techniques developed in intensive studies of communities and small-scale societies, to the study of modern institutions. (Lacey, 1970, p. xiii)

Apart from these brief remarks on the approach used, the only other comments on 'fieldwork' in Lacey's study consist of a brief description of the way in which the research was established and a timetable detailing the fieldwork which was conducted in different periods (Lacey, 1970, pp. xii–xv). Indeed, it was not until six years after *Hightown Grammar* had been published that Lacey provided an autobiographical account of his involvement in this research project (Lacey, 1976). Meanwhile, Hargreaves had published as an appendix to his secondary modern school study, an account of role conflict in participant observation research with special reference to the teacher role (Hargreaves, 1967, pp. 193–205).

When I began to prepare to do my research I was advised by Valdo Pons to read some of the anthropological accounts of urban settings (Pons, 1969; Mayer, 1971), studies of 'communities' in Britain (Williams, 1956; Frankenberg, 1957; Stacey, 1960; and Littlejohn, 1963), and studies of other social institutions such as factories where an ethnographic approach had been used. It was and still is good advice for research novices to read a large number of ethnographic studies outside the field in which they intend to work, as wide reading beyond the field of education may generate issues, ideas and insights that can be applied to educational settings. For example, Delamont (1981) cites the way in which Macintyre's work on the social construction of biological events relating to pregnancy (Macintyre, 1977) may be applied to teachers' ideas about physical and biological aspects of pupils' aggression, and how Newby's ideas on deference and patriarchal structures among agricultural workers (Newby, 1977a) can be used to examine relations between teachers and pupils and teachers and headteachers. She also demonstrates how an analysis of disputes in Malta (Boissevain, 1969) may help to generate ideas for analysing disputes in schools. Certainly, in my own study anthropological analyses of social dramas (Turner, 1957) were used to examine how crises were handled in the school (cf. Burgess, 1983, pp. 84–119). In addition, I read studies within the substantive subfield in order to anticipate the main issues and problems that might be examined. Certainly, this is also apparent in Stephen Ball's study (Ball, 1981) in which he highlights how Lacey's concepts of differentiation and polarisation (Lacey, 1966, 1970) were used to orientate his own work.

However, background reading is not all that can be used, for researchers can make links between their familiarity with a social setting and the literature within the field of study. My knowledge of schools, of pupils, of teachers and teaching together with my knowledge of the sociological and educational literature was therefore utilised in establishing a project that would focus on a comprehensive school. In common with many field studies my work was 'exploratory'. It had no well worked out hypotheses that were to be refined and tested. However, in common with all researchers I did have a set of questions to address which were generally framed. A similar position has been reported by Melville Dalton who indicates that in his study *Men Who Manage* (Dalton, 1959) he did not have any hypotheses because:

1   I never feel sure what is relevant for hypothesising until I have some intimacy with the situation – I think of a hypothesis as a well-founded conjecture;
2   once uttered, a hypothesis becomes obligatory to a degree;
3   there is a danger that the hypothesis will become esteemed for itself and work as an absurd symbol of science. (Dalton, 1964, pp. 53–4)

If a researcher enters a field setting with a set of hypotheses it may result in some misconceptions about the situation which will need rapid revision on the basis of the early observations that are made. In this respect, some commentators (cf. Moore, 1978; Ditton and Williams, 1981) have indicated that this particular problem means that it is difficult for field researchers to establish a detailed research design in the manner required by the Social Science Research Council (SSRC, now the Economic and Social Research Council, ESRC). Indeed, Ditton and Williams have mounted a critique of the SSRC's demands that grant applicants should be able to specify in advance their concepts, theories, and methods of research together with the practical application of their research in particular circumstances. Such problems have also been apparent to ethnographers working in the USA where these issues have been well summarised by Agar who writes:

> "How do I write a research proposal?" It's not necessarily that ethnographers don't want to test hypotheses. It's just that if they do, the variables and operationalisations and simple specifications must grow from an understanding of the group rather than being hammered on top of it no matter how poor the fit. You can't specify the questions you're going to ask when you move into the community; you don't know how to ask questions yet. You can't define a sample; you don't know what the range of social types is and which ones are relevant to the topics you're interested in. None of this goes over well with the hypothesis – testing fanatics. (Agar, 1981, pp. 69–70)

While these comments contain important points about the difficulties involved in preparing for field research, they do to some extent overstate the case. A cursory glance at these remarks might lead a research novice to conclude that there is no way in which preparation and research design can be achieved. While I would agree with Mills (1959) that a neat tidy application for funds is dishonest, pretentious and contrived, there is a middle course in which researchers can provide a minimum amount of information. Moore (1978) points the way towards this stance in his commentary on attempts to obtain funds to study developments in the North Sea Oil industry off the North East coast of Scotland. He indicates that given the difficulties involved in specifying precise locations, problems and methods it was hard to write research proposals for funding by the SSRC. However, he does indicate that it would be reasonable to put forward:

> a research strategy which is flexible as to precise location and method and which aims to compare the usefulness of various theoretical approaches for understanding what is happening rather

than to impose a set of narrowly defined theoretical questions.
(Moore, 1978, p. 272)

But we might ask: how can this be done? There are no guides
available on how to submit a successful application for funds (cf.
Eggleston, 1980). Furthermore, if we turn to the research reports and
published monographs we find that there are few details provided on
the initial research proposal and few clues about funding and the
politics of research funding. Some comments in the light of personal
experience have been provided by Stenhouse (1984) who indicates
that the art of writing a research proposal to engage in case study
research is to give the funding body what it requires while leaving
sufficient flexibility for the researcher to carry out the exploratory
programme of research.

An extract from a successful grant application written by Margaret
Stacey to the Nuffield Foundation for funds to support the second
study of Banbury (Stacey *et al.*, 1975) is one of the few publicly
available examples of research design that have been used in grant
applications. Here, Stacey outlined her aims and objectives together
with an indication of methodology. As far as objectives were
concerned she indicated that she wished:

(i) (a)   to assess the social systems present in Banbury,
          particularly those associated with class and tradition and
    (b)   to assess the social changes which have taken place in
          these systems since 1950 when the previous study was
          made. Specifically the object would be to test certain
          predictions that were made in that study about likely
          future changes.
(ii) to observe the new immigration which is now taking place
      and which will continue for the next four years.

Linked with these objectives was the methodology. Here, Stacey was
able to specify her methods and the purposes for which they would be
used:

(i)   By examination of documents, interviews with officials, town
      leaders and others, to gain some knowledge of the social
      developments of the period 1950–1966.
(ii) By participant observation by a number of research workers,
      who would be required to be resident in the Banbury area.
      Each would participate in different areas of the life of the
      town, their pooled data providing a qualitative assessment of
      the way the social system works.
(iii) By sample schedule to ascertain certain social characteristics

of the population, where this is necessary to supplement the census. Place of origin, length of residence, place of work, whether in or outside Banbury, associational allegiances, kin connections are examples of the information likely to be needed. This data would give some estimate of the size of the social systems isolated.

(iv) By examination of the local press and by interview of key informants to plot the leadership of the town's associations, in particular to ascertain the extent to which these overlap and cluster, thus providing indicators of the social system.

(v) By interview of selected sub-samples to analyze relationships within the extended family, which vary with membership of different social systems, particularly between the locally-based and those which are not locally based. (Stacey quoted in Bell, 1977, pp. 48–9)

These elements of the research proposal are instructive in a number of respects. First there is a broad indication of the theoretical concepts that are to be used; that is the basic framework within which research questions are to be generated. Secondly, there is an indication of the kinds of question that need to be addressed and the kinds of data that are 'likely to be needed'. Finally, there is a clear indication of the field methods that are to be used and the way in which these are to be complemented by a social survey. In these terms, Stacey was able to specify the aims, objectives, methods and questions that were to be used in her study. Her proposal highlights the relationships between problems, theories and methods and indicates the control which at least one sociologist attempts to have over the collection of her data.

While these elements of the research design provide a minimum amount of information to judge the quality of the proposed research, other components can be specified and lend a tone of 'firmness' to proposals for research using field methods. First, an indication of the way in which data are not only to be collected but also analysed and reported. Secondly, a research timetable to indicate a time budget for the collection and analysis of data together with sufficient time for report writing. Report writing is particularly important since too many projects finish without reports being produced, as research staff (regrettably lacking tenured positions) have to move to other jobs (cf. Platt, 1976). Thirdly, the division of labour between project staff needs to be included and, finally, some indication of the pattern of dissemination. The last point becomes particularly important in applied fields. For example, in the field of education, Cane and Schroeder (1970) found it was unlikely that teachers would read the technical and theoretical journals whose articles were intended for an 'academic' audience (cf. Burgess, 1980; Nixon, 1981) with the result that more wide-spread dissemination in non-technical language becomes essential.

If these elements were considered in all research designs for field research projects they would not limit the field of social inquiry, nor would they superimpose preconceptions or misconceptions on the field of study. Rather such research designs would provide a framework within which theories, methods and problems could be monitored throughout the research process. The research design would not be a static model of the research indicating procedures which were to be followed doggedly, but a base against which modifications could be made as the research continued. Among those elements which need to be specified is the access that is required to institutions and to individuals. Accordingly, researchers need to consider how access can be achieved. Yet this is not just a theoretical question, for the tactics and strategies that are used to gain access hold implications for the research, the researcher and the research process. The remaining part of this chapter will focus on problems and procedures involved in gaining access, drawing on issues that relate to the study of schools. I shall also review my experiences of gaining access to Bishop McGregor Comprehensive School and finally I shall consider the themes that arise out of my research experience and the extent to which similar issues and problems have arisen in other projects and how they have been handled by researchers.

Gaining Access to Schools

Access has, until relatively recently, not been regarded as a problem by many researchers and has received little attention in basic methodology texts (cf. Bailey, 1978; Moser and Kalton, 1971). In some studies access has been taken for granted or ignored completely. Such a stance has in the past been taken by many researchers who conducted studies in schools and classrooms utilising questionnaires. Teachers and pupils were regarded as a docile and accessible population on whom to administer numerous tests and questions (cf. Wax and Wax, 1971). This approach has reduced the knowledge that we have of schools, and oversimplified the procedures involved in starting an investigation. For as Wax (1971) has indicated, the processes of initiation and resocialisation of the researcher that occur at the beginning of a research project influence the outcome of the final research report.

At its most basic, access involves gaining permission to do a piece of research in a particular social setting or institution (cf. Brown, Guillet De Monthoux and McCullough, 1976). However, there is really no way in which a school study can be done openly without seeking permission from the headteacher concerned (Wolcott, 1971). Indeed, in the USA access to schools has not only to be obtained through the principal but also through parents' groups and local school boards, while in England some local education authorities insist on being approached before research begins. However, as Wolcott indicates, the level at which researchers enter a school will influence research relations and the kind of data that are obtained. We already have accounts from British researchers involved in studying schools (Hargreaves, 1967; Lacey, 1976) about the way in which initial entry to their research schools, through the officers of a local education authority and individual headteachers, influenced the ways in which their studies were subsequently explained to teachers and received by them. In these accounts there are no discussions of the *actual* strategies involved in negotiating access with teachers, or with pupils. Nevertheless, Walker (1980) has reminded us that:

> To gain access to the school you need to first approach the Local Education Authority; to gain access to the staff, you need to approach the Head; to gain access to the pupils you need to approach the staff. Each fieldwork contact is thus sponsored by someone in authority over those you wish to study, and relationships between 'sponsors' and researchers cannot be broken if the research is to continue. (Walker, 1980, p. 49)

While this provides a guide for the researcher it omits general questions about relationships and particular questions about trust between the researcher and the researched. For if, as Walker suggests, the researcher enters a setting through someone higher in the hierarchy than the individual to be researched it raises questions about the trust teachers might put in a researcher who enters the school via the headteacher or the trust that pupils might put in a researcher who enters a school via the teachers. Indeed, Corrigan (1979) and Birksted (1976) have raised questions about using the teacher role to gain access to pupils. In particular, Corrigan points out that certain kinds of data will not be accessible to researchers who take a teacher role. Furthermore, he raises a series of ethical dilemmas that will confront those who teach: what happens if a pupil smokes? What happens if a pupil really hates a teacher? What does a researcher do if it is discovered that a pupil intends to burn down the school? Such issues, Corrigan believes, are too difficult to handle from the teacher role with the result that he took an alternative role of Cockney writer. While this resolved some of the problems to which he alluded, it did not bypass all the issues. Corrigan indicates that while he was accepted by the pupils, there was still the question of acceptance by the teachers together with day-to-day issues concerning his dress and his behaviour.

Just as Corrigan indicates that entering a school via the teachers and the teacher role poses problems, so in turn questions can be raised about the relationships between researcher and researched when access is negotiated through a headteacher. Researchers have to consider the extent to which they rely on a headteacher for initial sponsorship within the school. Some consideration has also to be given to the extent to which sponsorship by the headteacher will involve some limitation being placed on the study, or in turn the extent to which the researcher may become a consultant to the school and to the headteacher (cf. Richardson, 1973, 1975; Collier, 1978). Furthermore, the question has to be posed about the extent to which a headteacher can grant access to the whole of a school site, to classrooms, to teachers, to pupils and to documents (cf. Burgess, 1980). In short, the negotiation of access, while being fundamental to the research process, can also reveal to the researcher the pattern of social relationships at a research site.

Gaining Access in Bishop McGregor School: An Empirical Example

At McGregor, access could not be negotiated on a single occasion but involved negotiation and renegotiation in different phases of the research process with different members of the school (cf. Geer, 1970). Initially, I negotiated with the Headmaster by requesting permission to join the teaching staff and work part-time in the Newsom Department. The Head was prepared to give me access to the school but made several suggestions. First, he would discuss my position with his senior teachers which would, he hoped, help to establish my role as a part-time teacher in the school. Secondly, he thought I would have to establish contacts with individual teachers whom he considered should have the right not to participate in the study. Thirdly, he explained that while he did not personally have any objections to me conducting interviews with pupils in the school, he wanted pupils to have the right of veto over whether they should or should not be interviewed and whether the interviews should be tape-recorded. I was, therefore, asked to let the pupils know that they could refuse to participate in my project. The Head also suggested that teachers and pupils should be told about my study before agreeing to participate in it. In these terms, he was suggesting that there should be informed consent among participants (see Chapter 9). Finally, he asked that I should make myself available, not only to teach in the Newsom Department but also to take substitution lessons when teachers were absent as he believed that this would be appreciated by his staff and would help to establish my position with individual teachers. Meanwhile, he had no objections to the study and agreed that the work could proceed. However, he wanted me to allow a few days for him to discuss the idea of my research with his senior teachers after which he suggested that I should return to negotiate my work with members of the Newsom Department.

A week later the Head contacted me to say that all was well and that I could now go along to the school to see the Deputy Head and the Head of the Newsom Department to discuss my research. I went to the school expecting to find that these teachers were acquainted with the aims of my study, since the Head indicated that he would be circulating copies of a document that I had written outlining the aims and objectives of my research. Instead, I found that the Head had just mentioned to these teachers that I was coming into the school. Furthermore, neither of them had been provided with a copy of my research proposal, with the result that I had to begin by explaining the kind of work I wanted to do. This I found was the start of a very regular process, as whenever I encountered teachers for the first time I had to define for them what I was doing in the school. Inevitably, I found that over time the emphasis that I gave to certain dimensions of my study changed.

I found few difficulties with access to the school site and to teachers. This might be explained by the way I defined the study and in terms of my previous experience as a teacher which helped me to identify with teachers and for them to identify with me. However, I found that it was not easy to negotiate access to classrooms where teachers were working with Newsom pupils. When I asked teachers if I could go and observe their Newsom classes I found that they became very defensive. On reflection, I think this might be accounted for in several ways. First, the kind of activities that occurred in Newsom classes (that is, pupils not working, playing cards, and running around the room (cf. Burgess, 1982b, 1983)) did not lend themselves to the presence of an observer. Secondly, teachers do not normally have another adult in the classroom other than in team teaching situations. Thirdly, many teachers equate the presence of another adult in the classroom with the time when inspectors or advisers call on them for the purpose of assessment (cf. Shaw, 1969). Here, I found that I had to consider other ways of gaining access to teachers' classrooms. One way in which I could gain access was through team teaching arrangements which were part of the Newsom Department programme. In addition, I also got teachers to keep diaries (see Chapter 6) of what occurred in their Newsom classes. However, the researcher needs to consider the extent to which these activities involve covert observation on the part of teachers who agree to complete the diaries but who do not inform their pupils that they are recording observations on the lessons for the purpose of research (cf. Burgess, 1981a, 1981b).

Gaining access to pupils took various forms. Access to all pupils in the school could be obtained through collective situations: in assembly, during lunch breaks and break times. However, in these settings pupils participated in the research without knowing they were part of it. Access to specific groups of pupils could be obtained by teaching classes. To this extent, the formal teacher role provided access to pupils. However, access to individuals could only be gained outside the framework of formal lessons. Conversations with individual pupils could be conducted at break times, in lunch hours, on journeys to and from school by public transport and at other times that provided some break from the school's formal programme. However, when I came to interview pupils in the Newsom Department, I found that the access situation was more complex.

The only time that I could interview Newsom pupils or rather when pupils were prepared to be interviewed was during lessons (and preferably those lessons that they disliked). I therefore became involved in obtaining permission from teachers for pupils to be absent from classes to come and talk to me. However, in no case did I find a teacher who refused to allow Newsom pupils out of their classes, in fact the opposite was often true as several teachers asked, 'Would you like a few more?' This in itself testified to the reputation of Newsom pupils in the school (cf. Burgess, 1983). For the pupils used the research situation to their advantage by getting me to negotiate their release from particular classes that they disliked. In this respect, it was an extension of the process of negotiation that normally took place between Newsom pupils and teachers (cf. Burgess, 1983, pp. 208–35). This also illustrated the close links between data collection and methodological concerns and how access itself may be the consequence of negotiations between parties on the research site.

As I arranged for all interviews to be conducted in the fifth year core course time when English, Mathematics, Religious Education and Physical Education were taught, no pupils refused to be interviewed. To begin with, some of the pupils asked if the tape recordings that I made of our conversations would be played back to other teachers. I assured them that anything they told me would only be used for the purposes of research. However, some consideration needs to be given to the point that while my study does not give access to the identities of particular pupils, it will nevertheless give teachers in general public access to the 'private' world of Newsom pupils. In these terms, teachers may utilise this knowledge to handle pupil strategies, while pupils will not read a field study of a school to gain knowledge on how they might handle teacher strategies in the classroom. The public accessibility of data on schools and classrooms appears therefore to give even greater power to teachers than to pupils, regardless of the safeguards provided by researchers (cf. Burgess, 1984c; Davies, 1984).

Although I gave pupils my word that I would not tell their teachers about the things that they told me during interviews and conversations, there were still doubts. I was a part-time teacher as far as they were concerned and my word had to be 'tested'. Pupils, therefore, 'tested' me out by giving me information that to begin with was fairly innocuous and in some cases inaccurate to see if it would 'get back' to teachers. It was, therefore, not until later in the research period when I had passed their 'tests' that they would discuss their activities in any detail with me and I was given access to aspects of their lives in the school and classroom.

Finally, there was the question of access to documents. The Head had given formal agreement saying, 'You can see any documents that I've got except staff confidentials'. However, I found that all his documents (apart from confidential files on the staff) were located in the school secretary's office. On the first occasion that I visited the office I found that things were not as straightforward as the Head had suggested. After I had explained to the secretary what I was doing, I told her that the Head had agreed that I could use any of the files in her office. However, access was not immediate as she had not been told by the Head that I could use this material. Furthermore, she considered that 'There will be bloody hell to pay if the staff found out that you knew all about their salary scales'. She was not prepared to let me look at any files before checking with the Head to see if I did actually have access to 'her files'. Some days later when I was in the school, I went to the main office where the secretary told me that she had checked with the Head and I could look at whatever files I wanted. Access to documentary materials had, therefore, not been simple and straightforward as I had needed to renegotiate access with the secretary having initially negotiated access with the Headmaster. However, the situation was even more complex.

The files that were kept in the main school office were not neatly ordered. In this respect, I found that it was essential to sort much of the material into chronological order if I was to make sense of it. The school secretary was so appreciative of the fact that I had tidied up these files that she started to discuss some of the materials with me and to give me her version of the context in which some of the documents had been written. In addition, she could also provide the responses that had been made by some of the teachers. One day when the Headmaster was out of the school, she remarked, 'I bet you'd like to read some of the notes that the staff write to him [the Head] about all this'. I indicated that I had seen some notes from teachers to the

Head as they were located in various files in her office. However, she claimed that I had seen relatively few as the Headmaster kept most of the correspondence from individual teachers in their confidential files in his office. 'Wouldn't you like to see those?' she asked. I reminded her that the Head had said that I could read any files except the staff's confidential records. At this she laughed, went into his office and returned with a file. She started to read bits aloud from an individual teacher's confidential record and then passed it to me to read. In these circumstances, I considered that I had few options. If I had refused to read the file the secretary might have felt vulnerable as I could have told the Head about her action, but in turn I would also be vulnerable as she could claim that I had asked to read the file. There were also further problems for me if the Head returned while I was reading this file (cf. Burgess, 1981b). In this situation, I was confronted with an ethical dilemma which involved my relationship with the Headmaster and the secretary, both of whom I relied on for access to different dimensions of the research situation. Here, I decided that I had few choices but to break my agreement with the Head, as I thought that if I refused to read the file the secretary might discredit me with other members of the teaching staff. Certainly, I am open to criticism here for breaking my research agreement. However, in real research situations it is not possible for the researcher to follow a 'set of rules' to do research. Furthermore, I have not used any of the material that was lodged in that file during the course of writing up my study. Nevertheless, it can be argued that my interpretation of situations and of the roles that participants took within the school has been influenced by what I had read within the confidential file. Furthermore, questions can be raised about using this situation to illustrate methodological points in the text.

The main office contained only a selection of documents within the school, for files on individual pupils, copies of school reports and House business were kept by Heads of Houses. I decided that I needed to gain access to this material if I was to gain detailed documentary evidence on pupils. I began by approaching the Headmaster for permission to examine files kept by House Heads. While he had no objections to me seeking permission to examine files, he explained that he could not insist that I should see House files. Indeed, he explained that he always had to ask permission to read pupils' files. In these circumstances, access to House documents had to be negotiated with the six House Heads on six separate occasions. Here, I was given different degrees of access. In two Houses, I was merely left to sort through filing cabinets in order to decide what I wanted. In another House, I was given what the House Head described as 'juicy files' containing material such as educational welfare officers' reports, psychologists' reports and court records that she considered would be useful for my study. A further House Head requested that I should provide in advance details of individual files that I wanted, in order that they could be retrieved from the general system for my use on specified days. A fifth House Head gave me files on pupils in the Newsom Department, while the sixth House Head gave me access to all pupils' files but no other House documents. When the researcher obtains access to different kinds of data as in this situation, questions need to be raised concerning comparability (cf. Stacey, 1969c; Gittus, 1972).

Issues in Gaining Access

My research experience alerted me to several problems involved in starting research projects in general and in a school in particular. First, that access is not a straightforward procedure. Indeed, in the school, different approaches had to be made to individuals at different levels in the organisation. Access, therefore, involved negotiation and renegotiation. Secondly, that access influenced the kind of investigation which could be done and the position that I could take. Finally, that access occurred throughout the research process and as such generated other problems involved in doing field research (that is, selecting informants and observing situations). It is to these and other issues involved in gaining and managing access that I now turn using not only my research experiences but also those of other researchers in order to put the issues relating to access in a broader context.

Gaining access is an essential phase in the research process. For access is a prerequisite; a precondition for research to be conducted. Secondly, access influences the reliability and validity of the data that the researcher subsequently obtains. The points of contact which the researcher has with an institution, organisation or group will influence the collection of data and the subsequent perspective that can be portrayed. Finally, the activities that occur during this key phase of the research process will influence the ways in which those who are to be researched define the research and the activities of the researcher. The key issues involved in this phase of the research concern initial contacts, ethical considerations, gatekeepers, the presentation of the study and the research bargain, all of which are considered in turn.

Initial Contacts

In numerous studies the reasons for the selection of a particular research site are often quickly passed over. The only information that we are given is that access was 'gained' or 'presented no difficulties'. Yet in these circumstances, we need to consider *why* access was so straightforward. In some cases, the researcher already has contacts in a setting, as for example Otto Newman's contacts who gave him access to the betting shop in which he conducted the bulk of his observations (Newman, 1973). In other situations, individuals already have knowledge of the setting, as in Ditton's case where he had worked in the bakery in which he conducted his research (Ditton, 1977). Meanwhile, in some studies researchers have used their knowledge of a broad category of settings as a basis for negotiating access to a particular situation. Indeed, I would claim that this applies to my own study as I found that my former teacher status and my knowledge of schools facilitated access to Bishop McGregor School. Similarly, McNally (1979) reports that her experience as a 'temp' in several offices during her vacations helped her to gain access to secretarial staff who were 'temping' in offices. Finally, in some situations individuals' research work arises out of the situations in which they find themselves. A classic example of this would be Roth's experiences as a tuberculosis patient in a hospital. His patient status on the hospital ward gave him an opportunity to begin a study concerned with the organisation of life on the wards (cf. Roth, 1963, 1974).

However, there are also classic instances of failures to gain access that are reported in the literature (cf. Argyris, 1952; Blau, 1964; and Diamond, 1964). These cases are important as they allow us to consider what can be learned from the initial failure. For example, Blau (1964, pp. 24–7) discusses some of the blunders that he made during his initial entry to an organisation. In particular, he discusses how his failure to clarify his identity in the first two weeks of his work in that organisation resulted in a number of rumours circulating about him and his study. At this stage, he had not started to engage in observation but members of the organisation were already observing him. The result was that Blau learned from this experience how important it is for a field researcher to explain the purposes of a study from the first day in an organisation.

As well as researchers learning from their errors in the field, there is also the question of the implications that flow out of initial failures for subsequent approaches and the handling of field relations. Whyte (1955) reports in detail on one of his numerous false starts in beginning his classic study *Street Corner Society*. He writes as follows:

He [a researcher who was advising Whyte] also described how he would occasionally drop in on some drinking place in the area and strike up an acquaintance with a girl, buy her a drink, and then encourage her to tell him her life-story. He claimed that the women so encountered were appreciative of this opportunity and that it involved no further obligation.

This approach seemed at least as plausible as anything I had been able to think of. I resolved to try it out. I picked on the Regal Hotel, which was on the edge of Cornerville. With some trepidation I climbed the stairs to the bar and entertainment area and looked around. There I encountered a situation for which my adviser had not prepared me. There were women present all right, but none of them was alone. Some were there in couples, and there were two or three pairs of women together. I pondered this situation briefly. I had little confidence in my skill at picking up one female, and it seemed inadvisable to tackle two at the same time. Still, I was determined not to admit defeat without a struggle. I looked around me again and now noticed a threesome: one man and two women. It occurred to me that here was a maldistribution of females which I might be able to rectify. I approached the group and opened with something like this: 'Pardon me. Would you mind if I joined you?' There was a moment of silence while the man stared at me. He then offered to throw me downstairs. I assured him that this would not be necessary and demonstrated as such by walking right out of there without any assistance. (Whyte, 1955, p. 289)

This situation resulted in Whyte reconsidering his field tactics. Indeed, he also learned about certain features of the area that he was to study and in particular that no individual from Cornerville visited the Regal Hotel. As a consequence, he had to consider other ways in which he might gain access to the area and to the individuals which resulted in an approach through a settlement house that in turn brought him into contact with Doc (a key informant) who subsequently introduced him to other individuals within the area. Similar approaches have also been used by Patrick (1973) and by Pryce (1979) whose key informants have brought them into circulation within a particular area. However, in contrast to Whyte's study, both Patrick and Pryce have acted covertly, a situation that raises ethical issues to which we now turn.

Ethical Considerations in Gaining Access
Fundamental to the ethical questions surrounding research access is the dichotomy between covert and overt research. This debate will be discussed in greater detail in relation to the whole of the research process in Chapter 9. Meanwhile, in this instance we shall consider the implications of overt as against covert research activity in relation to gaining access.

The decision to do covert research is often posed as an alternative to overt research. However, I do not think it is as straightforward and simple as this would suggest. In some instances where access is openly negotiated not all individuals will know about a piece of research, nor will they all hold the same or similar interpretations about what is being done. Furthermore, some researchers may establish open access with some groups while closing off details about the research to other groups.

The cases of research access that are best known are those where covert research has been done, that is, cases where the researcher did not indicate his or her real intentions for being present in the group. In Britain, James Patrick's study of a Glasgow gang (Patrick, 1973) was done covertly as only Tim (his key informant) knew of his research intentions. Another case of covert activity is Wallis's study of the Church of Scientology (Wallis, 1976) in which a covert role was taken at the beginning of the research to see the ways in which scientologists processed an individual coming 'off the street' into their organisation. However, eventually Wallis decided that he could no longer continue with the deception and later returned to the organisation's headquarters and 'owned up' to the fact that he had been conducting research (Wallis, 1977).

Both instances together with classic examples of covert research in the USA (cf. Humphreys, 1970) are justified by the researchers concerned on the basis that the activities that they wanted to observe would be interrupted by overt research; that is, that the acknowledged presence of an observer would interfere with the 'normal' course of activities that were to be observed. Yet as Wallis (1977) indicates, the use of such a research stance limits the range of research activities. If a study is covert then the researcher only has access to those situations which are observed. In these circumstances, it is not possible to conduct interviews, collect life-histories or documentary evidence that is produced by the group. In short, covert research places limitations on the conduct of an investigation while bypassing the negotiation of access with a gatekeeper.

Gatekeepers

Gatekeepers are those individuals in an organisation that have the power to grant or withhold access to people or situations for the purposes of research. Some commentators (cf. Bogdan and Taylor, 1975) indicate that the researcher usually gains access to an organisation through the person who is in charge. However, as my field experience indicates, this is not always good advice. First, as in the case of school classrooms, it was not the headteacher who could grant or withhold access to these situations. Secondly, with regard to requests for documentary evidence, it was not just a question of dealing with the Headmaster. Here, the individuals who had control over different kinds of documentary materials had also to be negotiated with if access was to be achieved. In these terms, we cannot talk of *a* gatekeeper and *a* point of access. Instead, we need to think in terms of gatekeepers who can grant permission for the researcher to study different facets of the organisation. There are, therefore, multiple points of entry that require a continuous process of negotiation and renegotiation throughout the research. Research access is not merely granted or withheld at one particular point in time but is ongoing with the research (cf. Geer, 1970).

However, there are settings in which no gatekeeper, in the sense of an individual occupying a designated position in an organisation, is present. In particular, public settings involving street gangs have demanded a change in tactics. Whyte (1955), Liebow (1967), Patrick (1973) and Parker (1974) have all indicated how such research involves befriending an individual or a number of individuals who will sponsor them into a group and within the locality.

Finally, there are public settings such as towns, football matches, church services, school assemblies and parents' evenings when access cannot be successfully negotiated with all participants. In each instance, there is no opportunity for the researcher to have full permission to observe for research purposes in such settings. Indeed, even if formal announcements are made or negotiations conducted with town councils, football managers, the clergy or headteachers it still leaves vast numbers of people outside the research bargain. Negotiating directly with those on whom researchers intend to focus their studies is a difficult requirement to fulfil in a public setting.

In gaining access through different individuals detailed field notes need to be kept, for these initial encounters will help researchers to develop their research designs and to modify the questions that are posed within a field of study. The process of gaining access not only provides data that are of relevance in developing and understanding research methodology, but also yields data on the ways in which different individuals perceive an organisation or institution or neighbourhood (cf. Geer, 1964). This initial entry will also indicate ways in which newcomers are processed into an organisation. For example, in studying a hospital Minocha (1979) comments:

Having chosen the hospital, I sought permission from the authorities to study it. This turned out to be complicated and time-consuming. It took nearly three months before I was able to enter the wards. But the very process of obtaining permission gave me an idea of the medical and administrative hierarchies, the complicated linkages between different departments of the hospital and their relative autonomy, and the status and authority enjoyed by the incumbents of various offices. (Minocha, 1979, pp. 202–3)

Presenting the Study and Establishing a Research Bargain

In the course of gaining access, researchers have not only to present themselves but also their studies. In these circumstances, the question arises as to what should be discussed. In particular, researchers who intend to give informants access to their research need to indicate who they are and what they intend doing. In these terms, the role of the researcher and the content of the research needs to be explained. However, as the research develops and the role of the researcher is modified accordingly, so the account that is provided will be subject to change.

However, informants should not be subjected to a theoretical treatise or a research design, for sociologists have indicated the hazards involved in presenting studies in these terms (cf. Voss, 1966; Kleinman, 1980). Instead, a clear indication should be given of those aspects of the setting on which you intend to focus and those individuals with whom you intend to work most closely. In particular, attention should be drawn to the implications of your work for the setting and those within it.

At this point, some consideration needs to be given to the agreement or research bargain that is established between researcher and researched. Researchers should not conduct research in order to spy on the activities of others on behalf of the gatekeeper. Anonymity and confidentiality must be discussed with all individuals who agree to co-operate with social researchers. In this respect, even at the point of access the researcher should be able to give some indication of the different ways in which the research results will be used, for it is important to be able to assure informants that the organisation and the real names of individuals will remain confidential. The researcher is, therefore, immediately confronted with ethical problems that have to be resolved to the satisfaction of all the parties involved in the research setting.

Conclusion

This chapter has focused upon those research activities that occur at the beginning of a research programme. Accordingly, there has been some consideration given to the ways in which research problems are selected, the design of investigations and the conditions that are involved in bringing about access. Throughout the chapter, the points that are made within the literature have been considered in relation to examples drawn from my own work and the work of others in order to illustrate that actual research situations are much more complex than the way in which they are presented in the literature.

Indeed, the central dilemma for the field researcher at the start of a research project is that a research design has to be established for presentation to a funding body and in addition an account of the research has to be provided for those individuals who are to be researched if access is to be obtained. Yet often the researcher only has a broad idea of the research problem and the access that is required as the research problem will unfold throughout the project. The result is that the researcher's conception of the project is continually being modified. In this respect, the researcher is not just concerned with research design and research access at the beginning of a project but throughout the research process.

The accounts of gaining access that are provided by the different contributors to Habenstein (1970) indicate that research access varies with the researcher, those who are researched and the research problem. Nevertheless, it is possible to extract a series of general principles concerning research access. First, that access should not merely be negotiated with those who occupy the highest positions in a social situation but with individuals at different levels so as to avoid misunderstandings. Furthermore, in situations where different groups are involved it is essential to negotiate with all the parties so as to avoid accusations of bias and to prevent the research report being considered partisan. Secondly, it is important to develop an account of the research that is plausible to those involved. In turn, it is important to indicate to individuals any major changes in the direction of the research. Thirdly, attempts should be made to present an accurate account of the research design although this may not always be possible and compromise may be essential. Fourthly, the researcher needs to establish a clearly defined role and a work routine to promote the research. Finally, researchers need to monitor their own activities not only to understand the research process but to deepen their own understanding of the relationship between research questions and analyses, for data are derived and shaped in all these initial encounters. Such strategies for gaining access are intended to assist the researcher in developing research activities whilst collecting valid data.

Suggestions for Further Reading

Methodology

Bell, C. and Newby, H. (1977) (eds), *Doing Sociological Research* (London: Allen & Unwin); provides a collection of papers on the conduct of research. In particular the papers by Bell (1977) on the Banbury project and Newby (1977b) on his study of farm workers provide discussions of the relationship between pre-fieldwork and fieldwork.

Burgess, R. G. (1982) (ed.), *Field Research: a Sourcebook and Field Manual* (London: Allen & Unwin). See section one on starting field research which contains articles by the editor on the main issues and questions, by Devons and Gluckman (1964) on demarcating a field of study, by Spencer (1973) on gaining access to an elite group (at West Point Academy), and by Pons

(1969) on starting research in Avenue 21 in Kisangani (formerly Stanleyville).

Burgess, R. G. (1984) (ed.), *The Research Process in Educational Settings: Ten Case Studies* (Lewes: Falmer Press); provides essays from British researchers who have engaged in the study of classrooms, schools and curricula. Among the topics on which the editor invited the participants to focus is research access.

Habenstein, R. W. (1970) (ed.), *Pathways to Data* (Chicago: Aldine). A collection of essays by American field researchers who responded to particular questions raised by the editor. Among the issues considered is the question of access.

Johnson, J. M. (1975), *Doing Field Research* (New York: The Free Press); chapter 3 contains a critical evaluation of the American literature on gaining and managing research entrée based on the researcher's own experiences.

Moore, R. (1978), 'Sociologists Not at Work – Institutionalised Inability: A Case of Research Funding' in G. Littlejohn *et al.* (eds) *Power and the State* (London: Croom Helm), pp. 267–302; provides a discussion of the problems of research design and gaining access to research funds for a project on the social impact of North Sea Oil.

Schatzman, L. and Strauss, A. L. (1973), *Field Research: Strategies for a Natural Sociology* (Englewood Cliffs, NJ: Prentice-Hall). Contains a review of the tactics that the authors have used to bring about access.

Shaffir, W. B., Stebbins, R. A. and Turowetz, A. (1980) (eds), *Fieldwork Experience: Qualitative Approaches to Social Research* (New York: St Martin's Press); contains first-hand accounts of field research that include discussions of access. In particular see Kleinman (1980) and Hoffman (1980); the latter is especially interesting on gaining access to élites and boards of directors.

Empirical Studies

This chapter contains an argument that research design and the granting of research access occurs *throughout* a research project. However, it is rare to find accounts of research design and strategies for gaining access neatly detailed. Often these elements of the research process are implicit within the studies. The following studies should, therefore, be examined with a view to considering what principles of research design were used and how access was achieved:

Ditton, J. (1977), *Part-Time Crime: An Ethnography of Fiddling and Pilferage* (London: Macmillan).

Patrick, J. (1973), *A Glasgow Gang Observed* (London: Eyre-Methuen).

Pryce, K. (1979), *Endless Pressure* (Harmondsworth: Penguin).

Roth, J. A. (1963), *Timetables* (New York: Bobbs-Merrill).

Shipman, M. (1974), *Inside a Curriculum Project* (London: Methuen).

Whyte, W. F. (1981), *Street Corner Society* (3rd edn) (Chicago: University of Chicago Press).

3

Selection Strategies in Field Research

Field research takes place in social situations in which the researcher participates. Here, it is the task of the researcher to observe and record the life of the people as it occurs. However, in these circumstances selection is inevitable as field researchers need to define their field of study and to narrow the focus of their work. In these terms, researchers must continually decide when, where, what and whom to observe and interview. It is these aspects of field research that are crucial throughout the research process and will be the subject of consideration in this chapter. One of the main problems that confronts researchers working in the field has been neatly summarised by Naroll and Cohen (1973) who remark:

> Unfortunately, the people do not have the responsibility of analyzing and categorizing their social and cultural experience and therefore cannot sort their own behaviour or responses to questions into neat packages for placement into a filing system or an analytical framework. (Naroll and Cohen, 1973, p. 9)

It is the focus upon natural settings which presents the field researcher with problems of selection and control over the data that are collected. Field researchers are therefore constantly having to select locations, time periods, events and people for study. The result is that while some elements of the situation and sections of the population are included in a study, others are excluded. It is this set of activities involving principles of selection that brings the field researcher directly up against a consideration of sampling. However, it is rare to find a systematic discussion of the principles of selection that were used in a particular study, as it is generally assumed that the 'sample' is broadly 'representative' of a larger universe of actions, events and people. Yet such a procedure automatically meets with objections concerning the representativeness of the units of study. Field researchers need, therefore, to defend their actions by discussing the principles by which they select some situations, events and people but reject others while working in the field.

It is never possible for the researcher to be able to study all the people and all the events in a social situation. While a researcher may have general access to a research setting, it may not automatically mean that access is given to every person and every event on a research site (see Chapter 2). Furthermore, there may well be restrictions of time and money with the result that sampling procedures become essential. The events, situations and people which a researcher decides to observe usually depend upon the researcher's theoretical and substantive interests which will result in the use of different sampling strategies. Accordingly, field researchers have engaged in probability sampling, non-probability sampling and theoretical sampling.

There are certain procedures and principles that are common to all these approaches. First, the researcher's observations should be theoretically directed. Secondly, it is important for the researcher to be able to locate and enumerate the main units of study. Thirdly, the sample must be representative of the universe from which it is drawn. Fourthly, researchers should remain in the field until a theory is adequately tested or developed. Fifthly, behaviour should be sampled in natural settings so that the observations which are made will be relevant to the theoretical perspective. Sixthly, sampling should whenever and wherever possible be comparative; and finally, researchers should make public their sampling procedures so that an assessment may be made of the selection procedures used (cf. Denzin, 1970a). Certainly these are principles which any field researcher would do well to keep in mind, but it is important to remember that different degrees of emphasis will be given to different principles depending upon the research problem which is to hand together with the substantive and theoretical interests of the researcher. With these principles in mind we turn to some of the main strategies of sampling involved in field research.

Sampling Strategies

There is a range of technical terminology used in discussions of sampling and distinctions are made between various forms of sampling procedure. This section will, therefore, provide a brief guide to this terminology drawing special attention to sampling procedures used in field research. The basic distinction that is made by researchers is between probability and non-probability methods of sampling. In *Probability Sampling* every unit in the universe under study has the same calculable and non zero probability of being selected. Meanwhile, with *Non-probability Sampling* there is no means of estimating the probability of units being included in the sample. Indeed, there is no guarantee that every element has a chance of being studied. While both these forms of sampling have been used by field researchers, it is non-probability sampling that is more often used and includes:

Judgement and Opportunistic Sampling. These forms of non-probability sampling involve the selection of actions, events and people. In judgement sampling informants may be selected for study according to a number of criteria established by the researcher such as their status (age, sex and occupation) or previous experience that endows them with special knowledge. The researcher therefore requires a detailed knowledge of the universe from which to draw individuals who have distinct qualifications as informants. Meanwhile, opportunistic sampling is used to refer to the process whereby field researchers find informants who provide them with their data. Here, the researcher selects individuals with whom it is possible to cooperate. In these terms, replication is impossible as the researcher selects individuals who are available and who are willing to cooperate with the research.

Snowball Sampling Once again, this relies on a researcher's knowledge of a social situation. This approach involves using a small group of informants who are asked to put the researcher in touch with their friends who are subsequently interviewed, then asking them about their friends and interviewing them until a chain of informants has been selected. As Coleman (1958) indicates, such a sampling procedure follows the pattern of social relations in a particular setting and therefore the population in the sample involves individuals *and* relations among individuals.

These non-probability sampling procedures are among the most common found in field research. However, there are great variations involved depending upon the researcher, the problem of study and the theoretical perspective used.

Glaser and Strauss (1967) have suggested that researchers can also use *Theoretical Sampling.* They define theoretical sampling as

> the process of data collection for generating theory whereby the analyst jointly collects, codes and analyzes his data and decides what data to collect next and where to find them, in order to develop his theory as it emerges. (Glaser and Strauss, 1967, p. 45)

In these circumstances, data collection is controlled by the emerging theory and the researcher has to consider: What groups or subgroups are used in data collection? For what theoretical purpose are the groups or subgroups used? Theoretical sampling therefore involves researchers in observing groups with a view to extending, modifying, developing and verifying theory.

It is this approach that Smith and Pohland (1976) consider to be one of the most significant contributions to field research. For in their view, Glaser and Strauss's term 'theoretical sampling' formalises various activities that they consider are important in field studies: having enough evidence, having enough data in a particular area, and deciding when to move on to other related problems. They indicate that in Smith and Keith's study of Kensington School this involved focusing on pupils of different age levels or divisions, examining independent study versus tradition versus basic skills and focusing on matters that were internal to the school and external to it (Smith and Keith, 1971).

A number of concepts are associated with theoretical sampling including 'saturation' and 'slices of data'. The term 'saturation' is regarded by many researchers as being particularly helpful as it refers to the fact that no additional data can be found that contribute to the categories being considered. However, the major problem associated with this notion is that it assumes that researchers know in advance what categories can be used in a study (Smith and Pohland, 1976). The way in which Smith and Pohland resolved this issue was by focusing on situations until no further insights could be generated. In turn, Glaser and Strauss's concept of 'slices of data' which they define as 'different kinds of data [that] give the analyst different views or vantage points from which to understand a category and to develop its properties' (Glaser and Strauss, 1967, p. 65) is of importance as it has much in common with a multi-method strategy that can be adopted by researchers (see Chapter 7). Indeed, Smith and Pohland (1976) indicate the way in which their studies have used this approach in order to obtain valid pictures of social settings.

Field researchers thus have a number of sampling strategies from which to choose. Researchers are, therefore, engaged in different activities depending on the sampling procedures they adopt. However, we need to consider how these different forms of sampling are actually used in field research, for special problems associated with natural settings mean that these sampling strategies cannot be directly applied to field research but require some modification on the part of the researcher. It is to the use of these strategies and the problems that are involved in applying them to field settings that we now turn.

The Problem of Sampling in Field Research

One of the clearest expositions of sampling problems in field research is provided by Becker (1970c) who discusses the key issues involved in the study of vice and crime. He begins by pointing out that in studying deviance there are no definitive lists of participants. Indeed, he considers that the limits, locations and units of study are only known to the researcher in a fragmentary way with the result that conventional sampling theory has not been able to address the problems involved. However, he considers it doubtful whether a mathematical approach would be appropriate in these circumstances and indicates how sampling strategies need to be based on the sociological characteristics of the population that are of interest to the researcher.

Becker (1970c) identifies six strategies by which the researcher may sample the group that is to be studied. First, he indicates that access through a role in private life may open up opportunities for snowball sampling. Here, he cites his own work on marijuana users (Becker, 1963) which was started by using contacts that he had made as a dance musician. Similarly, Polsky (1969) used his abilities as a billiard player to start to collect data on fellow players. In both these instances, the researchers knew individuals who could be observed and interviewed and who in turn were willing to pass the researcher through their social network in order to observe and interview their associates. However, in these circumstances the representativeness of the data collected depends upon the extent to which all those who should be studied exist in a complete social network. In such situations it is, therefore, more likely that a particular subgroup is studied (see the section below on locating people).

In studying deviance, a second strategy that Becker recommends for gaining access to a large sample is to study incarcerated deviants. However, bias exists in such a group, for the deviants that are studied are unsuccessful; they have been caught! The result is that the sample available may be unrepresentative of all deviant individuals. Furthermore, there is the question of the reliability of the data that are obtained from a group who are imprisoned – how far does what they say match up to what they *actually* did?

Thirdly, it is possible to utilise a random sample of the population to study particular activities but, as Becker indicates, this is a particularly wasteful method as some deviant activities such as heroin use and incest may not be sufficiently represented within a random sample of the population for this to be a good use of a researcher's time and resources. Such an approach is therefore only useful when a researcher is interested in the distribution of a variety of deviant activities or deviant activities that are common to large groups. A strategy that is a variant on the former approach is to advertise to interview deviants, but here one might consider the extent to which reliable data are obtained, for in these circumstances they are only obtained from willing volunteers. It is this approach that has been used by sex researchers (cf. Kinsey, Pomeroy and Martin, 1948; Kinsey, Pomeroy, Martin and Gebhard, 1953; Hite, 1977) who have been criticised on the grounds that their work does not include all those experiences and types of individuals who might be found in the universe (cf. Geddes, 1954 on the Kinsey report). This approach may, therefore, be of limited use. A further variant of this approach is to provide some service for the individual in return for research data. For example, Bogdan (1974) provided legal services for the transsexual Jane Fry. However, doubt can be cast upon the representativeness of the individuals who participate in such relationships with researchers.

Finally, Becker suggests that one way to avoid the problems associated with the other procedures is for researchers to locate themselves in natural settings where observation can occur, a strategy that he considers neatly solves the problem of sampling. However, Becker appears to have overlooked several assumptions that are made here. First, that boundaries can be clearly established in a field of study. Secondly, that activities can be easily studied. Thirdly, that individuals who are representative of the group studied are present. Fourthly, that the setting remains 'natural' once an observer becomes involved and, finally, that the setting is 'representative'.

Researchers who have worked in natural settings and who have reflected on their selection strategies indicate that there are many problems to resolve. For example, Hammersley considers some of these problems in relation to his research in a school staff room (Hammersley, 1981). Here, the researcher spent break times and lunch times in the staff room on days when he was in the school. In addition, he also spent time (when he had no lessons to observe) sitting in the staff room. However, he indicates the problems involved with this approach in a reflective essay (Hammersley, 1984) when he states:

> There is unintentional and unprincipled sampling involved here: questions can be raised about how representative the exchanges I recorded were of the whole body of staff talk even during the two terms when I was in the school. (Hammersley, 1984, p. 52)

Hammersley continues by recommending strategies to overcome these problems. In particular, he suggests randomly sampling inter-action among staff over time, and using incidents from the staff room on randomly chosen days and at randomly chosen times. Such strategies as these highlight the fact that field researchers working in informal settings cannot obtain neat lists of names for the members of the groups they wish to study. Indeed, there are no neat boundaries to their research locations, and few fixed activities to observe at set times. In this sense, field researchers need to consider the locations, times, events and people that are studied. In turn this leads on to a consideration of sampling procedures that are used to study social situations and to a discussion of the control which the researcher has over the units of study. It is to these strategies that we now turn.

The Selection of Research Locations *A*

To begin a field study a research site needs to be selected. Indeed, those who fund research, such as the SSRC, insist as a minimum requirement that researchers should have access to a research setting. Here, it is important to consider why one location is chosen rather than another. Often field researchers indicate that their focus upon social processes means that they are not concerned about whether a site is 'typical' or 'representative'. As a result, research sites may be selected where individuals are willing to cooperate, where the situation is convenient for the researcher and where the researcher has some contacts already established. For example, my research was not initially planned to be conducted in a Roman Catholic school. I had decided that I wanted to focus on a comprehensive school and on work with non-academic pupils. However, in the first few months of starting my research I met the Headmaster of Bishop McGregor School who invited me to visit his school. McGregor was a comprehensive school that had made provision for non-academic pupils. Furthermore, the Headmaster was willing for me to join his staff in order that I could teach and do research. In these terms, the conditions seemed to provide a suitable research base since members of the school were interested in my project and the Headmaster was willing for me to do research in the school (Burgess, 1984c).

In a similar way, Shipman (1981) indicates how convenience determined his choice of a research site when he made a seven-year follow up study of the college of education in which he worked (Shipman, 1967). This he admits was an arbitrary choice which placed limitations on the extent to which generalisation was possible. There are also instances where researchers conduct studies in situations where access is relatively easy. For example, Wakeford (1969) reports how his study of an independent school was conducted in an institution which he had attended as a pupil, which his brother had attended and where he was a member of the old boys' association. These are but three examples from countless field studies where the willingness of members of the institution to cooperate with the researcher, convenience and ease of access influence the choice of the location.

Many field studies appear to be located on a single site: a factory, a hospital, a school or a town. Yet each of these sites may include numerous subsites whose choice may influence data collection. For example, Strauss *et al.* (1964) indicate that in studying a hospital a researcher will be continually confronted with questions of selection such as:

> Which wards should he observe? If one ward, should he stay at the nurses' station or move around to other locations on the ward? Should he make rounds of other locales? Should he attend meetings? Which ones? And where should he eat or have coffee? (Strauss *et al.*, 1964, p. 23)

Indeed, they go on to argue that studying a single location within a hospital allows the researcher to focus on the social rhythm, the pattern of events and expected behaviour as well as the crises that occur. However, they maintain that a number of locations need to be selected for study in order that a broad perspective of the institution can be obtained. In these terms, researchers who select a single location need to consider the social networks and clusters of situations that are involved (Spradley, 1980).

My own study of a purpose-built comprehensive school located on one site may appear to involve research in a single setting. However, the school was divided into a number of separate buildings and included: six Houses as well as departments for academic, non-academic and practical subjects. In this sense, selection was involved in making decisions about working in particular Houses and certain Departments. At McGregor, the House Heads consisted of three men and three women and therefore intensive studies were done of one House that had a man as Head of House and one House that had a woman as Head of House. This allowed me to make some comparisons between two Houses and two House Heads. As far as departments were concerned, I made a detailed study of the Newsom Department for less able children as I was aware that many earlier studies of schools had focused on academic subject departments rather than non-academic departments (cf. Ball, 1984). However, in order to contextualise my observations in the Newsom Department I also took substitution lessons in a variety of other departments drawn from the Arts/Humanities group and the Science/Technical groups. Obviously such a selection was not strictly representative of the whole school but did allow some comparison to be made between the major groups.

As well as social situations being linked together by physical location, they are also connected because the same people participate in different locations (Spradley, 1980). For example, the Newsom pupils that I studied were all members of the school but they were also members of Houses, subject departments and the Newsom

Department. In order to study the network of social situations in which Newsom pupils were involved, I needed to focus on the different locations in which they worked (cf. Burgess, 1983; especially part two). Social situations can also be linked together on the basis of similar activities. For example, I found that the Newsom pupils had developed strategies for passing time in school that were common to many classrooms. Accordingly, I examined how the same group of pupils passed their time in different classes: Newsom classes, English classes (an academic subject in the core curriculum) and a Physical Education class (a practical subject within the core curriculum). Here, the focus was upon the activities that were common to the different locations.

The selection of research sites is, therefore, more complex than might at first appear. Five criteria can be identified in the selection of a research site (Spradley, 1980). First, simplicity; that is a research site that allows researchers to move from studying simple situations to those which are more complex. Secondly, accessibility; that is the degree of access and entry that is given to the researcher. Thirdly, unobtrusiveness; that is situations that allow the researcher to take an unobtrusive role. Fourthly, permissibleness; that is situations that allow the researcher free or limited or restricted entry. Fifthly, participation; that is the possibility for researchers to participate in a series of ongoing activities. However, it is rare for the researcher to be able to meet all these criteria in selecting a social setting and therefore some compromise is essential depending on the substantive and theoretical interests of the researcher together with the constraints on his or her work.

The Selection of Time: Time Sampling

The activities that occur within a social organisation may vary according to time, each organisation having its own social rhythm. The time dimension is ever present in all field situations. For example, hospitals have routines that are associated with set times: visiting hours, meal times, staff meetings and shift changes. It is rhythms such as these that need to be considered by the researcher. However, the researcher has to decide whether to make continuous observations or to engage in some form of sampling. In short, researchers have to monitor whether they focus upon continuous, regularly recurrent or irregular processes (cf. Strauss *et al.*, 1964).

Meanwhile, in schools researchers need to take note of the three-term cycle and its influence upon timetables and related activities. Here, there are differences between the activities of the autumn, spring and summer terms, between the beginning and end of term, between the start of a week and its end, and the beginning and end of days. Furthermore, within each day there are further subdivisions between morning and afternoon school, between lessons before and after break and within specific time periods in individual lessons.

Schools in common with many other social institutions have sets of activities that are determined by time periods. In these circumstances, researchers need to consider the way in which particular periods of time may influence the activities that are observed. For example, Ball (1980) has demonstrated the importance of research that involves observing the first classroom encounters between teachers and pupils at the start of a new term in a new academic year. In particular, he demonstrates how by focusing on this particular time period it may influence our understanding of teacher–pupil interaction. Meanwhile, Burgess (1983, pp. 101–14) has demonstrated how a detailed analysis of the last week of the academic year in the summer term may contribute to our understanding of the 'normal' pattern of social relations in a school. Such examples highlight the importance of considering not only *what* activities occur but *when* they occur.

Indeed, detailed accounts over short periods may chart particular activities in relation to time. For example, Cleary (1979) uses diary records to detail the time period of the distress symptoms of a 4-year-old boy who is moved from an individual cubicle on a hospital ward into the main ward. The time period of the child's distress is recorded as follows:

9.10 p.m.	Nurse to Richard for blood pressure, etc. He cries when disturbed, especially for bp.
9.20	Richard starts crying, 'Mammy'.
	Fat staff nurse: 'Do you want to wee-wee?'
	'No.'
	'What are you crying for, then?' 'Mammy.'
	'She'll be coming in the morning when it's light.'
9.32	Richard still crying.
9.35	Staff: 'Richard be quiet.'
9.40	Richard, crying more quietly for a little, now gets louder again. Michael (aged 11) calls to Richard, goes to him, offers water – 'No'. Tries to distract him by asking teddy's name, but he just calls 'Mammy' and 'Daddy'.
	Michael misunderstands – 'Mandy', 'Dandy?' – then realising says, 'Daddy can't come till you've gone to sleep, and I bet you he'll be here when you wake up'.
	Staff: 'Daddy will be here in the morning when it's light'. To observer: 'When they're in a cubicle you can shut the door and get a bit of peace'.

9.45	Richard still crying. (No one has explained to him that his bed has been moved from the cubicle while he was asleep; he is looking around anxiously as well as crying.)
9.55	Auxiliary to Richard, she strokes his head. Calming gradually. Staff stands by cot for a moment.
10.00	Auxiliary still stroking Richard. Staff and auxiliary talk to observer about night work; 'We've got three on tonight when it's quiet; would have been glad earlier in the week when we were busy'. Daniel starts making muttering noises, disturbs Michael and Richard, who was nearly asleep. Auxiliary goes to quieten Daniel and Richard starts crying hard again. Michael says: 'Be quiet, Daniel. There's a good boy, you just woke the baby up.'
10.05	Auxiliary leaves Richard and he cries again.
10.20	Staff is with Richard, reminds him that his mother gave him jelly today and he starts to cry for jelly, but when offered jelly he cries 'Mammy' again. Staff says: 'If you don't shut up I'll give you something to cry for'. Looks a bit sick when she remembers observer, but says, 'I've tried reason, now I'll try threats'. Night superintendent on round sits by cot, tries the usual line about Mammy coming tomorrow, talks about teddy and toy car. Asks Staff if he has been asleep and just woken up. 'Yes' (in fact just about an hour). Offers horse but he responds to everything with 'I want Mammy'.
10.30	Auxiliary back with Richard. He repeats continuously, 'I want my Mammy'.
10.35	She leaves him, he clutches the car, crying fairly quietly 'My Mammy, my Mammy'.
10.40	Richard sits up. Staff comes to look at him, does not go close – 'Better if they don't see us'. Observer asks if his being moved while asleep might have upset him. 'Of course, I didn't know that had happened. I wish they wouldn't do that. Often a child is worried that his mother won't find him when he's moved from a cubicle anyway.'
10.50	Richard quiet. (Cleary, 1979, pp. 119–20)

Such a detailed account over time allows the researcher to chart staff–patient interaction. Indeed, on the basis of this episode together with other sets of detailed observations over time Cleary (1979) is able to conclude that there is a time limit on reassurance and comforting. Furthermore, she is able to portray how distress gets redefined as naughtiness and therefore becomes undeserving of sympathy within a given period.

Even more detailed time sampling has been done by Pill and reported in Stacey *et al.* (1970) in studying hospital wards. Here, Pill devised a system to study children during the period 7.00 am to 7.00 pm which was defined as the children's waking hours. The time period was divided into twenty-minute intervals and during five minutes of each of these intervals the child's interaction was recorded in detail for a five-second period. Such a system required a detailed pre-coded observation sheet divided into sixty separate horizontal rows, an extract of which is provided in Figure 3.1.

Such a system of detailed systematic observation over time can also be made in structured time settings such as individual lessons in school classrooms in which interaction is recorded at pre-determined times using pre-coded categories. There are a number of systems that can be used, among which the best known in the USA are those devised by Simon and Boyer (1967, 1970) and by Flanders (1970) in which pre-coded categories of behaviour or check lists of events are provided for the researcher to use. The Flanders system involves a researcher watching a teacher during a lesson and every three seconds the researcher is required to write down the category number for the interaction involved. This involves writing down twenty numbers per minute. Obviously, such a system requires some training using audio tapes and videotapes before going into a classroom. The main categories established by Flanders are shown below:

Table 3.1   *Flanders's Interaction Analysis Categories* (FIAC)*

	1 *Accepts feeling.* Accepts and clarifies an attitude or the feeling tone of a pupil in a nonthreatening manner. Feelings may be positive or negative. Predicting and recalling feelings are included.
Response	2 *Praises or encourages.* Praises or encourages pupil action or behavior. Jokes that release tension, but not at the expense of another individual; nodding head, or saying "Um hm?" or "go on" are included.
	3 *Accepts or uses ideas of pupils.* Clarifying, building, or developing ideas suggested by a pupil. Teacher extensions of pupil ideas are included but as the teacher brings more of his own ideas into play, shift to category five.
Teacher Talk	4 *Asks questions.* Asking a question about content or procedure, based on teacher ideas, with the intent that a pupil will answer.

Table 3.1 (*continued*)

Teacher Talk (*contd.*)	5 *Lecturing.* Giving facts or opinions about content or procedures; expressing *his own* ideas, giving *his own* explanation, or citing an authority other than a pupil.
Initiation	6 *Giving directions.* Directions, commands, or orders to which a pupil is expected to comply.
	7 *Criticizing or justifying authority.* Statements intended to change pupil behavior from nonacceptable to acceptable pattern; bawling someone out, stating why the teacher is doing what he is doing; extreme self-reference.
Response	8 *Pupil-talk-response.* Talk by pupils in response to teacher. Teacher initiates the contact or solicits pupil statement or structures the situation. Freedom to express own ideas is limited.
Pupil Talk Initiation	9 *Pupil-talk-initiation.* Talk by pupils which they initiate; expressing own ideas; initiating a new topic; freedom to develop opinions and a line of thought, like asking thoughtful questions; going beyond the existing structure.
Silence	10 *Silence or confusion.* Pauses, short periods of silence and periods of confusion in which communication cannot be understood by the observer.

* There is *no* scale implied by these numbers. Each number is classificatory; it designates a particular kind of communication event. To write these numbers down during observation is to enumerate, not to judge a position on a scale.
Source: Flanders (1970).

This scheme makes certain assumptions that have been discussed by Flanders. First, that the system is designed for classifying interaction which is defined as public talk involving more than one person. Secondly, the analysis is based on teacher talk. As a consequence this pre-coded system when used will result in some elements of bias in the analysis as the focus is upon teachers' activities in classrooms that are formally organised.

However, as Delamont and Hamilton (1976) indicate, this style of work does have strengths and weaknesses. In positive terms such systems are simple, well tried and easy to use, especially when large numbers of classrooms are involved. Accordingly, statistical data can be produced which can refer to samples and populations. For example, on the basis of the data that are collected a researcher can compute the amount of time during the observation period that a particular kind of verbal interaction occurred and the strategies that a teacher used to initiate talk. Indeed, the Flanders system has the potential to address such questions as: how often do pupils talk in the classroom? How much do pupils talk in comparison with teachers?

Figure 3.1 Observation Sheet

NAME.. People in Ward at beginning of sample

Date.......................... Day.......... ....

....

Time	Child on own	Position	Interaction with other children	Interaction with nurses		Interaction with other people (doctors, sister, domestic, technicians, porters, parents – specify)		Who comes into Ward and who leaves
				As individual	As one of group	As individual	As one of group	
1								1
2								2
3								3
4								4
5								5
6								6
7								7
8								8
9								9
10								10
11								11
12								12
13								13
14								14
15								15
16								16
17								17
18								18
19								19
20								20

What is the pattern of pupil talk with each other and with the teacher? How does the teacher reinforce pupil verbal behaviour? What strategies does the teacher use to initiate pupil discussion? In this sense, the Flanders system would appear to have the potential to analyse communication strategies in the classroom. However there are a number of restrictions and limitations to such systems among which Delamont and Hamilton include the fact that the data gathered are divorced from their social and historical context, are only concerned with overt observable behaviour, are only concerned with what can be categorised or measured, are limited to the pre-defined categories and are static. In these terms, they have reservations about the origin, use and assumptions associated with interaction analysis. The use of such instruments by field researchers may, therefore, generate statistical data, but some consideration needs to be given to the problems which may accompany those data that are collected.

Meanwhile, in Britain systematic observation systems that utilise a twenty-five second time-sampling unit have been used on the Observational Research and Classroom Learning Evaluation (ORACLE) project on primary education (Galton, Simon and Croll, 1980). Here, separate systematic observation categories have been developed in a pupil record (see Table 3.2) and a teacher record (see Table 3.3).

Table 3.2   *The Observation Categories of the Pupil Record.*

Coding the pupil–adult categories		
Category	*Item*	*Brief definition of item*
1 Target's role	INIT	Target attempts to become focus of attention (not focus at previous signal)
	STAR	Target is focus of attention
	PART	Target in audience (no child is focus)
	LSWT	Target in audience (another child is focus)
2 Interacting adult	TCHR	Target interacts with teacher
	OBSR	Target interacts with observer
	OTHER	Target interacts with any other adult such as the head or secretary
3 Adult's interaction	TK WK	Adult interacts about task work (task content or supervision)
	ROUTINE	Adult interacts about routine matters (classroom management and control)
	POS	Adult reacts positively to task work (praises)
	NEG	Adult reacts negatively to behaviour, etc. (criticizes)
	IGN	Adult ignores attempted initiation

Table 3.2 (*continued*)

Coding the pupil–adult categories

Category		Item	Brief definition of item
4	Adult's communica- tion setting	IND ATT	Adult gives private individual attention to target pupil
		GROUP	Adult gives private attention to target's group
		CLASS	Adult interacts with whole class
		OTHER	Adult gives private attention to another child or group or does not interact
5	Target's role	BGNS	Target successfully begins a new contact
		COOP	Target co-operates by responding to an initiation
		TRIES	Target unsuccessfully tries to initiate
		IGN	Target ignores attempted initiation
		SUST	Target sustains interaction
6	Mode of interaction	MTL	Non-verbal, mediated solely by materials
		CNTC	Non-verbal, mediated by physical contact or gesture (with or without materials)
		VRB	Verbal (with or without materials, physical contact or gesture)
7a	Task of other pupil(s)	S TK	Same as target's task
		D TK	Different to target's task
7b	Sex and number of other pupil(s)	SS	Target interacts privately with one pupil of same sex
		OS	Target interacts privately with one pupil of opposite sex
		SEV SS	Target interacts publicly with two or more pupils having same sex as target
		SEV OS	Target interacts publicly with two or more pupils, of whom one at least is of the opposite sex to the target
7c	Base of other pupil(s)	OWN BS	From target's own base
		OTH BS	From another base

Coding the activity and location categories

8	Target's activity	COOP TK	Fully involved and co-operating on approved task work (e.g. reading)
		COOP R	Fully involved and co-operating on approved routine work (e.g. sharpening a pencil)
		DSTR	Non-involved and totally distracted from all work

Table 3.2 (continued)

Coding the activity and location categories

Category		Item	*Brief definition of item*
		DSTR OBSR	Non-involved and totally distracted from all work by the observer
		DSRP	Non-involved and aggressively disrupting work of other pupil(s)
		HPLY	Non-involved and engaging in horseplay with other pupil(s)
		WAIT TCHR	Waiting to interact with the teacher
		CODS	Partially co-operating and partially distracted from approved work
		INT TCHR	Interested in teacher's activity or private interaction with other pupil(s)
		INT PUP	Interested in the work of other pupil(s)
		WOA	Working on an alternative activity which is not approved work
		RIS	Not coded because the target is responding to internal stimuli
		NOT OBS	Not coded because the target is not observed for some reason
		NOT LIST	Not coded because the target's activity is not listed
9	Target's location	P IN	Target in base
		P OUT	Target out of base but not mobile
		P MOB	Target out of base and mobile
		P OUT RM	Target out of room
10	Teacher activity and location	T PRES	Teacher present with target through interaction or physical proximity
		T ELSE	Teacher privately interacting elsewhere with other pupil(s) or visitor
		T MNTR	Teacher not interacting but monitoring classroom activities
		T HSKP	Teacher not interacting but housekeeping
		T OUR RM	Teacher out of room

Source: Galton, Simon and Croll (1980), pp. 12–13.

Galton, Simon and Croll (1980) report that the pupil record was used to focus on eight previously selected 'target pupils' who were observed in order in each classroom and their behaviour was coded at twenty-five second intervals using a multiple coding method. In order that observers could code at designated time intervals these were pre-recorded on tape and fed to the observer through an ear piece attached to a tape recorder. Furthermore, during each observation session observers were required to observe pupils for ten time signals and teachers for forty-five signals. However, to observe teachers, the observers used the teacher record as shown in Table 3.3. This record was designed to focus attention on the teacher contact with pupils. Here, the same twenty-five second time intervals were used and at each signal the observer noted down the type of conversation and the silent interaction that occurred in the classroom. Such an approach demands a period of training (Galton, Simon and Croll, 1980, pp. 166–71) as it is a highly structured approach that has been conducted by ten observers.

Table 3.3   *The Observation Categories of the Teacher Record.*

Conversation		*Silence*
Questions		Silent Interaction
Task		Gesturing
Q1	recalling facts	Showing
Q2	offering ideas, solutions (closed)	Marking
Q3	offering ideas, solutions (open)	Waiting
Task supervision		Story
Q4	referring to task supervision	Reading
Routine		Not observed
Q5	referring to routine matters	Not coded
Statements		No Interaction
Task		Adult interaction
S1	of facts	Visiting pupil
S2	of ideas, problems	Not interacting
Task supervision		Out of room
S3	telling child what to do	Audience
S4	praising work or effort	Composition
S5	feedback on work or effort	Activity
Routine		
S6	providing information, directions	
S7	providing feedback	
S8	of critical control	
S9	of small talk	

Source: Galton, Simon and Croll (1980), p. 17.

It is this approach that has been used to conduct much of the research that is reported in the first three books on the project findings (Galton, Simon and Croll, 1980; Galton and Simon, 1980; and Simon and Willcocks, 1981). Meanwhile, as Galton and Delamont (1984) demonstrate, this approach has also been linked up with ethno-graphic observational data when school transfer was considered (Galton and Willcocks, 1983). At first sight it may appear that systematic observation using time-sampling has little to do with field research. However, it is in the ORACLE project that there is an attempt at establishing relations between 'systematic' and 'ethnographic' research and at using multiple strategies of research (Galton and Delamont, 1984). In these instances the researchers have taken account of time units in relation to the individuals and activities that were observed with the result that comparisons can be made between actions and activities over time and between data collected in structured and unstructured ways.

The Selection of Events

A further unit of study on which field researchers need to focus is the behaviour of those persons who are observed. Here, behaviour may, as with time-sampling, be examined in an unstructured or a structured way, each of which will be considered in turn.

Schatzman and Strauss (1973) have subdivided the behaviour that researchers can observe into three groups. First, routine events, that is activities that are part of the daily round of life. Within a school this could include such daily activities as school assembly (cf. Burgess, 1983; pp. 26–51 and 52–83) and break time conversation. At such times the researcher becomes involved not just in non-probability sampling of events but also in theoretical sampling. Hammersley (1984) demonstrates this point when he discusses how in focusing on staff room conversation he tried to keep notes on those conversations that were relevant to the school, to teaching and to pupils. As Hammersley indicates, this is a sampling process which is

intentional, systematic and theoretically guided

but he continues by pointing to the problems involved in this process as he remarks,

I may well have not recognised things which were actually very relevant or very useful indicators, and my conception of what was relevant may have changed over the course of the fieldwork (there is no solid basis for checking whether this is the case). (Hammersley, 1984, p. 53)

A second category of behaviour on which individuals may focus are special events which Schatzman and Strauss consider are fortuitous but anticipated. In terms of the cycle of events in the academic year of a school this may include the religious festivals of harvest, Christmas and Easter which may bring with them special services, concerts and charity collections. In Bishop McGregor School, Lent was not only a period when special Masses were held but also when the Lenten Charities Collection took place. By focusing on the Charities Collection I was able to highlight the relationships that existed between the six House Heads, their relationships with other teachers and with pupils (cf. Burgess, 1983, pp. 66–9). Similarly, if researchers focus on sports days and sports matches between staff and pupils, they may be used to highlight the pattern of social relations that occur in other areas of the school (cf. Woods, 1979, pp. 221–3). In short, special events in a school may lead a researcher towards focusing on ritual occasions associated with schooling and which may highlight aspects of school organisation: norms, values and routines (cf. Bernstein, Elvin and Peters, 1966).

Thirdly, researchers may focus upon untoward events which include emergencies, dramatic situations, and crises which are not anticipated. Here, researchers can utilise the extended case method (Gluckman, 1961) which, it is argued, allows us to examine a series of connecting cases to see the ways in which relationships develop, operate and change over time. This approach has been developed by Turner (1971, 1974) who argues that by focusing on events or crises that he terms social dramas we may follow changes in situations and social relations. Turner maintains that the main unit of study is the social drama which he indicates is

> not to present a reputedly objective recital of a series of events; it is concerned, rather, with the different interpretations put upon these events, and the way in which they express nuanced shifts or switches in the balance of power or ventilate divergent interests within common concerns. (Turner, 1971, p. 352)

Accordingly, if 'social drama' is taken as a major unit of study it allows the researcher to focus on the social processes involved in the operation of social structure; the processes that occur in day-to-day life. This approach has been used by Bell (1968) to look at social relations in middle-class families, by Morgan (1972) to look at sets of social relations in a factory and by Abner Cohen (1982) to examine social relationships that are highlighted by events within the Notting Hill Carnival. In my own study I used this approach to focus on three social situations: a series of bomb scares, a walk-out staged by 600 pupils and the events that occurred in the last week of the school year (cf. Burgess, 1983, pp. 84–119). In each case, these were single events that were used to discuss social relationships between teachers and pupils. By focusing on these social dramas I was able to examine the social processes involved when conflict occurred, how it was handled and the basis upon which it was handled. Each of these situations was isolated from the others in terms of the time when it occurred, but they were also linked together in a number of ways. First, they were all defined by the teachers as 'crises'. Secondly, they involved the same teachers and, finally, all of these events took place on a school-wide basis. Accordingly, they were used to examine the ways in which members of the school worked and the ways in which teachers and pupils reconciled different versions of school and schooling in the course of their work.

So far, we have focused upon events and activities which the researcher selects out from the total range of experience in an unstructured way. However, events and activities can also be systematically recorded as in interaction analysis where pre-coded categories are used in order to study small-scale units that can subsequently be tabulated. In such situations a researcher may record an event each time it occurs. The events that the researcher chooses to observe may depend upon the theoretical and substantive problems that are at the centre of the study. Here, although the researcher observes events as they occur, the units of study need to be specified ahead of time. For example, Boehm and Weinberg (1977) suggest that research on nursery school classrooms could focus on pupils' self-help skills: going to the toilet unassisted, washing hands, buttoning clothes, putting on shoes, tying up shoe laces and so forth. In this instance, records may be kept concerning when these events occurred. However, the use of such structured observation systems needs to be considered in relation to the problems posed in the course of the research (cf. Boehm and Weinberg, 1977, pp. 58–9).

The Selection of People: Key Informants

It is traditional in much sociological research for individuals to be selected for study using random sampling methods. In these circumstances, organisations such as factories, prisons, churches and schools may have lists of members which can be used as a sampling frame from which random samples may be drawn. However, some field researchers who have adopted random sampling methods have had to adapt this approach in order to avoid overlooking particular groups. For example, Becker *et al.* (1961) report that in conducting student interviews for their medical school study they used a random sample of fifteen students. However, they decided that four additional student 'freshers' also had to be interviewed as this group was omitted from the random sample. Many field researchers have also found other problems involved in random sampling as it relies upon lists of members from which the sample may be drawn. This results in the focus being upon formal rather than informal groups for which no lists of members are available. Accordingly, researchers who wish to focus on such groups have utilised opportunistic samples, judgement samples and snowball samples especially when working with informal groups such as deviants (cf. Becker, 1970c; Plant, 1975; West, 1980).

However, the best known approach for working with individuals in field research is 'intensive work with informants' (Conklin, 1968, p. 172). This approach has long been used by social anthropologists (Casagrande, 1960) and involves the selection of key informants. Indeed, sociologists studying industrial societies have followed the same strategy, for Whyte's key informant 'Doc' in the study *Street Corner Society* (Whyte, 1955, 1981) is as well known as the study itself. Other examples include Tim who introduced James Patrick into a Glasgow gang (Patrick, 1973), Tally who introduced Elliot Liebow (1967) into a group of black street corner men and five men in a factory who Nichols and Beynon (1977) claim

> we talked to from time to time over the first three years of the 1970s.

Indeed, they argue,

> They aren't 'special people' or people who we think have anything more special to say than anyone else; nor are they a 'representative sample'; they are simply five of the two hundred we talked to about their lives, their futures and their pasts. (Nichols and Beynon, 1977, p. 78)

Similarly, Ball (1984) indicates how his comprehensive school study involved the use of five informants who were not representative, or typical, or untypical teachers. However, they were individuals whom he got to know well and with whom he could discuss situations. In these terms we might ask: how are key informants selected? How are they used?

In reflecting on her work in social anthropology Mead (1953) argues that the selection of an informant demands that the researcher has a knowledge of the situation that is to be studied in order to evaluate the individual's position in a particular setting and their knowledge of that setting. The selection is made not just in terms of representativeness, as Mead remarks:

> the validity of the informant depends not so much upon the number of cases as upon the proper specification of the informant, so that he or she can be accurately placed, in terms of a very large number of variables – age, sex, order of birth, family background, life experience, temperamental tendencies (such as optimism, habit of exaggeration, etc.), political and religious position, exact situational relationship to the investigator, configurational relationship to every other informant, and so forth. Within this

extensive degree of specification, each informant is studied as a perfect example, an organic representation of his complete cultural experience. (Mead, 1953, pp. 645–6)

Informants need, therefore, to be selected using the researcher's judgement and can be used to portray aspects of the social situation. Indeed, Van Maanen (1981) indicates that informants that are used by sociologists may be selected on the basis of race, age, sex, size, socio-economic background and appearance as these factors will influence relationships. He considers that sociologists need to establish relationships with a number of informants as it is doubtful whether sufficient individuals are acquainted with all aspects of a cultural setting. He suggests, therefore, that researchers need to find informants who have knowledge about specialised interests and concerns in a social setting. He draws on his study of the police to show how he built up a range of police informants: the 'gung ho' type who were in pursuit of a good arrest, 'cabbages' who had a relaxed attitude to the job, 'high minded professionals', 'the cops cop', 'brown nosers' who were interested in advancing their position by whatever means possible and 'bent' policemen. Each of these informants gave Van Maanen a different perspective on the police. This highlights the importance of field researchers selecting a range of informants if they are to avoid partial accounts of a social situation. Indeed, other researchers have pointed to the advantage of using informants drawn from different status levels in organisations (cf. Strauss et al. (1964) on using informants in studying hospitals). Similarly, in my study, key informants were drawn from different groups: teachers and pupils; different subgroups: teachers in Houses and teachers in Departments, and teachers from different status levels: probationary teachers, scale post holders, teachers in charge of subjects and Heads of Departments, for they each provided a different account of the school and taught me about different elements of their culture and the cultural scene as they perceived it.

The selection of individuals in field studies is, therefore, a different procedure from the selection procedures associated with statistical sampling in survey research. For in field research informants are selected for their knowledge of a particular setting which may complement the researcher's observations and point towards further investigation that needs to be done in order to understand social settings, social structures and social processes.

Conclusion

Field researchers confront situations in the course of their studies in which there is considerable variability. Accordingly, this chapter has examined some of the sampling procedures that can be used by field researchers in attempting to focus their work. In turn, it is suggested that field researchers need to keep in mind four particular categories when sampling: research locations, time, events and people. However, it is well to remember Margaret Mead's comment on sampling in anthropological field research which she claims is not

> a version where *n* equals too few cases. *It is simply a different kind of sampling.* (Mead, 1953, p. 654)

It is this 'different kind of sampling' that has been adopted by field researchers studying their own cultures in order to address qualitative issues concerning what occurs and the implications of what occurs for social relations.

Suggestions for Further Reading

Methodology

There are relatively few direct discussions of selection/sampling strategies in field research as sampling is often discussed as part of survey research in general methodology texts. Accordingly, the following references have been specially chosen as they relate to specific issues of selection that can be used in field research.

Ball, S. J. (1984), 'Beachside reconsidered: reflections on a methodological apprenticeship' in R. G. Burgess (ed.), *The Research Process in Educational Settings: Ten Case Studies* (Lewes: Falmer Press). A discussion of the author's *Beachside Comprehensive* (Ball, 1981) which includes a discussion of the use of informants.

Bennett, N. and McNamara, D. (1979) (eds), *Focus on Teaching* (London: Longman). See section two that deals with systematic observation and principles of sampling.

Burgess, R. G. (1982) (ed.), *Field Research: a Sourcebook and Field Manual* (London: Allen & Unwin). Section three deals with sampling and includes papers by Honigmann (1973), Brookover Bourque and Back (1966) and Tremblay (1957).

Casagrande, J. (1960) (ed.), *In the Company of Man* (New York: Harper & Row). A set of papers by anthropologists who discuss their work by focusing on their informants.

Glaser, B. and Strauss, A. L. (1967), *The Discovery of Grounded Theory* (Chicago: Aldine); includes a discussion of theoretical sampling.

Hammersley, M. (1984), 'The researcher exposed: a natural history' in R. G. Burgess (ed.), *The Research Process in Educational Settings: Ten Case Studies* (Lewes: Falmer Press); includes a discussion of the researcher's sampling problems while conducting a field study in a school.

Schatzman, L. and Strauss, A. L. (1973), *Field Research: Strategies for a Natural Sociology* (Englewood Cliffs, NJ: Prentice-Hall). Chapter 3 includes a discussion on the selection of locations, people and events.

Spradley, J. P. (1979), *The Ethnographic Interview* (New York: Holt, Rinehart & Winston). See the chapter on the location of informants.
Spradley, J. P. (1980), *Participant Observation* (New York: Holt, Rinehart & Winston); contains a chapter on the location of social situations.

Empirical Studies

Field studies seldom contain explicit discussions on selection strategies and the use of informants. The following studies should, therefore, be examined with these questions in mind in order to see the way in which such strategies are actually used.

Ball, S. J. (1981), *Beachside Comprehensive: A Case Study of Secondary Schooling* (Cambridge: CUP).
Burgess, R. G. (1983), *Experiencing Comprehensive Education: A Study of Bishop McGregor School* (London: Methuen).
Patrick, J. (1973), *A Glasgow Gang Observed* (London: Eyre-Methuen).
Roth, J. (1963), *Timetables* (New York: Bobbs-Merrill).
Stacey, M., Dearden, R. Pill, R. and Robinson, D. (1970), *Hospitals, Children and their Families* (London: Routledge & Kegan Paul).
Strauss, A. L., Schatzman, L., Bucher, R., Ehrlich, D. and Sabshin, M. (1964), *Psychiatric Ideologies and Institutions* (New York: The Free Press).
Whyte, W. F. (1981), *Street Corner Society* (3rd edn) (Chicago: University of Chicago Press).

4

Methods of Field Research 1: Participant Observation

In commenting upon the object of social scientific research Schutz (1954) makes a distinction between the physical reality described by the natural scientist and the social reality described by the social scientist when he writes:

> There is an essential difference in the structure of the thought objects of mental constructs formed by the social sciences and those formed by the natural sciences. It is up to the natural scientist and to him alone to define, in accordance with the procedural rules of his science, his observational field, and to determine the facts, data, and events within it which are relevant to his problems or scientific purposes at hand. Neither are those facts and events pre-selected, nor is the observational field pre-interpreted. The world of nature, as explored by the natural scientist, does not 'mean' anything to the molecules, atoms, and electrons therein. The observational field of the social scientist, however, namely the social reality, has a specific meaning and relevance structure for the human beings living, acting, and thinking therein. By a series of commonsense constructs they have pre-selected and pre-interpreted this world which they experience as the reality of their daily lives. It is these thought objects of theirs which determine their behaviour by motivating it. The thought objects constructed by the social scientist, in order to grasp this social reality, have to be founded upon the thought objects constructed by the common-sense thinking of men, living their daily life within their social world. (Schutz, 1954, pp. 266–7)

Such a perspective suggests that the social world is not objective but involves subjective meanings and experiences that are constructed by participants in social situations. Accordingly, it is the task of the social scientist to interpret the meanings and experiences of social actors, a task that can only be achieved through participation with the individuals involved.

Although social scientists have a range of approaches for studying the social world – experimental methods, statistical measures and survey research – none of these methods can fully encapsulate the subjective elements of social life. Accordingly, researchers have turned to observation and participant obervation in order to get access to the meanings which participants assign to social situations. In these circumstances, the researcher learns first hand about a situation by using participant observation. The tasks associated with the participant observer have been summarised by Becker in the following terms:

> The participant observer gathers data by participating in the daily life of the group or organization he studies. He watches the people he is studying to see what situations they ordinarily meet and how they behave in them. He enters into conversation with some or all of the participants in these situations and discovers their interpretations of the events he has observed. (Becker, 1958, p. 652)

In research involving the use of participant observation it is the researcher who is the main instrument of social investigation. On this basis participant observation facilitates the collection of data on social interaction; on situations as they occur rather than on artificial situations (as in experimental research) or constructs of artificial situations that are provided by the researcher (as in survey research). The value of being a participant observer lies in the opportunity that is available to collect rich detailed data based on observations in natural settings. Furthermore, the researcher can obtain accounts of situations in the participant's own language which gives access to the concepts that are used in everyday life. The researcher can, therefore, construct an account of a social situation on the basis of the various accounts that are obtained from informants. In these circumstances, there is an opportunity to collect the different versions of events that are available. Here, it is the researcher's aim to compare these accounts with each other, and with other observations that the researcher has made in the field of study. The result is that researchers can utilise their observations together with their theoretical insights to make seemingly irrational or paradoxical behaviour comprehensible to those within and beyond the situation that is studied. Observations can also be used to support or refute ideas about human behaviour and to generate questions that can be used in future research (cf. Emmett and Morgan, 1982, pp. 140–1; Anderson and Lee, 1982).

Such situations raise a series of problems that have been identified by various researchers. Schwartz and Schwartz (1955) recognised that participant observers are involved in face-to-face relationships with those who are researched, and that the observers are part of the context that is being observed. This results in the possibility of researchers modifying and influencing the research context as well as being influenced by it themselves. Automatically, this raises a series of common problems about the influence of the researcher on the researched that have been identified by different writers. For example, Howard Becker asks: 'to what degree is the informant's statement the same one he might give, either spontaneously or in answer to a question, in the absence of the observer?' (Becker, 1958, p. 652). While Janes (1961) asks: 'how does the community role of the investigator affect statements made by local respondents?' In short, these questions concern the researcher's participation and relationships with informants and their impact upon the data that are gathered. Such topics are frequently covered in the field research literature, especially in discussions of field roles and field relations which form the bulk of the abstract technical writing in this area. This chapter will be concerned with a review of some of the literature on field roles together with a commentary on the assumptions made and the procedures used while doing participant observation, drawing on examples from particular research projects.

Field Roles and the Participant Observer

Major distinctions have been made between active and passive roles (Schwartz and Schwartz, 1955), open and closed roles (see Chapter 9) and known and unknown participant observers (Schwartz and Jacobs, 1979). Whatever distinctions are made between the various roles, the basic typology involved is that devised by Gold (1958) in which he distinguished four *ideal typical* field roles: the complete participant, the participant-as-observer, the observer-as-participant and the complete observer. It is the first two of these four roles that are most often adopted by participant observers and which will, therefore, be given most detailed treatment in this section.

The *complete participant* conceals the observer dimension of the role with the result that covert observation is involved (cf. Bulmer, 1982). There are now several examples of the role being used by researchers such as Homan (1978) and Pryce (1979) in their studies of sectarian groups as well as by Humphreys (1970) and others while studying deviancy. A classic example can be found in the work of Festinger, Riecken and Schachter (1956) who were studying a small group that had predicted the end of the world. The sociologists entered this group on the pretence that they were genuinely interested in the group and its activities and soon became full members. The researchers provide a rationale for conducting their study without the knowledge or consent of the group when they state:

Our very first contact with the central figures of the group, their secrecy and general attitude toward non-believers made it clear that a study could not be conducted openly. Our basic problems were then obtaining entrée for a sufficient number of observers to provide the needed coverage of members' activities, and keeping at an absolute minimum any influence which these observers might have on the beliefs and actions of members of the group. We tried to be non-directive, sympathetic listeners, passive participants who were inquisitive and eager to learn whatever others might want to tell us. (Festinger, Riecken and Schachter, 1956, p. 234)

While such a role may seem appropriate to the research situation it is also apparent that several problems are involved. First, the researchers may alter the behaviour of the group they have entered. Secondly, the researchers may be handicapped by the assumed roles, as for example when one of the researchers in Festinger *et al.* was asked to lead a group meeting. Thirdly, the researchers may play their roles so effectively that they will 'go native' and no longer gather data or record the observations that are made. To overcome this problem researchers who have utilised this role recommend frequent breaks from the field in order that researchers can record, reflect and analyse the data that are collected.

Secondly, the *participant-as-observer* role involves situations where the researcher participates as well as observes by developing relationships with informants. A detailed discussion of this role is provided by Donald Roy (1970) in commenting on his study of southern labour union organising campaigns in the USA. Here, Roy indicates that it is this role that he has used most often and distinguishes it from complete participation in the following terms:

The main distinction between the two subtypes seems to lie in the matter of research role concealment. The participant-as-observer not only makes no secret of his investigation; he makes it known that research is his overriding interest. He is there to observe. To mention a second distinction that I regard as important, the participant-as-observer is not tied down, he is free to run around as research interests beckon; he may move as the spirit listeth. (Roy, 1970, p. 217)

It would appear, therefore, that this role has great potential for the researcher. Indeed, Roy outlines the kinds of situations in which he has deployed this role: hanging around union headquarters, observing mass meetings and other observational situations such as accompanying organisers on calls to the homes of mill workers to obtain signatures for a petition, standing at the mill gates to watch organisers distribute union leaflets to workers and joining picket lines. In these situations he indicates (1970, pp. 229–38) that the value of this role lies in the kinds of data that can be obtained.

Roy provides an evaluation of the participant-as-observer role. He highlights its advantage in providing the researcher with the freedom to go wherever the action is that is relevant to the investigation. However, he indicates that a disadvantage of this role lies in combining data collection with an area of social conflict especially in union–management relations where researchers will find themselves at odds with the opposition. Secondly, there is the problem of bias and, finally, the question of the extent to which a researcher participates. However, for Roy the participant-as-observer role has the advantage of allowing the researcher to penetrate social situations in order to establish relationships with informants so that some understanding of their world may be achieved.

Finally, Gold refers to two further roles that are not so frequently used in the course of field research. First, the *observer-as-participant* role which is used to refer to situations where contact with informants is brief, formal and openly classified as observation. In this situation, the observer role is made public and there is less chance that the researcher will 'go native'. However, the nature of this role is less satisfactory as the brevity of the relationship results in problems of bias arising out of the researcher's brief contacts. In turn, Schatzman and Strauss (1973) have indicated that such brief encounters will mean that the researcher will find difficulty in gaining access to the meanings that participants utilise in social situations. Finally, the *complete observer* role is identified with eavesdropping and reconnaissance in which the researcher is removed from sustained interaction with the informant. While Gold recognises that such a situation avoids 'going native', it does bring with it the problem of ethnocentrism as the researcher may reject the informant's views without ever getting to know them.

In many projects researchers have indicated that they have predominantly used one of these roles. For example, many studies of schools have been conducted by researchers who have used a participant-as-observer role. Hannan (1975) participated but did not teach in the secondary school that he studied, while Hargreaves (1967), Lacey (1970) and Ball (1981) took teacher roles within their studies. For as Hargreaves remarks:

Any adult (who is not dressed as a workman) appearing in school must in their [the pupils'] eyes have some strong connection with the teaching profession. (Hargreaves, 1967, p. 201)

In contrast, King (1978) took an observer role in his study of infant school classrooms. He explains how he established this role in the following terms:

> I rapidly learnt that children in infants' classrooms define any adult as another teacher or teacher surrogate. To avoid being engaged in conversation, being asked to spell words or admire pictures, I evolved the following technique. To begin with I kept standing so that physical height created social distance . . . Next, I did not show immediate interest in what the children were doing, or talk to them. When I was talked to I smiled politely and if necessary I referred the child asking a question to the teacher. Most importantly, I avoided eye contact; if you do not look you will not be seen. (King, 1978, p. 4)

In other situations, researchers have taken participant observer roles with pupils, as Spindler has remarked on his Schönhausen study:

> Though it may seem incongruous to think of a middle-aged, 200-pound male anthropologist being a participant-observer in third- and fourth-grade classes, this was actually the case. I sat at a desk in the back of the room and did the same things the children did insofar as my ethnographic recording activities permitted. The children accepted me and my role much more quickly than did the teachers, but both seemed to adapt to the incongruities after a period of several weeks. I can think of no other way that I would have come to an understanding of what the third and fourth grade in the Schönhausen Grundschule were like. (Spindler, 1974, p. 385)

However, other researchers have rejected the idea that adults can take on the role of a child or a pupil given their size, their age and their status (cf. Corrigan, 1979; Fine and Glassner, 1979). However, for most researchers the dispute is over *which* role is adopted.

This idea of taking *a* role oversimplifies the situation, for Junker (1960) argues that while

> it is made to appear that the four roles can be sharply distinguished and that the fieldworker will find himself cast in one and only one position, with its opportunities and limitations as indicated . . . the practising field worker may well find his position and activities shifting through time from one to another of these theoretical points, even as he continues observing the same human organization. (Junker, 1960, p. 38)

The field researcher may, therefore, find that these different roles are used in different phases of the research over a period of time, or for that matter these roles may be used in different moments in the course of research. For example, in studying curriculum change by focusing on the Keele Integrated Studies Project Shipman (1974) indicates that it would be misleading to maintain that his role was consistent throughout his research. He demonstrates how he began as a sociologist who was present with the project team and whose task was to observe, question and test. However, he indicates that during the study he became a participant observer, a participant who did not observe and a consultant to the project team. His relationship with the team is summed up by David Jenkins who comments on Shipman's account in the following terms:

> Shipman does injustice to the complexity of his relationship with the course team. He began as wallpaper, making unthreatening non-noises, but soon his dormant position came under pressure from two directions. First, the methodology of participant observation became a team in-joke, attracting banter ('Why is Shipman covering up his notes with his hand?'). Second, the team saw Shipman as a person well able to work his passage. Invitations to participate rather than observe were parried in crucial areas, but accepted in others. The knife-edge walked by this particular 'detached-observer' is insufficiently acknowledged here. In general he tried to keep his counsel in meetings, but offer support outside, e.g. with in-service training to encourage the social science contribution. The occasional doubt persisted ('Do you think Shipman *really* believes in what we're doing?'). (Jenkins in Shipman, 1974, pp. ix–x)

Such an account highlights how a researcher cannot merely choose to adopt one role that is adhered to throughout a project but that several roles are developed throughout an investigation (cf. Patrick, 1973).

Indeed, Janes (1961) has argued that field roles are developed in five separate phases which he identifies as: newcomer, provisional acceptance, categorical acceptance, personal acceptance and imminent migrant. Similarly, Olesen and Whittaker (1967) have discussed the ways in which field roles are developed and the implications this has for data collection. Olesen and Whittaker utilise their own experiences of research on student nurses to discuss the processes involved in role definition. They argue that in the course of a social research project roles are established on the basis of exchanges taking place between the researcher and the researched. The result is a process of role making which they consider passes through four phases:

1 *Surface encounter* which involves initial encounters with the other's research and life roles.

2 *Proferring and inviting* involving mutual exchange in definitions of self by the parties involved.

3 *Selecting and modifying* involving the reciprocal selection of meaningful and viable research roles and life roles of participant and observer.

4 *Stabilizing and sustaining* involving the achievement of balance within and between research and life roles.

While Olesen and Whittaker indicate that these phases highlight the flow of role making they also maintain that the roles are not clear cut in research experience. Indeed, they point towards roles existing simultaneously and overlap occurring between roles. The result is that there may be discrepancies between the phases and researchers may not be in the same phase with all those who are researched simultaneously; a point to which we now turn.

Developing Field Roles in a Research Project

Research roles are constantly negotiated and renegotiated with different informants throughout a research project (cf. Schatzman and Strauss, 1973). In my own study I found that although I principally took a participant-as-observer role there were several different phases associated with this role over time and which varied with the individuals with whom I worked. As far as phases of the research role were concerned I found that I was in different phases with different individuals. Accordingly, Table 4.1 summarises the phases of my role relationship with three individuals with whom I was in daily contact during the first six months of my research project in Bishop McGregor School (Burgess, 1983). First, Sylvia Robinson who was Head of the Newsom Department during my first term in the school. Secondly, Roy Carey, the Head of the Mathematics Department who was a member of the House to which I belonged and, finally, Mrs Watson the School Secretary.

Sylvia Robinson made it her business to go around with me during the first week of my research introducing me to teachers and pupils as *another teacher* who had come to work in the Newsom Department. By the second week, she was asking questions about my teacher status. Indeed, she was concerned that I did not have sufficient classes to teach and invited me to take classes for her, a task that I wished to avoid as I did not want to be perceived as a student teacher by the pupils. However, I did agree to take substitution classes as this allowed me to demonstrate my competence to her and to other teachers as well as to pupils. As a consequence, I found that Sylvia and other teachers were willing to accept my teacher role and I was regularly given substitution classes to take when other teachers were absent from school. Indeed my work with classes in general gave me categorical acceptance as a teacher with many teachers, while my work with Newsom classes earned me personal acceptance from Sylvia and from other members of the Newsom Department. Indeed, when an outside activity was being organised for staff, Sylvia indicated, 'you can sign up for that as you're a member of staff. You can join in as well.' Furthermore, in the months that followed, her offers of advice and help both within and beyond the school indicated that she accepted me as an individual and as a teacher. Finally, when a rumour circulated among Newsom teachers that I might be leaving at the end of the Christmas term, Sylvia expressed her concern as she thought that my absence would create a gap in the Newsom timetable.

In contrast, Roy Carey took a different position. From the start he did not see me as a teacher, nor a part-time teacher in the school. For him I was a visitor which he made very clear. When I arrived one morning in the early days of my research before any other teachers were in the school he remarked, 'I expect the rest of the staff will be along shortly. It's bad when visitors arrive before the staff.' Indeed, throughout the first term when I was in daily contact with him I found that he placed me in the category of visitor rather than teacher. Indeed, by the time my research ended (just over a year later), it was doubtful if he saw me in any other position than that of visitor. Often in conversation I would be ignored by him. This was clearly illustrated by a situation in the penultimate week of my first term in the school when he brought a new mathematics teacher into the House to introduce to everyone. I was sitting in the middle of a group of staff. However, as he went around introducing each person in turn to the new teacher he missed me out completely – perhaps for him I did not exist at all!

While these two cases present polar opposites, the third case demonstrates how the same phases through which my role progressed with Sylvia Robinson took a longer period with Mrs Watson, the School Secretary. I had been given permission by the Headmaster to use the files in the school office as a resource for my research. However, when I went to ask the Secretary if I could use them she refused saying that she would have to ask the Headmaster to see if he had granted me permission to use this material. In this sense, I was put into the position of a newcomer. Indeed, it was not until almost a month had elapsed that she indicated her willingness for me to use these files (see Chapter 2). However, it was apparent that I was on trial during that period as far as she was concerned. In order to use the files effectively I found that I had to tidy up each file by sorting the

Table 4.1   Phases in the Development of Research Roles with Three Informants at Bishop McGregor School.

	Newcomer	Provisional Acceptance	Categorical Acceptance	Personal Acceptance	Imminent Migrant
Sylvia Robinson	Sylvia introduces me to staff as 'Mr Burgess who has come to work with our Newsom pupils'. (1.5.73)	Concerned that I might not have enough to do – attempts to get me into other classes so that I can teach and do research. (3.5.73)	Sylvia says that she sees me as a teacher who can teach Newsom classes and take substitution lessons. (22.5.73)	Sees me as a member of staff (5.6.73) Offers to lend me her car. (25.9.73)	Concerned that if I was to leave the school it would leave a gap in the Newsom time-table. (18.9.73)
Roy Carey	Perceives me as a visitor. (3.5.73) Perceives me as a visitor. (3.7.73)				
Mrs Watson (School Secretary)	Secretary refuses to allow me access to office files – she is uncertain about my role. (8.5.73)	Allows access to files only when she has checked with the Head – she has had some clarification of my role. (22.5.73)	Allows me to use office files and jokes with me. (6.9.73)	Secretary says she thinks of me as one of the staff. (4.10.73)	

Note: The dates associated with the various phases of my role were obtained from field notes.

material into chronological order. During this process I came across items that had been incorrectly filed and temporarily lost. It was this task of tidying the files which appeared to establish my credibility with the Secretary who after six months in the field was inviting me into the office to do this work. Indeed, by the middle of the second term in the school she indicated that she accepted me as a member of the teaching staff, with the result that I was now not only invited into the office but was also included on her list of teachers who should be circulated with information.

These three examples indicate the complexity involved in a research situation where the researcher may be simultaneously perceived in different terms by different members of the same institution. These three cases have been presented as they show how my role went through different phases during the same period of my research. In these terms, the literature oversimplifies the situation as it tends to be assumed that the researcher simultaneously goes through similar phases with all members of the situation studied. An ideal type of situation is presented rather than an actual situation. Furthermore, little account appears to be taken of the researcher's social roles and social characteristics and the ways in which these may influence the research. Indeed, the social characteristics of the researcher raise a series of questions: are the roles that are taken by the researcher dependent upon biographical experience? Are the roles related to the age, sex, and status of the researcher? It is to these issues that we now turn.

The Role of the Social Researcher

The discussion so far has made a series of assumptions about the researcher who, it is argued, merely takes or develops a role in research. Yet we need to consider the extent to which experience, age, sex and ethnicity will influence the field researcher's role, field relations and the research process. How far does personal biography and personal experience influence the research role? What is the significance of age on field relations? What is it like to be a female doing research in a male setting? What is the significance of being male or female for field roles and field relations? How does a white researcher work in a social situation involving blacks? It is to these questions that we now turn, for the range of roles that the researcher can take on, and the relationships that are established, are intertwined with personal characteristics. Indeed, as the contributors to autobiographical accounts such as Bell and Newby (1977), and Roberts (1981) have shown there are a range of social factors that have influenced the selection of research roles.

The researcher's experience The influence of the researcher's own experience upon research findings has been clearly argued by Dawe (1973) who maintains that sociologists are participants in their own analyses. For Dawe considers that any statement of subjective meaning will incorporate elements of the sociologist's experience as well as the experience of those who are studied. A brief glance at many ethnographic accounts testifies to the truth of this statement as the experiences of the researcher become crucial in the production of data. A classic example is found in Becker's *Outsiders* (Becker, 1963) where the researcher's ability as a jazz musician clearly influenced the selection of the research problem together with the collection and analysis of data. Further examples include Roth's experiences as a tuberculosis patient (Roth, 1963, 1974), Ditton's experiences on a baker's round (Ditton, 1977) and my own experiences as a teacher (Burgess, 1983), all of which influenced the subsequent direction of the research. Indeed, in my own research it was my experience of being a teacher in the school's Newsom Department that helped me to develop a set of questions about pupils and teachers in the Department and the relationships that existed between them (cf. Burgess, 1983, pp. 123–46).

The age of the researcher This aspect is rarely, if ever, taken into account, yet age influences the activities in which the researcher can and cannot engage. Many ethnographic studies with street gangs (cf. Whyte, 1955; Patrick, 1973; Parker, 1974) assume some correspondence between the boys concerned and the age of the investigator. For example, Patrick (1973) and Parker (1974) discuss their active participation with street gangs which involved a high degree of physical activity. Similarly, Moore (1977) in discussing his work on the study of Sparkbrook in Birmingham, indicates that the situations in which he became involved in the streets demanded physical activity as he reports:

> Another time I was crouched under a hedge with bottles and bricks flying overhead as West Indians and tinkers fought a pitched battle. The police arrived in force, and I was moved on. What does the eager researcher do when moved on? I ran around the block, took off my coat and strolled innocently into the middle of the battle again. (Moore, 1977, p. 87)

Such situations as Lofland (1971) indicates would be difficult for elderly researchers to be involved in. For Lofland suggests

> the liability of being older, male and 'professorial' in style in part

accounts for the relative absence of observational efforts among such scholars. (Lofland, 1971, p. 101)

In turn, we need to consider what social skills are required in projects involving elderly participants. Fairhurst (1981) indicates that she encountered several problems in doing research among the elderly as she not only had to cope with hospital routines but also with the patients' incontinence and the smell which accompanied it. In addition, she discusses how she thought there might be a problem coping with the age difference, remarking:

It seemed to me that introducing myself to patients might present a special problem. While my efforts to familiarise myself with the concerns of those caring for the elderly could provide a basis upon which to initiate conversations with staff, I did not feel I could pursue a similar course of action to facilitate interaction with patients. In particular, I was acutely aware of the considerable age gap between myself and patients and I pondered upon this as a potential barrier in establishing relationships. (Fairhurst, 1981, p. 75)

In this instance, the researcher was aware that age was a factor that might have to be overcome when establishing relationships with informants and in sustaining those relationships. Indeed, she contrasts her research role with staff and with patients. For she considers that while it was possible to do work with the staff, it was impossible to 'do' being an old person. Age was therefore a key factor in thinking about relationships between the researcher and the researched. However, she found that it was not a barrier that existed between herself and those that she researched.

Sex A further characteristic of the researcher that needs to be considered is the influence of sex and gender on field research. Much of the literature considers how gender influences the questions that are posed and the data that are collected in field projects (cf. Golde, 1970; Warren and Rasmussen, 1977; Wax, 1979; Roberts, 1981). Indeed, much of the discussion focuses upon how being female influences the roles to which the researcher is allocated and how this may limit or impede the progress and process of research (cf. Easterday *et al.*, 1977). In particular, they indicate how young unmarried women are often allocated to a series of roles which are consistent with a stereotypical picture of women. Indeed, if women are allocated roles where they are subordinate to men it may mean that they do not have access to certain situations (cf. Dua, 1979; Gupta, 1979). In these circumstances, it is essential for researchers to reflect on the way in which sex and gender may promote or impede data collection when doing participant observation. Indeed, Wax (1979) suggests that research on a 'whole' culture demands teams of individuals of both sexes.

Meanwhile Frankenberg (1976), and Morgan (1981) have considered the extent to which 'men' and 'masculinity' pervade sociological inquiry and the way this influences the topics that are selected for research. It has been suggested that ethnography 'has its own brand of *machismo* with its image of the male sociologist bringing back views from the fringes of society, the lower depths, the mean streets, areas traditionally "off limits" to women investigators' (Morgan, 1981, p. 87). Certainly, the analyses provided by Frankenberg and by Morgan would suggest that this image of the male researcher influences topics that are chosen for research, research roles and data collection and analyses. In particular, Morgan analyses how his own role influenced the way in which he perceived gender in a factory (Morgan, 1969, 1972, 1975). He indicates that gender differences do not merely exclude researchers from certain areas but are a source of knowledge about a particular field. The gender identity of the participant observer is, therefore, crucial in the study.

Ethnicity   Finally, there is the question of race and ethnicity. Often situations in which whites conduct research with blacks are presented as a language problem with the result that the participant observer has to work through an interpreter (cf. Werner and Campbell, 1973). However, this oversimplifies the situation as linguistic problems could occur when whites conduct research with whites in different European countries or in different geographical areas within the same country where differences exist in language and dialect. In the USA Suttles (1968) has indicated how racial and ethnic boundaries were difficult to surmount when studying a Chicago slum where Italians, Blacks, Puerto Ricans and Mexicans lived. He comments:

As I acquired friends and close informants, my own ethnicity became a serious problem. A few people worked over my genealogy trying to find some trace that would allot me to a known ethnic group. After close inquiry, one old Italian lady announced with peals of laughter: 'Geraldo, you're just an American'. She did not mean it as a compliment and afterward I remember being depressed. (Suttles, 1968, p. 10)

Similarly, in situations where whites do research with blacks the individual may become a friend, but a friend who is always an outsider. For example, Elliot Liebow who conducted research among black street corner men comments that the

> brute fact of color, as they understood it in their experience and as I understood it in mine irrevocably and absolutely relegated me to the status of outsider. I am not certain but I have a hunch that they were more continuously aware of the color difference than I was. When four of us sat around a kitchen table, for example, I saw three Negroes; each of them saw two Negroes and a white man . . .
>
> Whenever the fact of my being white was openly introduced, it pointed up the difference between me and the other person, even when the intent of introducing it was, I believe to narrow that distance. (Liebow, 1967, pp. 248–9)

Indeed, Liebow indicates how colour was used to allocate him to a particular role of outsider, a role, he argues, which did not make him a competitor and which facilitated observational work. In this sense, colour like biography, age and gender can influence the tenor of relationships which the researcher establishes whilst doing participant observation.

Developing Relationships

In doing participant observation it is the researcher's aim to observe events while causing as little disruption as possible in the social situation. In this respect, developing trust and establishing relationships are a crucial part of a researcher's involvement in the social scene. The participant observer needs to blend into the situation if observations are to be made of the participants in their natural settings. Polsky (1969) advises that if the researcher wishes to observe a criminal in a natural setting it is important to follow that individual's routine, as he remarks:

> If he [the criminal] wants to sit in front of his T.V. set and drink beer and watch a ball game for a couple of hours, so do you; if he wants to walk the streets or go barhopping, so do you; if he wants to go to the racetrack, so do you; if he indicates (for whatever reason) that it's time for you to get lost, you get lost. (Polsky, 1969, p. 134)

This position advocated by Polsky has applicability to other social settings as it highlights how it is essential for the researcher to follow the informant's way of life. However, Polsky (1969) indicates that the researcher needs to decide on the extent to which he or she will participate otherwise it may mean that researchers will be drawn into forms of participant observation which violate their own ethical position. In short, whilst doing participant observation it is essential for participant observers constantly to monitor the differences between themselves and their informants. The researcher has, therefore, to be able to exercise control over the relationships that are established for research purposes.

An important dimension in developing rapport with informants involves learning their language. In particular, attention should be given not only to the words and phrases that are used but the circumstances in which they are used, especially if the researcher intends using the vocabulary in the course of the research. For example, Patrick (1973) indicates the importance of understanding the language of the Glasgow gang with whom he did research. He explains how the boys bragged of their extensive knowledge of 'kip shops' (brothels). However, he indicates that he was originally unsure about the meaning of this term, as he comments:

> I must confess that the first time the gang said they were heading for a kip shop, I thought we were on our way to buy fish suppers in a chip shop. (Patrick, 1973, p. 109)

Similarly, in a study of workplace crime, Mars (1982) indicates the importance of understanding the difference between the vocabulary of fiddle groups and the vocabulary of the law. He indicates that the 'otherness' of a fiddle group is sustained by a special language,

> a vocabulary which reflects the nature of the group's relationships with its own members and with other outsiders. Words which seem overtly innocent to outsiders must covertly alert insiders and raise the awareness of their obligations to each other. (Mars, 1982, p. 177)

In this respect, goods are only 'stolen', 'pilfered' or 'thieved' in the vocabulary of official groups. It is not a vocabulary that is acceptable to those who are engaged in fiddling. As Mars indicates, 'alerting phrases' are useful to induct a newcomer into fiddling. In such situations it would, therefore, be essential for a researcher to learn the vocabulary in order to understand the situation.

However, learning the language that is appropriate in different social situations is not merely relevant to those who study deviancy. For Becker and Geer (1957) indicate that in their study of medical students they needed to understand the word 'crock' if they were to appreciate the actor's perspective of a situation:

> I first heard the word 'crock' applied to a patient shortly after I began my fieldwork. The patient in question, a fat, middle aged

woman complained bitterly of pains in a number of widely separated locations. When I asked the student who had so described her what the word meant, he said that it was used to refer to any patient who had psychosomatic complaints. I asked if that meant that Mr X – a young man on the ward whose stomach ulcer had been discussed by a staff physician as typically psychosomatic, was a crock. The student said that that would not be correct usage, but was not able to say why.

Over a period of several weeks, through discussion of many cases seen during morning rounds with the students, I finally arrived at an understanding of the term, realizing that it referred to a patient who complained of many symptoms but had no discoverable organic pathology. I had noticed from the beginning that the term was used in a derogatory way and had also been inquiring into this, asking students why they disliked having crocks assigned to them for examination and diagnosis. At first, students denied the derogatory connotations, but repeated observations of their disgust with such assignments soon made such denials unrealistic. Several students eventually explained their dislike in ways of which the following example is typical: 'The true crock is a person who you do a great big workup for and who has all of these vague symptoms, and *you really can't find anything the matter with them*'. (Becker and Geer, 1957, p. 29)

By focusing on the word 'crock' during their observations, Becker and Geer indicate how they discovered the way in which this term was used to describe patients who took a great deal of student time, a discovery that suggested a perspective which could be used in their study. Similarly, in my research, I found that learning the vocabulary that was appropriate to various settings helped me to understand what behaviour was appropriate in particular circumstances. For example, distinctions were made between 'a common room' that teachers used for relaxation only and a 'staff room' where exercise books could be marked and lessons prepared. In each case, the terms defined the ways in which certain behaviour was appropriate to a particular setting. Furthermore, I found that in discussions of courses, criticisms were reserved for discussion among colleagues, while a different vocabulary to convey success was used with the Headmaster (Burgess, 1983, pp. 226–7).

So far, we have examined several aspects of participant observation but we might ask: how does a participant observer conduct research? Among the classic discussions are reflections on the research experience provided by Whyte (1955) and Liebow (1967) in the appendices to their studies of street corner gangs. Liebow discusses the way in which he entered a setting and established a role which assisted him in making a series of observations. He began by mingling with a small crowd in order to watch the police make an arrest. A day later he returned to the same location and stopped to help three 'wino's' feed a puppy which led to a conversation with Tally who was with this group. After this meeting, Liebow accompanies Tally to a Carry-out where he reports that he spent the time talking, drinking coffee and watching people entering and leaving the small restaurant that was to be his research base. Here was an opportunity to observe the hangers on, the friendly banter, the 'horse play' and the dancing. By the end of the day he reports that he had learned the names of waitresses, names or nicknames of other people and had a biographical sketch of Tally. It was this small restaurant which Tally frequented that became the setting where Liebow spent the next month meeting people, learning names and developing a sense of belonging.

However, Liebow's role and rate of data accumulation changed when he became involved in transporting Tally to a court room where a friend (Lonny Small) was on a murder charge. Liebow reports:

Almost imperceptibly, my association with Tally, and through him with Lonny, was projecting me into the role of principal actor in Lonny's life. By being with Tally through the trial, I found that first Tally, then Lonny, were looking to me for leadership and, as in the question of waiving extradition, for decision making. Court officials, apparently taking their cues from Lonny began looking to me as his spokesman. (Liebow, 1967, p. 244)

As Liebow indicates, this court case and the subsequent follow-up gave him a major role that took him into numerous places and provided contacts with a range of people that facilitated the collection of data first hand.

Meanwhile, in some settings it is the informants who provide the researcher with a guided tour of the setting. Clearly, Doc in Whyte's *Street Corner Society* (1955) is a classic example. However, other researchers such as Sudnow (1967) have reported that they developed friendships with informants who provided information on technical matters, the practices of others and information about situations at which the researcher was not present. In this way, informants can assist a participant observer in collecting data about core features of the setting under study. Researchers who become participant observers are, therefore, principally involved in observing daily life while collecting accounts from informants. However, in order to give some precision to their data they need continually to ask questions about the situations that they observe and the conversations in which they become involved.

Collecting Data

Having discussed roles and relationships we now turn to examine the kind of data for which this research method is ideally suited and which is collected by the participant observer. In particular, attention will be given to the observations that are made. At this point we might ask: what constitutes data? Spradley (1980) presents three types of observation: descriptive observations, focused observations and selective observations which he links to the kinds of questions that are posed by the participant observer.

Table 4.2   *Features of a Social Situation: Studying a School.*

Features Identified		*Features of a School*
1 Space	1	Identification of the layout of classrooms, offices and cloakrooms on the school site.
2 Actors	2	The people involved in the situation and their names.
3 Activities	3	The various related activities of people in the setting – teachers and pupils.
4 Objects	4	The physical elements present, for example the furniture and its layout in a particular office or classroom.
5 Acts	5	Actions of individuals – teachers and pupils.
6 Events	6	The particular activities of individuals in for example school assembly.
7 Time	7	The time sequence in the school – mornings and afternoons – lessons, breaks and lunch hours.
8 Goals	8	The activities people are attempting to accomplish in particular situations. Differences between teachers and pupils in a lesson.
9 Feelings	9	Emotions in particular contexts.

With descriptive questions the basic aim is description of the setting, the people and the events that took place. These elements constitute the basic units of field data which can be subdivided into discrete categories. For example, people may be described in terms of their age, sex, dress, numbers and physical appearance. Settings may include what is seen *and* what is heard, while events include work and play and related elements of discussion. The purpose of these descriptive observations is to act as a basic guide; to provide background to further observations. In particular, Spradley has identified nine major dimensions of a social situation on which data may be collected. In Table 4.2 I have illustrated these various dimensions of data collection by making reference to the kinds of data that could be collected in the study of a school. In addition to these nine dimensions that can act as a basic guide in making observations in a particular setting, more detailed questions can be followed up in relation to a particular action or event or period of time. For example, if we focus on mid-morning break in a school common room we might ask:

1 What occurs in the time period before the break begins?
2 What happens from the time the first person enters until the last person leaves?
3 What do people do?
4 What do people talk about?
5 What is the atmosphere in the room?

With these descriptive questions in view it is possible to build up a detailed portrait of a social situation which may lead on to more focused questions in particular situations. For example, the differences between descriptive and focused questions can be illustrated by reference to my work with Newsom teachers and pupils as I found that:

My early impressions of the school, the Newsom Department, its teachers and its pupils, raised several questions which I used to orientate my study. I began by asking: what is the Newsom course? How is this course seen by different members of the school (that is, the headmaster, Newsom and non-Newsom teachers and Newsom pupils)? What counts as working on the Newsom course? What are the patterns of social relations that occur between the teachers and pupils in the Newsom department? Do the work and the relationships within the department influence patterns of teaching in other departments of the school? (Burgess, 1983, pp. 208–9)

However, on the basis of my observations, the comments that were made by informants and my general interest in symbolic interactionism I focused my questions still further to include:

How do teachers define the Newsom course? How do pupils define and redefine the course? What strategies, negotiations and bargains are used by the teachers and pupils? To what extent do activities in the Newsom department influence work within the core courses which Newsom pupils attend? (Burgess, 1983, p. 209)

These questions allowed me to move from a detailed description of a particular setting towards making a series of observations that had a particular focus. In making these observations I needed to take account of the actions and activities of a range of teachers and pupils in order to avoid bias. Secondly, it was important to consider perspective, that is the angle from which observations could be made. In this instance, my perspective was that of a teacher. However, I took into account the perspectives of teachers in different status positions in the school who did and did not teach in the Newsom Department. Furthermore, the pupil perspective (seen from a teacher's point of view) was also considered (cf. Burgess, 1983, pp. 208–35). Finally, there was the question of the theoretical framework that was used. As I have indicated, I used a set of concepts derived from interactionism: negotiation, strategy and bargain which in turn led towards a series of grounded concepts, that is concepts that were used by the participants to come to terms with the situations in which they were located (cf. Burgess, 1982b, pp. 115–35).

Conclusion

This chapter has looked at the principal method that is used in field research: participant observation. This method of investigation involves the researcher in taking a particular role within a culture in order to examine at first hand a social situation from a participant's point of view. Essential to this method of investigation is role taking and role making which will influence the degree to which the researcher participates, the relationships that are developed and the data that are collected. However, participant observation is but one approach that is used in field research and has to be complemented by other methods that are discussed in subsequent chapters.

Suggestions for Further Reading

Methodology
There is a vast literature on participant observation, much of which is abstract. I have, therefore, selected particular items that have *relevance* for the *conduct* of field research.

Burgess, R. G. (1982) (ed.), *Field Research: a Sourcebook and Field Manual* (London: Allen & Unwin). The second section contains a range of papers on sex and gender (Easterday *et al.*, 1977) on roles (Frankenberg, 1963;

Gans, 1968) and on the ethics of doing participant observation (Jarvie, 1969).

Denzin, N. (1970) (ed.), *Sociological Methods, a Sourcebook* (London: Butterworths). Section 9 on participant observation contains the papers by Gold (1958) and by Olesen and Whittaker (1967).

Filstead, W. J. (1970) (ed.), *Qualitative Methodology: Firsthand Involvement with the Social World* (Chicago: Markham); contains a range of American papers on the conduct of participant observation, some of which are also included in McCall and Simmons (1969).

Frankenberg, R. (1982) (ed.), *Custom and Conflict in British Society* (Manchester: Manchester University Press); contains a set of papers from researchers who were influenced by Max Gluckman. In particular, attention is drawn to the way in which observational methods can be used to study institutions in industrial societies. See especially Cunnison (1982), and Emmett and Morgan (1982) on factory workshops and Lacey (1982), and Lambart (1982) on studying schools.

Johnson, J. M. (1975), *Doing Field Research* (New York: The Free Press). An account based on the researcher's own experiences in a social work agency. In particular, there are chapters on trust and on developing relationships.

Junker, B. H. (1960), *Fieldwork: an Introduction to the Social Sciences* (Chicago: University of Chicago Press); contains a classic discussion of the major roles that can be adopted by participant observers.

McCall, G. J. and Simmons, J. L. (1969) (eds), *Issues in Participant Observation: A Text and Reader* (Reading, Mass.: Addison-Wesley). A set of American papers that provide an outline of the main issues as seen by American sociologists in the 1960s. It includes the papers by Gold (1958) and Janes (1961).

Schatzman, L. and Strauss, A. L. (1973), *Field Research: Strategies for a Natural Sociology* (Englewood Cliffs, NJ: Prentice-Hall). A textbook discussion of the strategies that can be used by the participant observer in the field.

Spradley, J. P. (1980), *Participant Observation* (New York: Holt, Rinehart & Winston). A text in which the author outlines the main stages that he considers are involved in doing participant observation. This approach needs careful evaluation as the steps and stages cannot be mechanically applied in a field project.

Empirical Studies

There is now a vast range of British and American studies where participant observation has been used to study aspects of the researchers' own society. The following texts should be read with a view to considering the *roles* that were adopted within the studies and the ways in which these roles influenced the collection and analysis of data:

British Studies

Atkinson, P. (1981), *The Clinical Experience* (Aldershot: Gower).

Burgess, R. G. (1983), *Experiencing Comprehensive Education: A Study of Bishop McGregor School* (London: Methuen).

Cavendish, R. (1982), *Women on the Line* (London: Routledge & Kegan Paul).

Corrigan, P. (1979), *Schooling the Smash Street Kids* (London: Macmillan).

Cunnison, S. (1966), *Wages and Work Allocation* (London: Tavistock).

Ditton, J. (1977), *Part-Time Crime: An Ethnography of Fiddling and Pilferage* (London: Macmillan).

Hargreaves, D. H. (1967), *Social Relations in a Secondary School* (London: Routledge & Kegan Paul).

King, R. (1978), *All Things Bright and Beautiful? A Sociological Study of Infants' Classrooms* (Chichester: Wiley).

Lacey, C. (1970), *Hightown Grammar: the School as a Social System* (Manchester: Manchester University Press).

Lupton, T. (1963), *On the Shop Floor* (Oxford: Pergamon).

Patrick, J. (1973), *A Glasgow Gang Observed* (London: Eyre-Methuen).

Shipman, M. (1974), *Inside a Curriculum Project* (London: Methuen).

Woods, P. (1979), *The Divided School* (London: Routledge & Kegan Paul).

American Studies

Becker, H. S., Geer, B., Hughes, E. C. and Strauss, A. L. (1961), *Boys in White: Student Culture in Medical School* (Chicago: University of Chicago Press).

Cavan, S. (1966), *Liquor License* (Chicago: Aldine).

Festinger, L., Riecken, H. W. and Schachter, S. (1956), *When Prophecy Fails* (New York: Harper & Row).

Gans, H. J. (1967), *The Levittowners* (London: Allen Lane).

Humphreys, L. (1970), *Tearoom Trade* (London: Duckworth).

Liebow, E. (1967), *Tally's Corner: A Study of Negro Street Corner Men* (Boston, Mass.: Little Brown).

Olesen, V. and Whittaker, E. (1968), *The Silent Dialogue* (San Francisco: Jossey Bass).

Roth, J. A. (1963), *Timetables* (New York: Bobbs-Merrill).

Smith, L. and Keith, P. M. (1971), *Anatomy of Educational Innovation* (New York: Wiley).

Spradley, J. and Mann, B. (1975), *The Cocktail Waitress* (New York: Wiley).

Strauss, A. L., Schatzman, L., Bucher, R., Ehrlich, D. and Sabshin, M. (1964), *Psychiatric Ideologies and Institutions* (New York: The Free Press).

Whyte, W. F. (1981), *Street Corner Society* (3rd edn) (Chicago: University of Chicago Press).

Wolcott, H. (1973), *The Man in the Principal's Office* (New York: Holt, Rinehart & Winston).

5

Methods of Field Research 2:
Interviews as Conversations

Interviews are so extensively used by sociologists that Benney and Hughes (1956) have referred to modern sociology as 'the science of the interview'. Indeed, a brief glance at texts and monographs devoted to methodology and to empirical research confirms this point. However, close inspection reveals that there is a considerable difference between the interviews that are discussed in standard methodology texts (cf. Goode and Hatt, 1952; Moser and Kalton, 1971; Selltiz *et al.*, 1976) and the practice of interviewing that has been discussed by Corbin (1971), Oakley (1981), Platt (1981c), Finch (1984) and Stenhouse (1984) based on their experiences of conducting empirical studies. The divergence involved reflects opposite ends of the research continuum.

Text book writers have placed emphasis on the structured interview in the context of survey research. Here, there is no long-term relationship between the researcher and the researched. It is assumed that the interviewer can manipulate the situation and has control over a set list of questions that have been formulated *before* the interview and which are to be *answered* rather than considered, rephrased, re-ordered, discussed and analysed. In short, the interviewer is assumed to have power over the respondent who is given a subordinate role in this context. The result is a situation where, it is argued, there should be some rapport between the interviewer and the respondent but there are numerous warnings about the dangers of over rapport (Goode and Hatt, 1952; Moser, 1958; Selltiz *et al.*, 1976). It would, therefore, appear that there are 'rules' about 'proper' interview behaviour which should be friendly but not over-sociable in order to overcome problems associated with 'bias'. The structured survey interview is, therefore, presented as a data collection device involving situations where the interviewer merely poses questions and records answers in a set pattern. Sociologists such as Oakley (1981) and Wakeford (1981) have been critical of this model which, they argue, puts the interviewer in an unnatural relationship with those who are researched. Certainly, few field researchers have followed the structured approach, preferring to use an informal or unstructured or semi-structured style of interviewing which employs a set of themes and topics to form questions in the course of conversation. This strategy, it is argued, gives informants an opportunity to develop their answers outside a structured format. It is this style of interviewing, which I refer to as the 'unstructured interview', that will be focused upon in this chapter.

Unstructured Interviews in Social Research

There is a long tradition in social science research where interviews have been perceived as 'conversations with a purpose'. An early user of the unstructured or informal interview was Mayhew in his report *London Labour and the London Poor* which was published in four volumes from 1851. For Mayhew comments in the preface of his book:

> It surely may be considered curious as being the first attempt to publish the history of a people, from the lips of the people themselves – giving a literal description of their labour, their earnings, their trials, and their sufferings, in their own 'unvarnished' language; and to portray the condition of their homes and their families by personal observation of the places, and direct communication with the individuals . . . (Mayhew, 1851, p. iii)

This approach to interviewing has been utilised by other social scientists engaged in social research. For example, in discussing the interview as a technique of social research Sidney and Beatrice Webb regarded it as a conversation in which the interviewer should

> Bear in mind that it is desirable to make the interview pleasing to the persons interviewed. It should seem to him or her an agreeable form of social intercourse. (Webb and Webb, 1932, p. 139)

Indeed, the Webbs demonstrated how conversations were of greater value than straight question and answer sessions as they provided rich detailed data that could be used alongside other materials. Ferdinand Zweig (1948) indicated in his *Labour, Life and Poverty* how informal or unstructured interviews could be substituted for questionnaires and formal interviews. For Zweig considered that questionnaires and formal interviews would not provide the detailed data he required. Accordingly, he remarks:

> I tried a new and unorthodox technique . . . and, as far as I can

judge, it was not unsuccessful. I dropped the idea of a questionnaire or formal verbal questions put forward in the course of research; instead I had casual talks with working class men on an absolutely equal footing and in friendly intercourse. These were not formal interviews but an exchange of views on life, labour and poverty. (Zweig, 1948, p. 1)

The approach seems to have met with some success, as Zweig remarks:

I made many friends, and some of them paid me a visit afterwards or expressed a wish to keep in touch with me. Some of them confided their troubles to me, and I often heard the remark: 'Strangely enough, I have never talked about that to anybody else'. They regarded my interest in their way of life as a sign of sympathy and understanding shown to them even in the inner circle of their family. I never posed as somebody superior to them, or a judge of their actions, but as one of them, although a foreigner. (Zweig, 1948, pp. 1–2)

Here, Zweig highlights some of the key characteristics of the researcher who engages in unstructured interviews. For him the researcher is a friend and a confidant who shows interest, understanding and sympathy in the life of the person with whom a conversation occurs; a marked contrast to the interviewer who is portrayed in the texts on formal structured interviewing. However, Zweig indicates that this style of interview cannot be started without detailed knowledge and preparation. He recommends that it is essential to observe people before a detailed conversation can occur. He indicates that detailed knowledge is essential before questions can be framed and before individuals are prepared to give detailed information on their way of life. On this basis he argues that it is possible to obtain a series of deep insights into the people's way of life.

The Interviewer in Field Research

Zweig's work illustrates the conflict between the 'scientific objectivity' of the textbooks and the experiences of a researcher who engages in a series of friendly exchanges in order to find out about people's lives. This approach has been defended by Corbin (1971), Oakley (1981) and Finch (1984) who indicate that it is impossible to control the relationship between the researcher and the researched but that it is vital to develop the trust and confidence of those with whom interviews are used. Oakley (1981) and Finch (1984) draw on their experiences of interviewing women and suggest that textbook recipes for interviewing provide particular problems for feminist interviewers who wish to validate women's subjective experiences as women and people. It is, they argue, preferable for women to interview women. However, Finch qualifies the argument by indicating that this is not to say that men do not make good interviewers as she argues that male social workers and counsellors often get men and women successfully to talk about their lives. Such remarks highlight the importance of gender in interpreting the relationship between researcher and researched in interview situations.

Finch indicates how being a woman resulted in the young mothers in her study of playgroups giving her access to views that it would have been highly unlikely for a man to obtain. She provides an illustration from an interview with a young mother to whom she talked:

Self: [Janet Finch]	I know that the children are sort of small at the moment, but do you ever have any sort of hopes or dreams about what they might do when they grow up?
Interviewee:	Yes, I'm always – Don't get married for a start. (To child) Not to get married, are you not! And have a career, with some money. And don't have a council house. Bet there's no such thing as council houses when they get older. But I don't want them to get married.
Self: [Janet Finch]	No.
Interviewee:	No but I don't, because I think once you get married and have kids, that's it. To a lot of women round here – when you see them walking past – big fat women with all their little kids running behind them. And I think, God. That's why I want to go to College and do something. But fellas don't see it like that, do they? Like, he thinks it's alright for me just going back to work in a factory for the rest of my life, you know. But I don't want that. (To child) You have a career, won't you? Prime Minister, eh? (Finch, 1984, p. 77)

In particular, Finch highlights how the remarks that this mother makes about her daughters and about their future would have been unlikely to have been made to a male interviewer, especially as the woman had remarked, 'fellas don't see it like that, do they?', a question that would never be raised with a man.

For Oakley (1981) the experience of being a mother was crucial in her project on motherhood (Oakley, 1979, 1980) as this allowed her to answer questions about birth and babies that many women asked her. However, this use of personal experience is not confined to research on women. In the course of my own research I found that teachers and pupils often asked me for information during the course of interviews. I was asked about my biography, about my previous teaching experience and my views about schools and schooling just as I posed questions to teachers and pupils. To have avoided these questions would have provided the 'sanitised' interview demanded by the textbook writers but would have ruined my relationships with the teachers and pupils. In addition, I also discussed situations with my informants who invited me to comment on events that we had all observed. In such situations the researcher is often advised in the name of research to avoid such invitations. However, my participation in the school meant that I could hardly claim that I had no knowledge of the situation in which we were all located and the events within which we were all involved. The result was that some of my unstructured interviews became discussions in which some evaluation of social situations took place.

In addition to issues of gender and personal experience, a number of other overt characteristics of the interviewer are involved in these situations – age, social status, race and ethnicity (cf. Chapter 4). Such characteristics create an immediate impression of the interviewer and will, in part, place limits on the roles that an interviewer may adopt. The age of an interviewer may influence the roles that are used and the status that the individual has in an interview. Despite the textbook suggestion that interviewer and informant should when possible be matched by age, it is clearly not possible in some projects. This was apparent in my school study where I was about ten years senior to the pupils that I interviewed, but twenty years junior to some of the teachers. In such circumstances, it is not only age but also status that is involved. I had been a teacher before starting research but I had not been a Head of Department, Head of House or senior teacher. Furthermore, I was not only junior to them as a teacher but I no longer held the status of full-time teacher. Here, I had to cope with my new role and new status as a part-time teacher in the school who was also a postgraduate student. Another major characteristic of the interviewer that other researchers have reported on is the role of race and ethnicity in conducting interviews (cf. Pryce, 1979). Many racial and ethnic cultures are distinct from middle-class white cultures with the result that this difference may impede communication between the researcher and the researched. However, as Schuman and Converse (1971) have shown, the effect of the race of the interviewer depends on the kinds of questions that are posed. Furthermore, in the conduct of field research much will depend on the questions that are used, the meaning of race in the social context being studied and the relationship between the researcher and those who are researched. In short, researchers who conduct interviews in field research need to consider the extent to which their personal characteristics will influence the practice of interviewing.

The Use of Unstructured Interviews

The unstructured interview is rarely conducted in isolation; it is often part of a broader programme of research and draws on the knowledge that the researcher has of a social situation. Finch illustrates how her interviews with the wives of clergymen drew on her own experience of being married, at the time, to a clergyman, while her interviews with young mothers who attended preschool playgroups drew on her knowledge of the playgroups she was observing. Similarly with my own study, interviews with pupils in the Newsom Department were established on the basis of the participant observation that I had done, while my interviews with teachers and with the Headmaster drew upon my participation in the school and on my earlier teaching experience.

Interviews can also be used to complement participant observation; they can help the researcher to gain access to situations that through time, place, or situation are 'closed'. In this sense, interviews might be used to gain access to the biography of an individual or to obtain a career history (cf. Woods, 1984). Secondly, they may be used to obtain details of situations which the researcher did not witness (cf. Burgess, 1983; especially pp. 84–119). Thirdly, they may be used to gain entry to situations such as classrooms where teachers may not wish the researcher to be present (cf. Burgess, 1983; especially pp. 208–35). Here, interviews may be related to other research approaches such as the informant diary (cf. Burgess, 1981a) in order to gain access to a situation (see the following chapter). However, in all these contexts it is essential for the researcher to establish procedures around which the interview is based and to which we now turn.

Interview Procedures

So far, we have examined some of the issues and problems that arise in the practice of conducting unstructured interviews. Accordingly, this section of the chapter deals with some of the procedures involved in unstructured interviewing. Many of the issues are considered in relation to previously published work and to examples drawn from my own research experience of interviewing pupils in individual and group situations. Several unedited extracts of interviews are provided in order to demonstrate the procedures adopted and to illustrate the difficulty, not to say impossibility, of rigidly following any preconceived plan.

Establishing Relationships

In any project involving unstructured interviews the relationship between the researcher and those who are researched is crucial. Usually it is assumed that this relationship is established by the researcher. In these circumstances, it is essential that the researcher conducts the interviews rather than 'farming out' the task to a number of hired hands who are unfamiliar with the setting and the personnel (cf. Roth, 1966). Certainly, in my own work I had developed relationships with pupils who were in the school's Newsom Department with the result that no interviews were conducted where I had not met the pupils before. Nevertheless, I still considered that it was important to explain *why* I wanted to conduct interviews with them and what would happen to the interview material.

I decided to use individual unstructured interviews and group interviews in my project. Usually group interviews took place before any individual interviews as I considered that in a group situation pupils would have the potential power to redefine the topics of conversation. Furthermore, it allowed spontaneity so that pupils could enter into debate and discussion with their friends. In these circumstances, they could take the conversation in directions that were meaningful to them and develop a story about their lives in school (cf. Askham, 1982). However, I maintained a topic list as I wanted to cover a range of themes in all the interviews that could subsequently be compared.

Before each interview began I explained that I had an 'agenda' of topics that I wanted to cover. However, I indicated that there was no requirement for us to cover all my topics and themes in one session nor to cover these topics in a particular order. I indicated that I would like to tape-record the interviews so that I would have an accurate account of what they had to say. Finally, having explained something of the aims of my interview and the manner in which I would like to record it, I indicated that they were free to seek clarification of any of the points that I had made and to decide whether they wished to participate.

There were no pupils who refused to be interviewed. However, several indicated that this was nothing to do with a latent desire to be interviewed but because talking with one another was better than being in classes for English and Mathematics. Before the interviews commenced I was asked several questions. What would happen to the tapes? Would I play the tapes in the staff common room? Would particular teachers be allowed to listen to the tapes? I explained that all the tapes would be kept by me and would not be played or loaned to teachers. Furthermore, I indicated that the only other person who would be allowed to listen to the tapes would be a secretary who might be asked to transcribe the tapes for me. Further questions followed about what I would do with the material when I had it transcribed. I indicated that it would be used to write a book about their school lives. This in turn prompted the question, 'will we be named?' When I indicated that pseudonyms would be used in my study they expressed disappointment. Indeed, in some cases there was considerable discussion about pseudonyms and anonymity that related to themes covered by Barnes (1979) and which are considered in Chapter 9. Many pupils saw an opportunity for instant fame if I were to publish a book about them, and considered it unfair if their real names were not to be included. In these exchanges I always made it clear that pseudonyms would be used because I had made this agreement when joining the school. However, I know this did not resolve the situation, for while some teachers wanted confidentiality, there was no individual pupil who wanted anonymity in published work. Yet these two requirements could never be satisfactorily resolved (cf. Klockars, 1977). Nevertheless, interviews were granted in all cases.

The Aide Mémoire and the Interview
At the start of each interview I explained that I had an 'agenda' which included topics or themes that I would like to cover in our discussion. This agenda acted more as an *aide mémoire* which I could use to ensure that similar topics were covered in all interviews. My agenda or list of topics was structured around the chronology of the pupils' school lives. Accordingly, I planned to start with a statement about the names of the pupils I was interviewing and the dates when they were leaving school followed by a review of their junior school careers which would lead into a discussion of their lives in the secondary school from years one to three. Finally, I wanted to focus on their upper school careers and plans about jobs they would take up on leaving school. While many of these themes were covered I found that the order in which they occurred was different in each interview as these pupils had considerable freedom to develop strategies for answering my questions. For example, in one interview two boys immediately seized the opportunity to talk about what they planned to do on leaving school, as shown in the following extract:

RB.   Now we've got John Slattery and David Owen.

John	That's right.
RB.	And John you're leaving at Easter and David you're leaving in the Summer?
John	That's right.
David	Unless I get a job and then I can go on a three day week.
RB.	Oh, I see.
John	Peter Vincent, you know Peter Vincent don't you, he's got a job on a three day week until he leaves school.
RB.	How's he getting on?
John	Well, he's getting on all right, he's getting just under £10 a week [in 1974].
David	£10?
John	Yes.
RB.	That sounds good.
John	I tried at the place but I never got a job. I've got a job now for when I leave school.
RB.	What are you doing?
John	In this car factory place making the seats for the cars and the tractors and all this rubbish.
RB.	Are you pleased about that?
John	Not really, no. It's only a job see 'cos I'm trying to get some money to go on my holidays. I'm getting this job see and me brother-in-law's getting me a form to fill in for his firm. If I can get in there I'll pack this job in.
RB.	But anyway you have got something to go to as soon as you leave.
David	I tried for four jobs last week, I went to three interviews, to a toolmaking place.
John	Good job toolmaking.
David	Yes, I know. They all said the same thing you know, they can't insure me until I'm 16.
RB.	Yes.
David	You know the toolmaker said that if I wanted to go back when I'm 16 I'd be starting off on £18 a week and I went down another place and they said they can't insure me until I'm 16, they said the same thing. I'd get about £10 or £12. When I'm going to start work the wages are secure on £10 a week. Piece work you see so it depends on how much you do, so you can earn up to £1 an hour.
RB.	That's okay.
John	As long as you work hard.
David	But I am guaranteed £10 a week.
RB.	That's all right. Well that's about when you have left school. Let's go right back to the schools that you went to first.
John	This school?

RB.   Well before you got to this school. Schools that you went to before you came here.

At the beginning of this interview the boys immediately started to talk about the topic that I had planned to cover last. However, to have stopped them talking about this topic would have prevented spontaneous conversation and broken the flow of discussion that the boys quickly established. I therefore put the topic I had planned last at the top of the agenda before working my way back to the question I wanted to ask first about their early school experiences. In this sense, the actual questions did not follow a preconceived list but revolved around topics of conversation. While I had decided the main topics to be covered the actual direction of the conversation was partially determined by the pupils.

A similar approach was taken by Corbin (1971, pp. 279–85) in interviewing managers and their wives. In addition to drawing up topics and themes she also devised some questions that could be used to start an interview or to start a particular topic. An example of the kind of list that she worked with is shown in the following extract of the topics and themes that she used in the wife's interview:

WIFE'S INTERVIEW

1 *What sort of person do you see yourself as?*
   How do you think these other people see you? Husband; parents; siblings; best friend (specify); neighbours; other members of clubs to which you belong (specify); work colleagues (if applicable); boss; tradespeople (check alternative reference groups). (Try to explain any discrepancies in above role identities. Try to get some *hierarchy of role identities* as she sees them.)
2 *Do you think you have been, or will be, a different person at different times in your life?*
   What were you like, or would you like to be like, if it is in the future, before marriage, after marriage but before having children, when you had young children, with older children, when the children have left home, when you husband retires? (Try and get her self-conception at appropriate stages in her life cycle.)
3 *From what do you get your chief sense of security?*
   Husband, parents, children, home, social standing, education, jobs, looks, money, beliefs, friends? (An alternative approach to her conception of herself and her central life interests.)
4 *Socialization*
   What sort of person was your mother/your father? With which did you get on better? How did you get on with siblings? Who really was the strongest influence on you when you were a child?

What sort of a home was it, e.g. cultural and social atmosphere? What sort of situation was it in, e.g. country, suburb, etc.?

What time before you left home was the happiest, and what was the unhappiest?

In what ways do you feel yourself to be most like, or most unlike your parents? And in what ways does life in your home resemble or differ from life in your childhood home? (Biography affecting self-conception; relationship between family of origin and family of procreation.)

5   *Aspirations* (Actual or Hypothetical)
What would you like *your daughter* to be like? What sort of job do you expect her to do? What sort of person would you like her to marry? What would you expect to be her chief source of happiness? (How much mental mobility? Is she fixed in her cultural patterns and expectations over three generations? How much awareness and acceptance of *change*? Aim at *daughter* as means of self-identification. If no children ask *if* she had a daughter.)

What sort of *education* do you want for your children? What sort of qualifications would you like them to end up with? Do you think you have different ideas about education from your own parents? (Corbin, 1971, pp. 279–80)

However, as Corbin notes, no individuals think about themselves and their lives in the terms which sociologists use. Accordingly, this list merely indicates the kinds of topics, themes and questions that *might* be covered rather than the *actual* questions that were used.

Such an approach requires particular skills on the part of the interviewer. First, it is essential to listen carefully in order to participate in the conversation, to pose particular questions on topics that have not been covered or need developing. Secondly, it is important not to interrupt the person or persons who are being interviewed as in my interview with the two boys who wanted to talk about their work plans at the beginning of the interview. Thirdly, interviewers need to monitor their own comments, gestures and actions as these may convey particular meanings to those who are interviewed which may advance or impede the interview (cf. Bogdan and Taylor, 1975, pp. 111–14). Finally, interviewers need to ensure that similar topics are covered in interviews where the data are to be used to make comparisons.

The Questions

Crucial to the unstructured interview are the kinds of questions that are posed. Spradley (1979) has identified three main types of questions that are used. First, descriptive questions which allow informants to provide statements about their activities. Secondly, structural questions which attempt to find out *how* informants organise their knowledge and, finally, contrast questions which allow informants to discuss the meanings of situations and provide an opportunity for comparisons to take place between situations and events in the informants' world. These particular questions are used at different points in the interview while the interviewer probes for details about the informants and encourages them to discuss situations in their own terms.

While I could construct a hypothetical example of how interviews *should* be conducted, it is preferable to examine how an interviewer *actually* attempts to do all these things in the course of an interview. Accordingly, I have provided an extract from an unstructured interview that I had with a 16-year-old less able Newsom pupil in the course of my study. I have provided an extract from the interview together with a commentary on the style of interviewing.

The Unstructured Interview	*Commentary*
RB. What happens when anybody does anything really bad here then?	This section of the interview starts with a general *descriptive question* using my terms.
Sean You mean when people get into trouble?	The pupil defines the question in his terms and seeks reassurance from me.
RB. Yes.	
Sean I've been caned and I've been suspended twice.	He immediately equates 'really bad' with 'trouble' and 'trouble' with 'being caned' and 'suspended'.
RB. When was that?	I attempt to locate the time period he is talking about.
Sean At the beginning of the fifth year, in fact twice in the fifth year.	
RB. Why was that?	I attempt to get the pupil to talk about the context as well as the timing of these events.
Sean Something to do with a teacher.	
RB. What was this to do with the teacher?	
Sean Going on and on and blaming me for things.	
RB. And you got suspended for that?	

The Unstructured Interview	*Commentary*
Sean Yes.	
RB. Why did you get suspended the second time?	
Sean Mr Pennington caught me smoking and he said I was suspended.	The pupil talks about suspensions. I had already read an account of this on his file but I wanted to hear how he perceived it. I wanted him to *tell it in his own words*.
RB. So you just saw Mr Pennington?	
Sean No, I had to see Mr Goddard [the Headmaster] as well.	
RB. What did Mr Goddard say?	
Sean He said that I'd be suspended until we got a letter saying that I could come back.	Again, I had read what the Head had said but I wanted to check this account (the use of multiple strategies; see Chapter 7) and to get the pupil's perspective.
RB. What did you think of that then?	
Sean (smiling) It was all right, got two weeks off didn't I.	
RB. Have you ever been caned?	I move the conversation back to the topic of 'being caned' that Sean had initially raised now that he appears to have ended all he has to say on suspension and a *natural break* occurs in the conversation.
Sean Yes, I've been caned loads of times. Not long ago.	
RB. When you say not long ago, how long ago was that?	I use his phrases to keep the conversation going. I *repeat* his words here and at various points throughout the interview and I *probe* for further data.
Sean This term.	
RB. Who was it that caned you?	I ask a descriptive question.

The Unstructured Interview	*Commentary*
Sean	Goddard [the Head-master]. No, Mr Lloyd [the Deputy Head] did.	
RB.	What did you get?	
Sean	Two on each hand.	
RB.	What was that for?	I pose a further descriptive question which is designed to *probe* for further data.
Sean	For starting up a motor bike. Clive Smith bet I couldn't start the machine up and I said, 'yes, that's easy', and Wilkinson [a teacher] caught us.	
RB.	Did you think that was fair?	
Sean	Yes, I thought that was fair.	
RB.	When was this – during breaktime or lunchtime?	Here, the pupil has provided the context but not the time of the situation so I focus my question on time (cf. my earlier strategy where I moved from time to context).
Sean	No, during a lesson. We were painting boxes up there [in the workshops] and so we saw the bike and we just went and had a look at it.	
RB.	This was when you were painting the boxes for Mr Pennington when you were on an individual timetable was it?	I attempt to get the pupil to talk more about the event but without success. This leads to a further attempt.
Sean	Yes.	
RB.	Ah, yes I remember. So you started up this motorbike and you got caned?	I demonstrate my knowledge of the situation having been in the school.
Sean	Yes.	
RB.	You said you had been caned loads of times. What other things have	I introduce a *structural question* as I want to know the categories of misbehaviour for

The Unstructured Interview	*Commentary*
you been caned for?	which *he perceives* he has been caned.
Sean Messing about, cheeking teachers, being sent to Mr Pennington, being found out of school and that sort of thing.	
RB. And you've been caned for that?	I seek clarification.
Sean And for staying off school.	
RB. And you've been caned for staying off school? What do you think about this, do you think it is fair?	
Sean Probably. Some Houses don't give you the cane, some Houses just send a letter home.	
RB. So that means in Southwark House [his own House], Sean they send a letter home and you get caned. And you say that in other Houses they just send a letter home. What House is that?	I introduce a *contrast question* based on Sean's comment and my knowledge of the school. My aim is to get Sean to compare and contrast the activities of various Houses.
Sean In all the Houses. In Clifton and Lancaster they don't cane you.	
RB. I thought they did in Clifton. So that means you can be punished in different ways for the same thing depending on which House you are in. What do you think about that?	I provide some *commentary* on the situation that gives me an opportunity to pose a further question.
Sean Not right.	
RB. Well, why do you think it happens then?	
Sean Well some kids stayed off in Lancaster and nothing	

The Unstructured Interview　　　　　*Commentary*

	happened and I just stayed off for two weeks and I got caned for it.	
RB.	What do you think about being caned over and over again?	
Sean	You get used to it.	
RB.	Yes, you get used to it, but what do you think about it?	I *repeat* his words and bring him back to the question I posed. I give him a further opportunity to answer.
Sean	They just give you the cane and that's it, don't mind. Lloyd gave us the choice of getting the cane or doing an essay of so many words and I said I'd take the cane.	
RB.	The cane instead of doing an essay?	I express my ignorance here although I have a hunch about his reasons but I want to get the account *in his own words*.
Sean	Yes, it would take me ages to do an essay whereas the cane is just a couple of minutes.	
RB.	Just now you said that sometimes you got caned and sometimes you got suspended. Which do you think is worse?	I go back over what we have been talking about and indicate to Sean that he can still tell me more and I ask a *contrast question*.
Sean	Suspended – you've got to tell your parents about it and they worry about it. They wonder what you are doing during that two weeks. The cane, they just cane you and it's over with.	Sean talks generally about parents and I am uncertain whether he is talking about his parents.
RB.	What would your parents say if they knew you had got the cane?	I try to draw on information to which I have not got direct access and use it to pose a further *comparative* question which results in the parents'

The Unstructured Interview	*Commentary*
	perspective of suspension.
Sean Nothing.	
RB. On the other hand, you said you liked it when you were suspended, why do you like it?	
Sean Well, it's a couple of weeks off school. I like it, but my parents don't.	After a further question I get Sean's account of his parents' perspective.
RB. I see, so it's because your parents don't like it, that's what makes it worse is it?	
Sean Yes, I get trouble with me parents.	

This extract from an interview with Sean Kelly is included here not because I think it provides an illustration of what other interviewers should do but because it illustrates several features of unstructured interviewing. However, my commentary has focused on selected issues concerning the questions and strategies I used to encourage Sean to talk. In this extract I begin by talking about 'trouble' which I called doing 'anything really bad'. As far as I was concerned I was prepared to talk about a range of activities but Sean volunteers to talk about suspension and corporal punishment. As these two forms of punishment were frequently given to Sean and his fellow pupils I used this section of the interview for him to make a comparison between these two punishments. In the interview several approaches are used. First, in different sequences I start with simple questions that require description, move on to more complex structural questions before posing contrast questions where comparisons are required. Secondly, I make links between the comments by posing further questions in the boy's own words so as to encourage him to provide a portrait in his terms rather than my own. Thirdly, I repeat phrases in order to probe so that the informant will provide further information. Finally, this interview extract also illustrates how I made links between observations and interviews as I made comments on situations that I had knowledge about beyond the confines of this interview.

Group Interviews

So far I have focused upon the conversation between the researcher and the researched, but this overlooks the use of the group interview. As I have indicated, I also used group interviews with pupils as I believed this would give them some control over the discussion and over the questions posed. This is evident in an interview between Terry Nicholls, Malcolm Jackson and myself. Although I began by posing questions I found that gradually a discussion developed between the two boys as shown in the following extract:

Terry   They wouldn't let me take any exams. They said I were too much of a disruptive element so they chucked me in Newsom and I've been there ever since.

RB.   So this was when you got put into Newsom. Did you get put into Newsom, Malcolm?

Malcolm   No. I was in the exam course until Christmas in the fifth year.

RB.   So what is the Newsom course like that you are both doing? What about you Terry? You've had two years of Newsom. What's Newsom about?

Terry   I don't think it's about anything. You just sit around, drink coffee and do woodcarving, that's about it. It's boring.

Malcolm   Maybe it's boring but I think it's the only best thing really. Cos if you don't do your exams it's no use staying in hindering the exam people.

Terry   I think you should be made to stay on.

Malcolm   But you're only encouraging people to wag it; to play truant. If they stay in the exam courses and don't want to take exam courses they will play truant.

In this section of the interview my question led into a discussion between the boys. Here, I did not intervene as the discussion provides freedom for them to discuss the course in their terms and to cover themes that are important to them, rather than merely to address my questions. Similarly, at a later point in the interview I do not intervene when Malcolm starts to ask questions of his friend as well as answer them. Here, I considered that this provided the two boys with an opportunity to develop a theme that they considered worthy of discussion.

Terry   It's not the kids that need disciplining it's the method of teaching.

RB.   What method of teaching is there?

Terry   It's really taking any method, give them a book and let them sit around reading the book and making them read the book. In most schools they have the same method all the way through.

Malcolm   But would you want the same all the way through?

Terry	It wouldn't bother me. This way [Newsom work] is a sort of new method.
Malcolm	Did you wanna take exams?
Terry	I wanted to take them but they wouldn't let me take them. They chucked me out.

In this sense, the group interview provided the opportunity for a dialogue to take place between the participants. Such situations provided a further opportunity to examine the relationships between the participants and the perspectives that they used, both of which had been examined in my observational work with pupils.

Some Problems in Unstructured Interviewing

Any text on interviewing draws the researcher's attention to the problems involved in using interviews. Among the issues raised are: question wording, bias, rapport, and avoiding loaded questions. Certainly, some of these issues are also present in unstructured interviews. The following extract between Roy Nash and a boy called Bruce illustrates how even in these interviews, the interviewer can come very close to not only asking questions but also providing or imposing the 'answers':

RN	You know when you filled in that questionnaire for me, what did you say you wanted to do when you left school?
BM	Nothing.
RN	Nothing? No, you didn't. I meant to ask you about that. I said last night, you know, I said, 'I'm going to screw his ears off in the morning'. What – you never put your friends down either, did you?
BM	No. I've not got any friends.
RN	Why not?
BM	Because I haven't none.
RN	Got no friends at all?
BM	No.
RN	But you must have someone to play with?
BM	No.
RN	Well, you sometimes sit by Matthew, don't you?
BM	But I never see him. He always goes away and plays with somebody else.
RN	Does he?
BM	Yes.
RN	What do you do at playtime then, for goodness sake?
BM	Just sit there against the wall.
RN	Do you?
BM	Yes.

RN   Haven't you got *any* friends?
BM   No.
RN   Don't you want any?
BM   Not really.
RN   Did you have any friends at School E?
BM   Yes, I had a lot of friends at E.
RN   You had a lot of friends at E. Well, where are they now, then?
BM   I just sort of fell out with them.
(Nash, 1973, pp. 100–1)

This extract clearly demonstrates that question wording is an issue that interviewers using an unstructured approach need constantly to monitor. For it is evident from this example that Nash is attempting to get Bruce to give him a different answer to that provided. He indicates that negative answers are not acceptable. However, it is to Bruce's credit that he refuses to change his answers despite the pressure that is exerted upon him by Nash.

As well as problems that are common to structured and unstructured interviews, there are also problems that are special to unstructured interviews. Researchers need constantly to monitor the direction, depth, and detail of the interview, the topics to include and topics to avoid, together with question order. However, there are also problems concerning the length of the interviews, recording, transcription and subsequent analysis.

Interviews should be carefully planned and timed so that some estimate is made of the number of minutes that will be given to a particular topic or theme. The interviewer also needs to estimate the blocks of time that will be required adequately to cover the topics. Often, this will result in a personal decision on the part of the researcher. However, many writers advocate using no more than two-hour blocks, otherwise fatigue results among both parties. Certainly, I have found that one-and-a-half hours is the optimum amount of time for me in conducting unstructured interviews. However, within each block I need to estimate the amount of time that is to be devoted to key topics.

As far as data recording is concerned, most researchers advocate the use of a tape-recorder (cf. Schatzman and Strauss, 1973; Bogdan and Taylor, 1975; Gorden, 1980). Indeed, without a tape-recorder much important data would be lost. Whenever tape-recorders are used it is essential that the interviewer is familiar with the machine so that data is not lost because the researcher lacks knowledge about the way the machine operates. Indeed, some texts now devote space to discuss how tape-recorders work and strategies that can be used to check a machine that appears not to work (cf. Ives, 1980, pp. 3–32). Nevertheless, researchers need to evaluate the advantages and disadvantages of tape-recording interviews in each situation in which research takes place (cf. Bucher, Fritz and Quarantelli, 1956; Ives, 1980). Even when a complete tape-recording is made of an interview there is still the problem of transcribing and analysing the data. For researchers who transcribe their own tapes a series of strategies needs to be developed in order to avoid wasting time, for transcription work is a notoriously costly business as far as time is concerned. First, the interview needs to be played before transcription begins. Secondly, an index should be prepared using the counter on the tape recorder so that a record can be kept of the themes that occur throughout the tape. Thirdly, only relevant materials should be completely transcribed. Here, it is helpful to type up transcribed material so that several copies are available for researchers to use. For it is only when this material becomes accessible that data analysis can begin. However, transcription work is hard and long as many hours need to be spent on individual interviews, especially when preliminary categories and concepts are being developed from the available data.

Conclusion

As interviews are a key method of investigation used by sociologists there is a very large literature available. However, this literature has provided relatively little material for this chapter, as much of it deals with a structured approach. In contrast, field researchers use an unstructured approach that is based on developing conversations with informants. Accordingly, examples have been taken from my own research and that of others to provide an analysis of the issues and problems that need to be considered when using this style of interviewing in any project.

Suggestions for Further Reading

Methodology

The literature available appears very large, but field researchers need to focus on discussions of unstructured interviewing. Accordingly, the following materials are recommended:

Bogdan, R. and Taylor, S. (1975), *Introduction to Qualitative Research Methods* (New York: Wiley); contains a useful discussion of the practicalities involved in conducting unstructured interviews.

Burgess, R. G. (1982) (ed.), *Field Research: a Sourcebook and Field Manual* (London: Allen & Unwin); contains a set of essays in section four on unstructured interviews.

Finch, J. (1984), ' "It's great to have someone to talk to": the ethics and politics of interviewing women', in C. Bell and H. Roberts (eds), *Social Researching: Policies, Problems and Practice* (London: Routledge &

Kegan Paul); is a reflective essay on the author's experiences of conducting interviews in two projects. In addition, she discusses the influence of feminism on her interviewing style.

Gorden, R. L. (1980), *Interviewing: Strategy, Techniques and Tactics* (3rd edn) (New York: Dorsey Press); is a basic text that reviews a range of interviewing styles and has the virtue of looking at theoretical and practical issues involved in interviewing.

Oakley, A. (1981), 'Interviewing women: a contradiction in terms', in H. Roberts (ed.), *Doing Feminist Research* (London: Routledge & Kegan Paul); provides a feminist analysis of textbook accounts of interviewing.

Platt, J. (1981), 'On interviewing one's peers', *British Journal of Sociology*, vol. 32, no. 1, pp. 75–91; a discussion of the social, technical and ethical assumptions that surround unstructured interviews using the author's own research.

Simons, H. (1981), 'Conversation piece: the practice of interviewing in case study research', in C. Adelman (ed.), *Uttering, Muttering: Collecting, Using and Reporting Talk for Social and Educational Research* (London: Grant McIntyre); provides a useful discussion of the practicalities of conducting unstructured interviews.

Spradley, J. P. (1979), *The Ethnographic Interview* (New York: Holt, Rinehart & Winston); provides a detailed if somewhat schematic treatment of unstructured interviews.

Empirical Studies

There is a range of field studies that provide extracts from unstructured interviews. The following studies should be examined for the ways in which unstructured interviews have been conducted and used in the analysis:

Burgess, R. G. (1983), *Experiencing Comprehensive Education: A Study of Bishop McGregor School* (London: Methuen).

Corrigan, P. (1979), *Schooling the Smash Street Kids* (London: Macmillan).

Macintyre, S. (1977), *Single and Pregnant* (London: Croom Helm).

Nash, R. (1973), *Classrooms Observed* (London: Routledge & Kegan Paul).

Platt, J. (1976), *Realities of Social Research* (London: Chatto & Windus for Sussex University Press).

Pryce, K. (1979), *Endless Pressure* (Harmondsworth: Penguin).

Rainwater, L. (1970), *Behind Ghetto Walls* (Chicago: Aldine) (also published by Penguin, 1973).

Woods, P. (1979), *The Divided School* (London: Routledge & Kegan Paul).

6

Methods of Field Research 3:
Using Personal Documents

Early field studies conducted by social anthropologists rarely used written documentary evidence, as the societies they studied were pre-literate
and did not possess or spontaneously produce written evidence. However, when field research was utilised in the study of urban America in
the 1920s and 1930s documentary sources were added to the range of
evidence that could be used, for the people who were studied produced
and received written documentation that related to their own lives. The
documents that were utilised constituted natural subjective accounts of
the people's social world and included autobiographies, letters, diaries,
notes, memoranda, minutes of meetings, logs of decisions and official
records. In addition, there were also visual documents in the form of
photographs and films together with oral documents that sociologists,
anthropologists and historians invited the people to produce.

Despite the wealth of documentary materials that are available for the
social scientist to use, there are relatively few systematic accounts of
documentary evidence in 'methods' textbooks. Instead, documents are
usually dealt with in a brief way under such headings as 'official statistics', 'unobtrusive measures' or 'alternative sources of data'. Indeed, Platt
(1981a) found only seven accounts of documentary evidence in her
analysis of eighteen general methodology texts. However, the neglect of
these materials is not confined to 'methods' books, as introductions to
field research seldom contain any discussion of documents (cf. Lofland,
1971; Wax, 1971; Schatzman and Strauss, 1973; Johnson, 1975), nor do
field studies (cf. Whyte, 1955). As such this constitutes a major omission,
for as Plummer (1983) shows, the world is full of documents that people
write, send, keep, publish, display and screen. The range of written,
audio and visual material demands the attention of social scientists
including field researchers. However, if some benefit is to be gained from
documentary materials some classification is essential.

Classifying Documentary Evidence

A basic distinction has been made between *primary sources* and
secondary sources. Primary sources are materials that are gathered

first hand and have a direct relationship with the people, situations or events that are studied. Among the documents included as primary sources are: court records, minutes, contracts, letters, memoranda, notes, memoirs, diaries, autobiographies and reports. Each document provides a first-hand account of a situation. However, primary sources should not be viewed uncritically, for if such materials are to be used in studies it is essential to locate them in context. This often means looking at material that has already been published and which constitutes secondary sources. These sources may include transcripts or summaries of primary source materials. However, even though these materials are published, critical appraisal is essential as errors may have occurred when the materials were transcribed, summarised and edited. In the case of primary and secondary sources, the researcher needs to consider the perspective from which the materials are produced as they are versions of a social situation.

A second distinction that can be made is between *public documents* and *private documents* (Denzin, 1970a). Among public documents are included newspaper reports, court and police records. Webb *et al.* (1966, pp. 57–82) have identified four different types of public documents. First, actuarial records on the population, for example, certificates of births, marriages and deaths which yield large amounts of statistical data. Secondly, political and judicial records which include decisions by the courts, and by the government. Thirdly, other government records on the weather, parking meter collections, social welfare programmes, and hospital records. Finally, the mass media which can include analyses of newspaper editorials, advertising, and letters, as well as news content. Some of these items might also be included under the heading of private documents which have been taken to include letters, diaries, and autobiographies. However, researchers should note how these materials may start out as private personal documents and end up as public materials. For example, the letters that Margaret Mead sent to named individuals were subsequently made public in published form in reflections on her fieldwork (Mead, 1977). Similarly, Malinowski's personal reflections that were written in the diary he maintained on his field trips were later published (Malinowski, 1967).

Thirdly, a distinction is made between documents that are *unsolicited* and those that are *solicited*. Unsolicited documents are those that have been produced without research in mind. They have been produced for the personal use of the individual as in the case of a personal diary or a report. Meanwhile, solicited documents are produced at the request of the researcher, for example diaries that are kept to cover specific periods of time (Willmott, 1969) or specific activities (Burgess, 1983, pp. 229–32). In the case of unsolicited documents the researcher has to make use of what is available, while solicited documents allow the researcher some control over the material that is produced. In both instances some account needs to be taken of the perspective that is adopted by the writer, and the ways in which the materials have been selected, analysed and presented in the course of a study.

From a brief survey of documentary evidence it is apparent that there is a considerable range of material covered by terms such as 'personal document', 'life history', 'life story', 'human document', 'first person account' and 'autobiography'. No matter what form these various documents take, essential to them all is that they present an individual's subjective view of social life. In recent years many of these approaches have been neglected, yet the value of such documents is clearly revealed in classic accounts of sociological research. In the remainder of this chapter, I provide a brief survey of a range of personal documents together with some commentary on the ways in which these materials have been used in sociological research, including my own.

The Life History

The basic approach that has been used by sociologists engaged in the collection of historical materials is the life history which includes much autobiographical material presented in the informant's *own* words. Such material was used in classic studies such as Thomas and Znaniecki's *The Polish Peasant in Europe and America* (1918–20), in Shaw's *The Jack Roller* (1930) and Sutherland's *The Professional Thief* (1937). The argument for using life history data was clearly put by Thomas and Znaniecki when they wrote:

In analysing the experiences and attitudes of an individual, we always reach data and elementary facts which are not exclusively limited to this individual's personality, but can be treated as mere incidences of more or less general classes of data or facts, and can thus be used for the determination of laws of social becoming. Whether we draw our materials for sociological analysis from detailed life records of concrete individuals or from the observation of mass phenomena, the problems of sociological analysis are the same. But even when we are searching for abstract laws, life records, as complete as possible, constitute the *perfect* type of sociological material, and if social science has to use other materials at all it is only because of the practical difficulty of obtaining at the moment a sufficient number of such records to cover the totality of sociological problems, and of the enormous amount of work demanded for an adequate analysis of all the personal materials necessary to characterise the life of a social group. If we are forced to use mass phenomena as material, or any kind of happenings taken without regard to the life histories of the individuals who participated, it is a defect, not an advantage, of our present sociological method. (Thomas and Znaniecki, 1918-20, pp. 1832-3).

For these researchers life history data included autobiographies, letters and diaries which together constituted *perfect* sociological data. However, their view is not shared by all, for their study and the method of investigation has been the subject of a wide-ranging evaluation (Blumer, 1939). It seemed that the letters had been bought from individuals who responded to an advertisement in a Polish journal, that the newspapers were obtained by Thomas while visiting Poland, that documents were collected from an agency concerned with emigration from Poland and the autobiography had been obtained from a Pole who had recently come from Poland. While Blumer considered that these documents contributed to the subjective study of social life by providing theories, concepts, insights and observations, he was also critical of them. In particular, he argued that the reliability of these documents could be questioned as could their adequacy, representativeness and validity (Blumer, 1939). Researchers who use such documents therefore need to consider how they are gathered, how they are used and what their strengths and limitations are.

Autobiographies

Autobiographical data have taken various forms. Allport (1942) distinguished between three particular forms. First, the comprehensive autobiography which covers the main trends in an individual's life. Secondly, the topical autobiography which selects a particular theme around which an individual constructs a story. Finally, the edited autobiography where the researcher selects, monitors, and deletes items. In each case the autobiography provides individuals with an opportunity to give their own accounts of their lives. It provides an *insider's* point of view.

These documents are collected either by getting the individual to write out their own account as Sutherland got Chick Conwell to do, or by the researcher transcribing an oral account as Klockars (1975) has done. Klockars discusses the routine that he adopted with his informant Vincent. He explains that each meeting would begin with informal conversation over dinner in a restaurant after which we would drive to Vincent's home; there, in Vincent's consideration the 'real' interviewing would begin. This was signalled by my opening my briefcase and taking out my notebook and pencils. Vincent's part in the ritual was to settle in his large recliner chair and light his cigar. Quite often the topic which we would begin was carried over from our conversation at dinner.

By ten-thirty Vincent would usually grow tired; he started his day at five-thirty every morning except Sunday. Occasionally an especially productive interview would keep us going until midnight but usually I would leave by eleven. As I drove home I would dictate my comments, recollections and impressions into a small, battery operated tape recorder. (Klockars, 1975, p. 218)

In this instance the physical transcription is done by the researcher. Meanwhile, in Bogdan's study of the transsexual Jane Fry (Bogdan, 1974) the autobiography was obtained from 100 hours of tape-recorded conversation between the researcher and his informant.

In each of these cases the researcher has to decide what to ask, when to ask it, and how to ask it. In these terms, obtaining autobiographical data over a number of sessions allows the researcher to shift from the simple to the complex, and from the non-controversial to the contentious aspects of the informant's life. In my own study (Burgess, 1983) I wanted to obtain brief life histories from the teachers that focused in particular on their social background, their reasons for becoming teachers, their teaching experience in other schools and in McGregor School and in particular their contacts (of whatever kind) with the pupils who were in the fifth year Newsom group that I was studying. Accordingly, I produced a framework around which they could write a brief autobiography on two sides of A4 paper that was attached to the following note:

As part of my research I am interested in the kind of things you have done before coming into teaching, your teaching experience and the work that you do now. I am also interested in your contact with the 5th Year Newsom pupils.

In writing about these things on the attached sheet, the following suggestions might help:

The people in your family – the work they did, the area they lived in, their religion.
The schools you went to and what you did at school.
The college or university you went to and what you did.
Anything you have done other than teaching.
The places you have taught.

Your work in McGregor and your contact with the 5th Year Newsom pupils.

I hope this will help – if you would like to chat about this I shall be interested to hear from you.

Many thanks,

Bob Burgess.

These topics were specifically chosen as many of them arose out of my observational work in the school. Furthermore, I wanted all the teachers to write in these terms so that I could make some comparisons between the accounts and overcome problems of comparability between data sources that have been discussed by the contributors to Stacey (1969c) and Gittus (1972). The results of this approach are provided in the career biographies of two Newsom teachers that are reported in Burgess (1983, pp. 197–9) and which allowed comparisons to be made between their social and educational backgrounds, teaching experience and approach to teaching.

Although this approach does yield a range of data it also produces a number of problems. First, there is the problem of reliability: how do we know that the informant is telling the truth? In this instance, it is essential for the researcher to cross-check between autobiographical materials obtained at different times and autobiographical materials and other data (see Chapter 7). Secondly, there is the question of language. With written accounts this is not so problematic. However, researchers have to take account of the relationship between the informant's written words and spoken words. When a recording is made of an informant's life story particular attention needs to be given to vocabulary and the style of expression together with the rhythms and patterns of speech. In addition, there are also problems concerning authenticity, interpretation and presentation which are common to several documentary methods and which will be considered later in this chapter.

Diaries and Diary Interviews

Diaries are a further example of first-hand accounts which have been classified by Allport (1942) in terms of intimate journals, memoirs and logs. First, the intimate journal is for Allport the best form of personal document as it is here that the individual provides an account of thoughts, events and feelings which are considered important. It is a document that is produced spontaneously. However, such accounts have usually been produced by individuals from particular social groups, for they have rarely been produced by members of the working class. Secondly, there is the memoir which often shares much in common with the autobiography or career biography. A noted recent example is the diaries of Richard Crossman which discuss particular periods in his career such as his years at the Ministry of Housing (Crossman, 1975). Again, the extent to which these accounts represent particular sections of the population and omit particular social groups by class, race and gender should be noted. Finally, there is the log that Allport refers to as a record of events, meetings and visits. In my own research the school log book completed by the Headmaster provided this kind of account. Here, the entries were handwritten and covered various spans of time. I found that days, weeks, months and terms were not always written about with increasing detail. Indeed, in some instances there were as few details provided on a week's or term's events as on a day's events. This particular log provided examples of a number of problems associated with such documents. First, there is the practical problem of deciphering handwriting. Secondly, there is the question of selection on the part of the writer who has included, excluded and suppressed items or who has written in detail on some items and provided little information on others. Finally, there is the issue of relating data obtained in this way to other materials.

However, it is relatively rare to find diaries or logs being kept by individuals that are subsequently made public for research. Accordingly, researchers have persuaded their informants to keep diaries which can subsequently be used for research (Pons, 1969; Willmott, 1969; Burgess, 1983; Finch, 1983). In my own study, I used diaries to get access to events in classrooms. Here, I asked teachers who worked with Newsom pupils to keep diaries of what occurred within their classrooms. I adopted this approach as it is unusual (other than in team teaching situations) for another teacher to be present in the classroom (cf. Shaw, 1969) and I found that teachers were not always willing to have another adult in a classroom when teaching difficult pupils.

The type of diary that could be used might be highly structured with pages divided into particular sessions (morning and afternoon) with particular subdivisions for lessons and time periods within lessons. While this approach has been used by social scientists such as Maas and Kuypers (1974) to deal with problems of selection and typicality, I did not think that it was worth pursuing as it appeared to overlook spontaneity, detail and specific insights that individuals could provide about their encounters in the classroom. Accordingly, I adopted an unstructured approach. I gave each teacher who worked with Newsom pupils an exercise book in which to make their diary entries. Each book contained a note that provided a framework within which the teachers might consider making their entries and allowed some comparisons to be made between entries within a diary and between diaries. The note contained the following details:

DIARIES

I am interested in what actually happens in the course of your lessons with members of the 5th Year Newsom group. I would, therefore, appreciate it if you could keep this diary over the next four weeks. It would be interesting to know what the lesson is about, what members of the group say and do (or do not do). Finally, it might be useful to write up what one or two pupils (selected at random) do in the course of your lesson.

If you would like to chat to me about the notes you keep I shall be interested to hear from you.

Many thanks,

Bob Burgess.

These instructions were intended to get the teachers to provide a continuous record over one month that would address four questions: when? (the date and time of the lesson). Where? (the location; that is the Department in which the lesson took place). What? (the activities that did (and did not) occur). Who? (the individuals involved). Finally, I indicated that I would be willing to discuss entries in my informants' diaries which resulted in diary-interviews (cf. Burgess, 1981a; Zimmerman and Wieder, 1977).

The type of response that I obtained and the relationship between a diary and a diary-interview can be seen by examining extracts from Jane Adams's diary and a subsequent diary-interview that I held with her. Jane Adams taught English to the lowest ability group in the fifth year that contained a number of Newsom pupils. Her account begins with a discussion of the context before she provides individual entries. In the extracts that follow I provide a commentary on her entries which indicates the way in which the diary-interview was constructed.

Diary Entry	*Commentary*
5I English	
There are normally 25 in the class but fortunately they *are* [emphasis in original] never all here together. Five of the boys have been entered for CSE and one or two of them may have a slight chance. These five always sit at the back and are supposed to work on their own on a piece	This section provides the context of the classes and addresses the *who* question.

Diary Entry

Commentary

of work I set each week but they can't resist the comedy show put on by the rest of the class.

The underlining is my own and indicates an area that I would want to discuss in the diary-interview. In particular, I was interested in finding out about what constituted 'the comedy show'.

Only eight of the class are girls and they are generally quiet, either gossiping or sitting quiet or even working. They very rarely take the initiative in discussion or even trouble-making, though one or two sometimes reply vigorously to the boys' remarks.

The phrase 'trouble-making' was underlined by me to indicate that I would like to know what form this took.

Having provided the context of the classes there followed individual entries on particular lessons. I have chosen the following extracts from her diary as they are subsequently discussed in the extracts from the diary-interview.

6th March

Usually the best lesson of the week as it is the only one we have in the morning. Peter Vincent away to-day; Clive Smith asked permission to go to woodwork and brought me a picture of a bird he is carving, so I allowed him to go.

This section addresses the question *when*? This section also deals with *who* is and *who* is not involved in the class. In addition, this raises a question about why this teacher allowed this pupil to go to another class. I had found this occurred in other teachers' accounts and I wanted, therefore, to question her about this in the subsequent interview.

The work set was to finish writing on 'The person I will marry'.
This was begun on Monday but some people did no work at all then and others wrote only a few lines. I have marked what work they did and written in

This section addresses the question *what* is and is not happening in the class.

Diary Entry	Commentary
questions, hopefully (!) to provide further thought.	
The class worked quite well generally and most people wrote about half a page – then brought the book to me and I wrote in an extra question. For some reason this produces a better result than if I just say, 'Would you expect your wife to have a job?' 19 people in the classroom. Only 2 of the 5 CSE boys brought the books they should be studying.	The phrase has been underlined by me and indicates an area that I would like to follow up in a diary-interview. In particular, I decided that I would like to know what is the meaning of 'worked quite well generally'.
In all, quite a good lesson. Some laughing and gossip from the girls but boys wrote or talked very quietly. I didn't become angry or even annoyed.	Another phrase underlined by me as I wanted to find out in the subsequent diary-interview what 'quite a good lesson' is like. Here, I wanted to obtain further detail.
8th March Friday afternoon An unprepared and messy lesson – pupils and teacher feeling Friday-ish. Only 2 girls present. 1 CSE boy wrote diligently all lesson, 1 half concentrated. The former gave in his essay to be marked as he left.	The entry begins by providing the context and addresses the questions *when*? *what*? and *who*?
The rest of us discussed the boys' applications for jobs and the tests they are being given for apprenticeships. They are, or pretended to be, confident about these.	
Some noise and one or two minor tussles e.g. over a pencil.	
No serious trouble – a better result than I deserved, having prepared nothing for the lesson.	The phrase 'no serious trouble' has been underlined by me as I wanted to follow up the meaning of this phrase in a subsequent diary-interview in order to find out what constituted 'serious trouble' and what was 'no serious trouble'.

The extracts from this teacher's diary provide her account of her lessons. As I have indicated in my commentary I used her diary entries to construct a diary-interview with a view to obtaining a more detailed account of her lessons and in order to discover the meaning that she attributed to key words and phrases. To prepare for each diary-interview I began by going through each diary underlining phrases which I would like explained in greater detail and events that I wanted the teacher to describe. Secondly, I structured a series of discussion questions out of these diary entries which were then assembled with page references from the diary so that a diary-interview could take place in which relatively easy reference could be made to the diary itself. The particular section of the interview which relates to the extracts of the diary already quoted are given below together with my commentary.

Diary Interview

RB. For the 6th March in an English lesson where quite a few pupils did some writing you commented 'in all, quite a good lesson' and again in another section 'the class worked quite well generally' and then later that week you say 'there was no serious trouble'. I wonder if you could expand for example the phrase 'quite well' and 'no serious trouble' – what for you would count as 'serious trouble'?

Jane When I think that a lesson
Adams has gone well, I think what I mean is that if I have asked them to write they have done some writing, which certainly when I asked them to write not all of them always did. So, it was successful in that they did what I told them, which sounds dreadful, but also hopefully, to write they had considered the subject put forward and

Commentary

I provide details of the context in which the remarks were written before I use Jane's own words as a key to addressing particular questions. In addition, I bring together the comments on what was 'quite a good lesson' and where there was 'no serious trouble' to see if any comparison can be made by the teacher.

Jane begins by taking each phrase in turn. She explains the meaning she attaches to each phrase and provides further details about *what* was happening in this class.

Diary Interview

may have even thought about it a bit.

When I say 'there was no serious trouble' I would think that I mean if I introduce a subject for discussion some at least of the class talked about that subject and nobody disrupted the lesson by talking about something else or by being rude either to me or to each other to the extent that it became impossible to carry on that discussion.

RB.   What would count as being rude to you in the context of these lessons? Can you think of an example that has occurred this year?

Jane   That has occurred?
Adams

RB.   Yes.
Jane   I find that very difficult
Adams   because on the whole I don't tend to think in terms of being rude. I mean I was going to say if somebody said, 'Silly old bitch' to me but nobody did. I would have found that offensive.
RB.   Yes [said with interest].

Commentary

When the phrase 'no serious trouble' is explained Jane indicates by implication what would involve 'serious trouble' for her. Her discussion ends with a statement about 'being rude' which I subsequently use.

As with unstructured interviews (see Chapter 5) I take Jane's phrase and use it to form a question that keeps the conversation going. In addition, this brings in a further dimension which was not covered in the diary.

Jane seeks clarification from me. I indicate that I would like her to discuss an actual rather than a hypothetical example.

Nevertheless, she begins with a hypothetical example.

I use the word 'yes' with an expression and tone of voice that indicates interest on my part. I want to encourage her to continue talking.

	Diary Interview	*Commentary*
Jane Adams	Nobody did probably because they know that I would find that offensive. They did things that I didn't like. Like if I was talking about something that I thought was getting somewhere with somebody – somebody else interrupted me and said, 'That's a load of rubbish' I don't think I would say to them, 'That's rude' because that's a meaningless thing to say to them I find.	Jane provides an actual example of the kind of activity that occurs using the phrase 'meaningless' which I take up to pose a further question.
RB.	Why 'meaningless'?	

These extracts from a diary and a diary-interview indicate the use of these particular personal documents. The diary provides a first-hand account of a situation to which a researcher may not have direct access. Secondly, it provides an 'insider's' account of a situation and, finally, complements the materials that are gathered through observation and interview by the researcher. Nevertheless, diaries may vary in terms of depth and detail which may result in the researcher requiring more detailed data. In order to obtain the telling detail that is associated with field studies, the diary can be used as a resource to raise questions and queries that may generate further data.

Letters

Unlike autobiographies and diaries which are usually written with either the researcher in mind or as 'private' documents for the writer, letters are of a different nature. Letters are not written for research purposes but, unlike the other documents that have been discussed, are always written for an audience. In this sense, letters are indicative of different kinds of social relationships. The classic use of letters in social research is provided in Thomas and Znaniecki's study of *The Polish Peasant* (1918–20) in which they identify five major types of letter. First, ceremonial letters relating to births, weddings, and deaths and to particular periods of the year. Secondly, letters that are intended to provide information. Thirdly, sentimental letters. Fourthly, literary letters and, finally, business letters. These different kinds of letter are utilised in their study to discuss subjective elements of the society in which the letter-writers lived. However, an analysis of letters can reveal much about the two parties involved. Allport (1942) shows that letters may indicate the relationship between the letter-writer and the recipient. In particular, some note needs to be taken of the frequency with which letters are written, the style of address and the content of the letters.

During the course of my Bishop McGregor study I found letters to be indispensible. There were many different kinds available: letters between the Headmaster and external groups such as the governors and local education authority officials, letters from teachers to parents and parents to teachers, together with notes that took the form of letters for internal circulation among teachers. These letters could be used to help reconstruct events that occurred before my study began but which were relevant to the content, to complement observations that had been made in the school, or to complement data obtained in interviews. In addition, letters could also be used to shed light on social relationships. For example, I examined the letters that were written by the Headmaster about one boy's suspension from the school. There were copies of these letters on file that had been sent to the boy's parents, the chairman of the school governors and the director of education. In each instance, the letters were formal and the content was broadly similar. However, the terms in which the letters were written were different as emphasis was given to different points. To the parents the emphasis was upon the boy's misdemeanours and how he was to be excluded from the school until they had come to discuss his future with the Head. To the chairman of the governors there was a formal statement followed by a remark that indicated that teachers had persevered with the boy, while to the director of education the same letter ended with a note saying that the boy might have to be permanently removed from the school at a later date unless further support through the social services and through additional teaching staff was given to the school. In this instance, no individual letter standing alone adequately covered the suspension. Indeed, in order to construct an account about the issues and implications of the suspension all the letters had to be consulted (cf. the discussion of multiple strategies of research in Chapter 7). Furthermore, these letters could be compared with other letters to individuals and groups beyond the school to examine the nature of the Headmaster's relationships with parents, with the school governors and with local education officials.

While letters are a resource that the researcher can use, they do raise several problems. First, there is the problem of analysis. Letters need to be put in context. In these terms, individual letters need to be related to further letters either between the same people or to letters of a similar class. Secondly, researchers need to consider what right they have to use letters that they obtain in the course of research and whether they need to seek the permission of the writer and the recipient before they are used (cf. Burgess, 1981b). Finally, letters need to be examined in relation to other data (cf. Burgess, 1982b, 1983 especially pp. 147–80). In short, letters like other personal documents need to be evaluated, a subject to which we now turn.

Evaluating Personal Documents

In evaluating various forms of documentary evidence questions need to be raised about authenticity, distortion and deception, availability and sampling, and also presentation, all of which we shall examine.

Authenticity

Questions of authenticity may be seldom raised about personal documentary evidence that has been collected orally or that has been solicited from informants. However, where unsolicited written documents are used it is essential to establish their authenticity. Gottschalk (1945, pp. 28–34) indicates the criteria that need to be used in making a decision. First, there is the question of forgery or misrepresentation. Certainly, this problem had to be tackled when examining letters supposedly written by parents about pupil absences. In order to establish authenticity I looked at the handwriting (which could be compared between letters and in certain cases with the pupil's own handwriting (cf. Burgess, 1983, pp. 147–80)) and the type of paper which was used (lined or unlined writing paper or pages from a school exercise book). Secondly, I examined the mode of presentation, paying particular attention to the use of words and phrases and to spelling. Finally, there was the question of the meaning that could be attached to letters. This included making an assessment about home–school relations which could also be evaluated in relation to other data that I had collected (cf. Burgess, 1983, pp. 157–61).

Distortion and Deception

When considering distortion and deception on the part of the author some consideration needs to be given to an individual's motives for writing a particular document. Allport (1942, pp. 67–75) distinguished thirteen motives that individuals may have for producing particular documents. Accordingly, consideration needs to be given, especially when collecting autobiographical data, to points of exaggeration and misrepresentation (cf. Klockars, 1975, p. 224) as there may well be particular reasons why an individual would wish to reconstruct a situation or to exaggerate in order to propagandise. Furthermore, it is essential to consider if attempts have been made deliberately to omit materials or whether omissions have simply been made by the writer who assumes familiarity on the part of the reader with the cultural scene (cf. Chapter 1).

In short, the question that recurs when using various forms of personal document is: how do we know that the informant is not attempting to distort or deceive? Gottschalk (1945, pp. 43–4) has indicated five sets of circumstances in which he believes the researcher can assume that the informant is providing a credible account. First, when the writer is indifferent to the person or the situation. Secondly, when a statement is prejudicial to an informant. Thirdly, on matters of common knowledge. Fourthly, when situations are not well known but at least probable and, finally, when the informant makes statements which are contrary to the researcher's expectations. However, if these criteria are to be applied it would appear to assume that the researcher has a detailed knowledge of the informant from other sources.

Availability and Sampling

Once we begin to consider questions about the availability of documentary evidence we are also beginning to consider our sampling procedures as some account is being made of the materials that are and are not available for selection. In the course of examining the official school records I found that in some cases there were detailed syllabuses available for departments, yet in other instances no such materials were available. Here, several questions arise: is there any significance to be attached to the presence or absence of material? Does absence indicate that no such documents exist, or that no such documents exist for public consultation or that unlike the documents available some revisions are taking place? Finally, there are questions of typicality and the extent to which documents are representative or unrepresentative of a particular individual, group or situation.

In turn, there are also questions of selection and sampling. Platt (1981a, pp. 37–40) has indicated ways in which selection and sampling may be conducted in order to overcome bias. However, in the course of obtaining documents of the same class, for example pupils' files, one may find differences in the evidence that has been selected by those who maintain the files. At McGregor each House kept records on individual pupils. For each pupil there *should* have been a file that held: a primary school record card, a McGregor record sheet, copies of school reports, copies of letters to social agencies and parents concerning the individual pupil and letters received from home. However, there was no standard procedure for keeping and maintaining records with the result that different House Heads selected different material to keep on pupils. No House Head kept all the material on individual pupils. In Clifton House, every letter to and from parents was filed, while in Southwark House only letters from teachers to parents were filed. Meanwhile in Westminster House, in addition to the correspondence, a wide variety of ephemera had been collected about pupils: notes from teachers, commendation slips, notes initiated by the pupils to other pupils and in one case a copy of an obscene poem that the child had been found to be circulating in a class. The result of this range of material raises questions about quality as well as quantity and issues concerning comparability. In this instance it would be impossible to claim representativeness, but some control needs to be exercised over the data that are used. I attempted to come to terms with these issues by making comparisons between pupils for whom similar sets of documentary data were available in different Houses (cf. Burgess, 1983, pp. 147–80). In addition, I used documents as a resource from which social categories could be generated and subsequently checked against data that were obtained in other ways.

Presentation
A final problem which confronts the researcher is how to analyse, interpret and present the materials that have been collected. First, documentary evidence has to be interpreted in context. Secondly, some consideration needs to be given to the ultimate aims and objectives of the researcher in relation to the final research report, that is, the extent to which the material is to be used descriptively or in terms of making generalisations. Finally, there is the question of presentation. Some writers suggest publishing all the data that are collected (cf. Kluckhohn, 1945) or presenting all the instances that support a particular point (cf. Platt, 1976). However, these approaches are somewhat cumbersome with the result that Platt (1981b) suggests a series of strategies that are commonly used in field research. First, to use a systematic method and give a general account of it. Secondly, to give accounts of relevant aspects of methods in relation to conclusions or devising *ad hoc* means of supporting them. Thirdly, to provide illustrations representative of the data available. However, the problem here is that the reader has to trust the author unless all three strategies are used in any piece of work. It is a combination of strategies that is advocated by Platt, but this still requires the researcher to decide where the emphasis should be placed.

Conclusion

This chapter has provided a discussion and evaluation of some of the most common forms of personal documents that can be used by field researchers. As sociologists and social anthropologists have most often conducted life history studies using autobiographies, letters and diaries, particular attention has been given to these approaches. However, as Plummer (1983) has shown there is a range of other sources that can be used: oral history, journalism, photographs and films. Many of these have been discussed in greater detail elsewhere: oral history is reviewed by Thompson (1978) and by Bennett (1981), while journalistic accounts are available from Terkel in America (1967, 1970, 1977) and from Parker (1962, 1963, 1967) and Seabrook (1967, 1971, 1973) in Britain. In turn the importance of visual material in the form of photographic evidence is apparent in the work of Berger and Mohr (1967, 1975), Marsden and Duff (1975) and Walker (1984). Meanwhile, case studies are also available in a number of films. Ethnographic films are regularly reviewed in the *American Anthropologist*, and British television has screened documentary films produced by Roger Graef and 'narrative documentaries' by Richard Denton. British television producers have been able to make films that provide detailed case studies of prisons, the police, public schools, and comprehensive schools. However, no matter what documentary evidence is used there are problems concerning authenticity, availability, sampling, inter-pretation and presentation. All of these issues therefore need to be considered by researchers who use documentary evidence of any kind. However, the value of documentary evidence is that it provides data which may be used to examine social categories and social processes. In this sense, these data link up with other data that are obtained in the conduct of field research.

Suggestions for Further Reading

Methodology
There is a large literature on documents. However, it is *vital* to consider arguments that have direct relevance for the use of documentary materials in field research. Accordingly, the following books and papers should be consulted:

Allport G. W. (1942), *The Use of Personal Documents in Psychological Science*, Bulletin No. 49 (New York: Social Science Research Council); is a classic report on documentary research.

Bertaux, D. (1981) (ed.), *Biography and Society: The Life History Approach in the Social Sciences* (Beverly Hills, Calif.: Sage); contains papers on epistemological issues, life history as oral history and a range of empirical examples.

Burgess, R. G. (1982) (ed.), *Field Research: a Sourcebook and Field Manual* (London: Allen & Unwin). Section Five on historical sources in field research contains papers on written documents, oral sources and life histories (Mandelbaum, 1973; Thompson, 1972; Samuel, 1976).

Dymond, D. (1981), *Writing Local History: A Practical Guide* (London: Bedford Square Press). A short, well written guide on the conduct of historical research. It includes a discussion on the use of sources as well as on writing. This book should be read by all social scientists.

Gottschalk, L., Kluckhohn, C., and Angell, R. (1945), *The Use of Personal Documents in History, Anthropology and Sociology*, Bulletin No. 53 (New York: Social Science Research Council). A collection of essays that is a 'classic' in this field of study.

Graef, R. (1980), 'The case study as Pandora's box', in H. Simons (ed.), *Towards a Science of the Singular* (Norwich: Centre for Applied Research in Education, Occasional Publication No. 10), pp. 162–78; an account of doing case studies by a film-maker who has produced documentary studies of institutions. He raises questions about the ethics of observational film-making and the use of film.

Langlois, C. V. and Seignobos, C. (1898), *Introduction to the Study of History* (London: Duckworth). A classic statement on historiography. The focus is on written documents but their discussion is equally applicable to a range of documentary materials.

Platt, J. (1981), 'Evidence and proof in documentary research: some specific problems of documentary research', *Sociological Review*, vol. 29, no. 1, pp. 31–52.

Platt, J. (1981), 'Evidence and proof in documentary research: some shared problems of documentary research', *Sociological Review*, vol. 29, no. 1, pp. 53–66. Two related articles by the same author that provide a discussion of documentary evidence using a range of sources and examples. In particular, the relationship between documents and field research is explicitly discussed.

Plummer, K. (1983), *Documents of Life: An Introduction to the Problems and Literature of a Humanistic Method* (London: Allen & Unwin). A highly readable survey of documentary materials. It combines theoretical discussion alongside the practicalities of doing research together with critical commentary.

Empirical Studies

There is a range of studies in which life history and oral history documents are the major materials presented. Some of the main studies in these areas include:

Bogdan, R. (1974), *Being Different: the Autobiography of Jane Fry* (New York: Wiley).

Gittins, D. (1982), *Fair Sex: Family Size and Structure, 1900–1939* (London: Hutchinson).

Humphries, S. (1981), *Hooligans or Rebels? An Oral History of Working Class Childhood and Youth 1889–1939* (Oxford: Blackwell).

Klockars, C. B. (1975), *The Professional Fence* (London: Tavistock).

Shaw, C. (1930), *The Jack Roller, a Delinquent Boy's Own Story* (Chicago: University of Chicago Press).

Sutherland, E. (1937), *The Professional Thief* (Chicago: University of Chicago Press).

Thomas, W. I. and Znaniecki, F. (1918–20), *The Polish Peasant in Europe and America* (Chicago: University of Chicago Press).
Thompson, T. (1981), *Edwardian Childhoods* (London: Routledge & Kegan Paul).

In addition, researchers have used documentary evidence alongside other evidence. In particular, the following studies might be examined to see how documents are actually used:

Atkinson, J. M. (1978), *Discovering Suicide: Studies in the Social Organization of Sudden Death* (London: Macmillan).
Burgess, R. G. (1983), *Experiencing Comprehensive Education: A Study of Bishop McGregor School* (London: Methuen).
Goodson, I. F. (1982), *School Subjects and Curriculum Change* (London: Croom Helm).
Pons, V. (1969), *Stanleyville: an African Urban Community under Belgian Administration* (London: OUP for the International African Institute).
Willmott, P. (1969), *Adolescent Boys of East London* (Harmondsworth: Penguin).

7

Multiple Strategies in Field Research

In the course of most field studies, researchers use a variety of methods of investigation that are related to each other. For example, in my study of Bishop McGregor School (Burgess, 1983) I utilised participant observation, unstructured interviews and personal documents that were already available or which I invited members of the school to produce especially for my research. Although these methods were used alongside each other in the study, they have, for the purpose of description and discussion, been presented independently within the previous three chapters. However, no method is considered superior to any of the others, for each has its own strengths and weaknesses, especially when considered in relation tò a particular problem (cf. Trow, 1957). Accordingly, researchers need to take this situation into account and to approach substantive and theoretical problems with a range of methods that are *appropriate* for their problems. Such a perspective means that researchers cannot rigidly apply their methods but need to be flexible in their approach and utilise a range of methods for any problem. As Wax (1971) remarks:

> Strict and rigid adherence to any method, technique or doctrinaire position may, for the fieldworker, become like confinement in a cage. If he is lucky or very cautious, a fieldworker may formulate a research problem so that he will find all the answers he needs within his cage. But if he finds himself in a field situation where he is limited by a particular method, theory, or technique he will do well to slip through the bars and try to find out what is really going on. (Wax, 1971, p. 10)

The hallmark of being a field researcher is, therefore, flexibility in relation to the theoretical and substantive problems on hand. However, such a position leads to work of this kind being branded as subjective, impressionistic, idiosyncratic and biased. Field researchers are confronted with questions of validity for they are often asked: how far does the researcher's presence influence the generation of data? (internal validity). Can the data that are obtained in studying one situation be generalised to other situations? (external validity).

Many sociologists address these problems in their research by using what I have termed multiple strategies of field research (Burgess, 1982a, pp. 163–7) in order to overcome the problems that stem from studies relying upon a single theory, single method, single set of data and single investigator. As with many approaches, different sociologists have used different terms to describe what is broadly the same approach but with a different emphasis. The most widely used term to be found in the literature is *triangulation* which has been borrowed from psychological reports (cf. Campbell and Fiske, 1959) to refer to situations when

a hypothesis can survive the confrontation of a series of complementary methods of testing. (Webb *et al.*, 1966, p. 174)

It is this focus upon combining methods of investigation that is given a central position in the literature. However, triangulation can also be used to refer to a number of data sources, to a number of accounts of events. Indeed, in a study on the acquisition and use of language in the primary school in two school districts in Southern California, Cicourel and his associates (Cicourel *et al.*, 1974) collected several accounts of classroom activity by making audio and video recordings in the classroom. These were used when the researchers were talking to the children about their understanding of lessons. Later the teacher was interviewed and was asked to reconstruct the lessons. She was then shown the video of her lesson and asked to describe it, to comment on the children's activities and to provide her reactions. Such a strategy of investigation is referred to by Cicourel as 'indefinite triangulation' (cf. Cicourel, 1973) which, he argues, provides

details of how various interpretations of 'what happened' are assembled from different physical, temporal, and biographically provided perspectives of a situation. Comparing the teacher's accounts of the lesson before and after it was presented, and comparing the teacher's version with those of the children produced different accounts of the 'same' scene. It was sometimes difficult to recognise that the children and the teacher witnessed the same event. The children's responses during the lesson provided different conceptions of correct and incorrect answers which contrasted with the teacher's expectations stated prior to and subsequent to the lesson. The children seemed to receive and organize the lesson in terms of their own orientation at the time of the event, and these conceptions do not always match the teacher's account of the lesson's purpose and conduct. (Cicourel *et al.*, 1974, p. 4)

In this setting, the emphasis is placed upon data triangulation. Meanwhile, Denzin (1970a) has indicated that for him triangulation does not merely involve methods and data but also investigators and theories as well. Indeed, he indicates that there are four types of triangulation which include:

1 *Data Triangulation* which is subdivided into
   (a) time triangulation where the researcher attempts to consider the influence of time using cross-sectional and longitudinal research designs,
   (b) space triangulation by which researchers engage in some form of comparative study,
   (c) person triangulation at the following levels of analysis (i) the individual level, (ii) the interactive level among groups, (iii) the collective level.
2 *Investigator Triangulation* in which more than one person examines the same situation.
3 *Theory Triangulation* in which alternative or competing theories are used in any one situation.
4 *Methodological Triangulation* which involves 'within method' triangulation, that is the same method used on different occasions, and 'between method' triangulation when different methods are used in relation to the same object of study.

Meanwhile, other researchers have highlighted particular aspects of this approach. For example, Stacey (1969a) uses the term *combined operations* to refer to two kinds of research operation. First, the use of several methods of investigation within one research project to collect and check data and to test hypotheses. Secondly, the collaboration of researchers from other disciplines as in inter-disciplinary and multi-disciplinary research projects (cf. Gluckman, 1964; Devons and Gluckman, 1964). Finally Douglas (1976) refers to *mixed strategies* to refer to situations in which different methods of investigation are used. However, he indicates that researchers need to consider what mixture of methods can be used in relation to particular problems. He discusses three principles involved in using a mixture of methods. First, researchers should keep their options open at the start of a project. Secondly, flexibility should be maintained and, finally, uncontrolled methods should be used to determine how controlled methods can be used. The implication of these principles for the selection of the best mix of methods, Douglas argues, is that researchers should begin with as little control in their methods as possible and with as much natural interaction as they can. Any movement, he argues, should be from uncontrolled to controlled methods and from natural to less natural forms of interaction. It is these points that he illustrates by reference to his study of nude beaches (Douglas, Rasmussen and Flanagan, 1977) which began by the researchers interacting with the people in 'natural ways' before conducting interviews and engaging in natural experiments in the field setting.

Although these terms cover a range of research activities, they do not appear to me successfully to encompass the actual procedures involved in the practice of field research. For example, the term triangulation appears to imply the notion of three points of view within a triangle. Indeed, this view is taken by Elliott and Adelman (1976) who define the term in connection with studying classrooms in the following way:

> Triangulation involves gathering accounts of a teaching situation from three quite different points of view; namely those of the teacher, his pupils, and a participant observer. Who in the 'triangle' gathers the accounts, how they are elicited, and who compares them, depends largely on the context. The process of gathering accounts from three distinct standpoints has an epistemological justification. Each point of the triangle stands in a unique epistemological position with respect to access to relevant data about a teaching situation . . . By comparing his own account with accounts from the two other standpoints a person at one point of the triangle has an opportunity to test and perhaps revise it on the basis of more sufficient data. (Elliott and Adelman, 1976, p. 74)

Such a position while overcoming the problems that stem from the use of single methodologies appears to place certain limits on the number of approaches that can be used. Similarly, I consider that the terms used by Stacey and by Douglas while offering some flexibility for the researcher suggest little more than flexibility over methods. Accordingly, I suggest the term *multiple strategies* to allow the researcher to use a range of methods, data, investigators and theories within any study and so overcome any problems of bias. However, in using this term I have a further aim; that is not only to see different approaches used alongside one another but also to see them integrated within the course of an investigation (cf. Zelditch, 1962; Sieber, 1973).

Multiple Strategies: An Empirical Example

While the abstract methodological literature contains a number of discussions about the use of multiple strategies, it is not so apparent how these different approaches are explicitly used within a particular study without looking at the whole of an investigation. However, an account of some school-based research reported by Elliott and Partington (1975) that refers to one situation can help us to discuss the ways in which multiple strategies can be actually used.

The situation on which the researcher focused involves a lesson in which six fifth year secondary school pupils (boys and girls) taking a General Science course discuss their findings on an experiment which involves studying the effects of different treatments on plant growth. In this session John Elliott (the researcher) was present and made a tape-recording of the lesson (see A below). In addition, Elliott made some impressionistic notes in which he reported and interpreted events which seemed to him to be of major significance (see B). After making these observations John Elliott checked his interpretations of some of the events against those of the teacher and the pupils. This was done by holding an interview with the teacher immediately after the lesson (see D) and a further interview with the pupils (see E). Later, a discussion (see F) was held between the teacher, the pupils and the observer in order to compare and contrast the different interpretations. In addition, John Elliott also made a set of notes on the transcript of the lesson two-and-a-half months after it had taken place (see C). Finally, John Elliott reviewed all these documents that arose from his research in order to analyse the main teaching problems that were presented in this session. In the extracts that follow I have selected materials where the focus is upon the way in which the teacher gets the pupils to agree with him by using various verbal tactics including the phrase 'Do you all agree?'

A. An extract from the lesson where the pupils are completing an experiment

		Numbers on tape-recorder counter
Teacher	Great, great, so what would you do if I said to you now: Right you have just done an experiment, what are your conclusions – your obvious conclusion is the one we have just mentioned, about the paper pots, that they have grown and developed more – you've said that already, so that's one thing. What else would you say; would that be the only thing you want to know about a plant?	25
Pupil	How to condition it Sir?	26
Teacher	Yeh, do you all agree with that?	27

Pupil	Mm	28
Teacher	What do you think Derek? I mean are you bothered? I mean you look at yours there see – I think that is a tatty plant. (laughter)	29
Teacher	Now look at Kelvin's then. Now Kelvin's was the best. They are the ones that haven't so much brown in? What's made them go brown?	30
Pupil	Lack of nutrients. (Elliott and Partington, 1975, p. 5)	

B.   The observer's notes (written during the lesson)
Environmental Studies
Six pupils measuring height of leaves of Freesias. Pupils read out their readings. These are calculated by Dave Partington and averages worked out. Pots are grouped in different treatments.
Look at old tables of results. What's happened? Teacher asks specific pupils questions. When he disagrees raises his voice quizzically as if he disagrees. Question and answer. Hints. When right answer is given it is reinforced by the teacher. Right. (Guessing game.)
Do you all agree with that? Reply by one boy 'Mm'. When boy responds in a way which doesn't fit what teacher wants it is chopped. People not encouraged to elaborate on ideas. Wants to get them critical of John Innes compost manufacturer. John Innes made by pupils promotes growth better than commercial product. Asks why paper pots are better than plastic pots. Often makes an interpretation. Asks pupils if it is a 'reasonable guess'. Someone murmurs again 'yes'.
Asks 'Do you agree' quite a number of times. 'What have you learned then Derek?' Checks with only one pupil.
'Do you think it's worthwhile doing?'
Attempts to have some evaluation. When girl criticises he argues against. (Criticism silenced.) (Elliott and Partington, 1975, p. 13)

C.   Extract from the observer's notes on the transcript (written two and a half months after the lesson)
Note: These notes relate to the extract provided in section A.

| | Numbers on tape-recorder counter |
| 'Great, great' indicates that he now has the | 25 |

answer he wanted to (20). He also admits that the explanation they offered has some credibility, but is obvious compared to the one he has now 'guided them to'. So ideas selected by the pupils themselves have been made legitimate to some extent but not to the extent of the teacher's own ideas. Yet no reason is given by him as to why his idea is any less obvious than theirs.

A pupil gives him what he wants.   26

The 'yeh' indicates that the answer required has been   27
achieved, and that the question following requires
agreement to (26).

'Do you all agree with that?' is met with silence and an   28
odd Mm. Does this indicate pupils are afraid to
express disagreement or a lack of understanding as to
how the conclusion is arrived at?

Could Derek have drawn the required conclusion   29–30
from his specimen? It seems that he couldn't from the
teacher's remark '. . . that is a tatty plant'. Yet surely
the fact that it is 'tatty' might be seen by Derek as a
reason for disagreeing with the acceptable conclusion?
The teacher's remark and the subsequent laughter it
generates effectively rules criticism of the conclusion
'out of bounds'. Instead the teacher moves to a
specimen (30) which clearly supports the conclusion
he wants. The teacher's remark (29) clearly would
make it difficult for Derek to feel free to answer his
question 'What do you think Derek?' To have
resisted making such a remark might not only have
enabled Derek to disagree but to have opened the way
to an understanding of why individuals may vary
within a sample which have all received similar
treatments. (Elliott and Partington, 1975, pp. 15–16)

D. Extract from an interview between the teacher and John
   Elliott

Interviewer   Do you know that you use the words 'Do we all
              agree' quite a lot?
Teacher   No I didn't (pause) OK – I know I use that a lot.
Interviewer   Three or four times.
Teacher   I am asking for assent.
Interviewer   Are you? Is that what you are asking?
Teacher   I think probably I am. I think possibly I use that
              when I don't get . . . if I make a statement and I
              haven't got a . . . I don't know sometimes if it is a

rhetorical question or whether it is a question I want an answer to or whether it is just a statement, but I make a statement and I hope the response will come from it. If a response doesn't come from it, you either repeat it in a different way to a single individual and put them on the spot, or you perhaps get over it by saying OK or 'Do you all agree with that'. I suppose they can possibly con me by saying yes and carry on. It is something I hadn't thought of.

Interviewer   Do they all say yes?

Teacher   Well they didn't all say no. I reckon if you take a non-negative approach to be an affirmative, which is perhaps a big thing to do. I don't think you ought to do that really. Yes that's naughty isn't it!

Interviewer   Well the thing is I suppose when you say 'Do we all agree' they can say no.

Teacher   I give them the opportunity to say no.

Interviewer   They can say no, but how do they see it. If they see it as your seeking agreement –

Teacher   I think a lot of the time one must be seeking agreement. There is a basic thing that everybody wants to be loved and everybody like them and so on, and this even goes with this lot; I want the least problematic situation or antagonistic situation as possible and maybe this is a way of getting over it – saying 'Do you agree' and maybe having a head nod or a possible one saying yes and taking that as everyone agrees. Logically it's stupid because they can't all agree – they must all have slightly different ideas and yet at the same time what I am trying to put forward is what I feel to be a reasonable statement, a true statement. Although I didn't today, I do in fact sometimes put forward daft statements and you do usually find that they disagree if there is something stupid. It was a bit tame today – I mean you were coming in part way through a situation which wanted finishing and therefore I finished it. In terms of them going away and doing things – and I thought you would be more interested in discussion because of the material you had got – your recording technique. I didn't know I was going to do that for ten minutes, I hadn't prepared anything, well half an hour or more. (Elliott and Partington, 1975, pp. 22–3)

E. Extract from an interview between the pupils in the lesson
    and John Elliott

Pupil	But he wouldn't ask you what you think your conclusions were, he'll put his own conclusion up on the board, and you have to write it. He says do you agree, not always, but he don't want to rub it off so you just say yes to keep him quiet.
Interviewer	You say yes to keep him quiet.
Pupil	Keep him happy . . .
Interviewer	There was a time when he said he was making a guess and he asked you if you agreed whether it was a reasonable guess. I don't know if you remember that?
Pupils	Yes.
Interviewer	And one person said yes and everybody else kept quiet. Now what I want to know is whether the person said yes really did agree with him or just said yes because they thought he wanted them to say yes, and why everybody else kept quiet?
Pupil	Well he would have liked us to say yes, really, 'cause I mean you could see it.
Pupil	If you'd said no you'd waste time arguing wouldn't you.
Pupil	Yeh, if you ever say no he'll stand there and just keep on and on.
Pupil	He'll keep on till you come to his way of thinking.
Pupil	So it's best to say yes to start with.
Interviewer	So even if you did disagree when he said 'Do you all agree' you wouldn't.
Pupil	If you said no he'd keep on to you until you said yes.
Pupil	If you said no he's going to say why not.
Pupil	And if you argued with him he'd come round to the same point where you left off.
Pupil	Back to his way of thinking. (Elliott and Partington, 1975, pp. 28, 30–1)

F. Extract from a discussion between the teacher, his pupils and
    John Elliott

Note: This discussion followed the interview between John
Elliott and the pupils. The recording of the interview having been
played back to the teacher with the pupils' permission.

Teacher	Now I would have thought we would have wanted to wonder whether we want them to go all together or whether we ought to put them in bigger pots

	outside in the same compost as we had before. Interesting comments there about the way you say yes when I ask a question. A bit frightening really, because at one stage you said there that I ask you questions and you say yes to shut me up and yet at the same time a few minutes later you say he never gives us a chance to say anything about the lesson, which I thought was a bit unfair because in fact I usually do.
Interviewer	How do you respond to that? (pause)
Teacher	You know you put forward two opposite arguments there in one tape-recorded comment. Do you agree you did? At one stage somebody said, I think I am right if I remember, I don't give them a chance to say something about the lesson, and yet earlier on they say they don't say anything about the lesson because you don't want to be involved in it. It seemed a bit...
Interviewer	Who was it who said – was it you?
Pupil	Mm.
Interviewer	What do you think about what Mr. Partington has said there? (pause)
Interviewer	Do you still disagree with him?
Pupil	Yes – not all that much...
Interviewer	Come on then, say what you disagree.
Pupil	Well I disagree with him a little bit, not all that much, because four or five weeks ago when we started this experiment, and he wrote something up on the board and we...
Pupil	It wasn't none of our ideas was it?
Pupil	No.
Interviewer	You what?
Pupil	He wrote it on the board but it wasn't nothing we thought about. (Elliott and Partington, 1975, pp. 34–5)

The material that has been provided from Elliott and Partington's study focuses on the way the teacher attempts to control the content of the class discussion and the order in which the discussion occurs. On the basis of the material he has collected John Elliott concludes that the teacher's verbal acts and tactics prevent pupils from expressing and developing their own ideas through discussion because they perceive that the teacher controls the conversation in favour of his own ideas. Furthermore, he also concludes that the pupils find it difficult to understand ideas introduced by the teacher because their perception of his authority prevents them from feeling free to interrupt and request clarification. These conclusions that Elliott draws from his material are based on the degree of congruence between the account of the teacher and the pupils, together with his own account based on his observations in the classroom and the transcriptions that he has made. In short, multiple strategies of data collection assist in data analysis and the subsequent generation of hypotheses in this study.

The Use of Multiple Strategies

Multiple Methods of Investigation

The use of multiple methods of investigation takes two forms: within methods and between methods. When the researcher takes one method and utilises multiple strategies it is usually for reliability. It can be used to check data quality and to confirm validity. For example, in the Elliott and Partington study two sets of materials are derived from tape-recording the lesson: the transcript (A) and the observer's notes on the transcription of the lesson (C). Yet in these circumstances, researchers need to heed a warning concerning the use of one method:

> Every data gathering class – interviews, questionnaires, observation, performance records, physical evidence is potentially biased and has specific to it certain validity threats. (Webb *et al.*, 1966, p. 35)

The result is that Webb *et al.* recommend the convergence of data from different classes as well as convergence with different data from a single class. In this way, the researcher is advised to use different methods to look at the same situation. In Elliott and Partington's study we can see how different methods of investigation are used to focus on an individual lesson. The methods include participant observation and interviewing which give rise to: a transcription of the lesson (A), a set of field notes (B) that were written during the lesson, a set of notes from the observer on the transcript (C), and three further sets of transcripts that arose from interviews with the teacher (D), the pupils (E) and the teacher and the pupils (F). As well as observing lessons and interviewing, field researchers can also utilise audio-visual methods where a teacher wears a radio-microphone which picks up interchanges with pupils and the observer takes photographs which are subsequently pulsed on to the tape and help place the classroom talk in a visual context (cf. Walker and Adelman, 1975). In this respect, a document can be produced concerning the sequence of activities that occur in a classroom or in other social situations such as the exchanges between a local education authority adviser and educational personnel or the exchanges between teachers and pupils in the classroom (cf. Walker, 1981, 1984).

As well as different methods being used in one situation they can also be used to focus on events. For example, in my Bishop McGregor study, events were examined on the basis of my observations, accounts that were obtained from interviews and conversations with teachers and pupils and from documentary evidence. No individual method alone could yield the 'truth' about a situation. For example, when I discussed suspension and corporal punishment with pupils I was aware that exaggeration was possible. In an interview with John Slattery he discussed suspension and corporal punishment in relation to an incident in which he claimed that he had 'beat up a kid'. The particular discussion took the following form:

RB.   Have you ever been sent home?
John   I have Sir!
RB.   When was that?
John   When I beat up a kid. Peter Vincent put Mark Ball into hospital by smashing his ribs.
RB.   That was in the fourth year?
John   Yes.
RB.   And you got suspended for that?
John   No, I never but Peter did.
RB.   Why didn't you get suspended?
John   Cos Peter started it and I sorta helped him out.
RB.   So you came to school and he didn't. Have you ever been suspended?
John   No I have not because I'm a good lad.
RB.   Have you ever been caned?
John   Oh yes.
RB.   What have you been caned for then?
John   Burning a girl's tights, helping Pete Vincent in a fight (as I said).

This material referred to an incident that many teachers had talked to me about when I joined the school. The staff had told me that this attack on a fellow pupil was so extreme that the Head had produced a set of documents on the incident that were publicly displayed. I decided, therefore, to obtain the Head's account in order to compare it with John's story. The Head's account read as follows:

Account of an incident at Bishop McGregor School, Merston, Friday 23rd March 1973 – 9.00 am. Taking part – Peter Vincent, Mark Gibson, John Slattery and Mark Ball, all fourth formers in

Hexham House. (All will be referred to by surname since two have the same Christian name.)

Immediately after Friday morning House assembly, Gibson and Ball were showing each other a 'Faked Blow'. Vincent asked to be shown. They refused. Vincent tried to get hold of Gibson's football badge at which point Ball thought Vincent was attacking Gibson. Ball then jumped on Vincent's back to pull him away from Gibson. Slattery pulled Ball by the hair and kicked him. Ball fell to the floor. Vincent turned round and he kicked Ball several times with considerable force. Slattery had also kicked Ball 'to make him let go of my sleeves'.
Ball went to hospital with Gibson.
Ball's parents informed.
All witnesses questioned and statements taken.
Vincent and Slattery questioned and statements taken.
Both kept on the site and given lunch at House expense.
Messages received from hospital. Ball bruised about body. No bones broken; no apparent serious internal injuries.
Action ordered by Head.

Friday: Vincent and Slattery each to receive three strokes of the cane. This is to be the immediate punishment for the violence *after* Ball was on the floor. Slattery taken home by Head of House and a verbal warning to be given to parent that any further involvement in violence will be met by the Head with suspension.
When Slattery was taken home, parents were not in. Evidently, the father is in hospital, and the mother was visiting him. Slattery was brought back to school and a note from Head of House was sent home with him.
Note: this is being followed up by a formal letter from the Head of confirmation to the parents.
Vincent will be suspended for the rest of this term as a punishment for disobedience to the Head. On returning from his last suspension, the Head laid it down as a condition of his return that if there was an episode of serious violence, suspension would be used for disobedience in addition to any punishment for the violence.
Action being taken on Monday 26th March 1973 by Head.

1   Letter to the LEA informing them and associated departments of action already taken by Head.
2   Letter to the Chairman of Governors informing him of action taken by Head.
3   Letter to Mr and Mrs Slattery confirming the warning already given about future violence offered by their son to others.

4   Letter to Mr and Mrs Vincent confirming present suspension
and stating conditions for readmission after the Easter holiday.
(signed) G. Goddard
Headmaster

This second method of obtaining data on the same situation provides
a difference in emphasis and detail. Here, we are told of how the Head
perceived John's part in the episode, the corporal punishment he
received and how it was that he was sent home but not suspended.
Neither account provided 'the truth' about the incident but the
degree of cross-checking that could be done allowed me to validate
the two accounts and use them in discussing how reputations were
established by pupils (cf. Burgess, 1983, pp. 127–30). The accounts
that I was given by teachers (in conversation) could be cross-checked
with the pupil's account (in interview) and further checked with
documentary evidence from the Head and in the school punishment
book. In this case, different methods were combined in order to
pursue a particular line of inquiry and to maximise the validity of the
data collected. Here, the methods used related to the research
problem, the accounts available from participants in the research
setting and the substantive and theoretical concerns of the study.

Multiple Sets of Data
As Denzin (1970a) has indicated the collection of multiple sets of
data brings the researcher back to a consideration of the units of
analysis and to questions of sampling (see Chapter 3) by time, by
person and by situation. If we return to our two examples from the
work of Elliott and Partington and from my own research we can see
how the use of different methods of investigation gave rise to different
sets of data; that is to different accounts of the same situation.
However, the key issue involved in obtaining such accounts using
observations, interviews and documentary evidence is to relate what
people do; for example in Elliott and Partington's work, the teacher's
use of the phrase 'do you all agree' with what the teacher claims to do
and what the pupils perceive. Adelman (1981) has outlined four
stages involved in the collection of such accounts to go alongside the
observer's account. First, the observer makes a recording of the lesson
using field notes, tape-recordings and photographs. Secondly, pupils'
accounts of the lesson are obtained. Thirdly, the pupils' accounts are
played back to the teacher in order to obtain the teacher's account
and finally the observations of the lesson and the various accounts
from the participants are transcribed and placed alongside one
another. While this presents a strategy for the collection of different
sets of data, it still leaves the researcher with the problem of how to
integrate the data that are obtained.

A further problem is the extent to which the researcher's data and the researcher's account can be substantiated by the participants. Marten Shipman indicates that a lone researcher can take up different substantive concerns and different theoretical perspectives that exist among participants. He suggests that researchers should get their informants to comment upon their accounts and to publish these remarks in the final project report (cf. Shipman, 1974). In the course of studying the Keele Integrated Studies Project he obtained comments on his manuscript from David Bolam, the Director, and David Jenkins, the Deputy Director of the curriculum project, and also from Geoffrey Hartley and Alan Townsend who were two of the project co-ordinators. Such remarks help to provide an account not only from a researcher's angle but also from insiders in the project team. For as Shipman remarks:

> One advantage of including comments from insiders is to highlight this difference [between researcher and researched] which is rarely examined in the reports of observational studies. Another is to show that the views of those on the inside also differ between themselves. (Shipman, 1974, pp. viii–ix)

In this respect, Shipman highlights a strategy that has the potential to bring together researchers and participants in a collaborative exercise in which different sets of data can be presented and different substantive and theoretical perspectives can be explored and developed within one project.

However, as we have seen from our two examples, there is often a lack of consensus about the actions and activities of participants. In these circumstances, comparison of the different accounts becomes possible but integration into a single narrative is difficult to achieve (cf. Gans, 1967). Here, the researcher needs carefully to focus on a unit of study. For example, in my own research I was interested in collecting data on strategies that were used by teachers and pupils. Accordingly, I focused on the strategies that were adopted by teachers who worked in different areas of the school and who were of different levels of seniority. Furthermore, I focused on the strategies used by the same group of pupils in a number of different classes that they attended. Here, comparisons could be made between the strategies that were adopted and an account developed. Similarly, Becker *et al.* (1961) in their study *Boys in White* examined study patterns in laboratories, fraternities and classrooms which subsequently allowed them to make comparisons not only of an activity, that is study patterns, but also of situations at different times. Such an approach involves a complex research design in order to get access to multiple sets of data but was greatly assisted by the fact that this was a multiple investigator study.

Multiple Investigators

The basic principle involved in multiple investigator studies is that more than one investigator is used in the research situation. As I have shown elsewhere (Burgess, 1982a, pp. 164–5) this can involve researchers in a variety of different relationships. First, partnership research where separate but co-ordinated activities occur in order for there to be some cross validation of data collection and analysis (cf. Davis, Gardner and Gardner, 1941; Fujisaka and Grayzel, 1978). Secondly, team-based research where a number of people work together to support one another and to cross-check each other's work. Such an approach has been used by Stacey in both her studies of Banbury (cf. Stacey, 1960; Stacey *et al.*, 1975) in which team members were drawn from different social classes and included men and women. Similarly, the study of nude beaches by Douglas and his associates operated on the same principles (Douglas, Rasmussen and Flanagan, 1977). In addition to research teams being comprised of individuals drawn from different classes, sexes, ethnic groups and age groups (cf. Mead, 1970; Wax, 1979), it is also possible to bring together researchers drawn from different disciplines with a view to integrating the data that are collected (cf. Stacey *et al.*, 1970; Hall and Stacey, 1979). Certainly, *Hospitals, Children and their Families* (Stacey *et al.*, 1970) represents such a synthesis where sociologists and psychologists worked together to understand different elements of children's experiences. Meanwhile, members from different disciplines can also be brought together to provide multi-disciplinary studies of a situation. For example, Hilton (1967) reports the work of colleagues from six disciplines who conducted a study of the Lower Swansea Valley.

Such use of multiple investigators would seem to hold much potential for overcoming the bias that may be associated with an individual researcher. This is indicated by Strauss and his colleagues (1964) in their study of a mental hospital when they report:

> There were three fieldworkers subjected for the most part to the same raw data. Search for pinpointing negative evidence was abetted by the collective nature of our inquiry. If a colleague reported the same kind of observation as another without prior consultation, confidence grew. If, after hearing the report of an observation, a colleague was himself able unquestionably to duplicate it, it indicated that our observational techniques had some degree of reliability. If no colleague did corroborate an observation – which did happen – if it seemed important then, or

later, further inquiry was initiated. Something like a built-in reliability check was thus obtained because several fieldworkers were exposed directly to similar or identical data. (Strauss *et al.*, 1964, p. 36)

While this study reports the successful use of several investigators, other researchers have pointed to the difficulties that have to be resolved when groups of people work together. For example, Bell (1977) comments on the problems that he confronted when working as a member of the research team that conducted the second study of Banbury (Stacey *et al.*, 1975). This project was directed by Margaret Stacey with Colin Bell as the 'foreman' who had the responsibility for seeing that the work was done in the field. However, Bell indicates that the organisational ambiguity that existed on the project resulted in serious authority problems among team members. As a consequence, Bell claims that he had doubts about the use of research teams until he went on to do work on East Anglian farmers (Newby *et al.*, 1978).

This theme of relationships between team members is also found in reflections from team members associated with other projects. In commenting upon a study of postgraduate education in Britain, Porter (1984) shows how for the researcher there is the problem of relating individual interests to those interests of the project director. Meanwhile, in relation to the same project, Wakeford (1984) points to the hazards that exist for the project director when appointing staff and developing a research project based on democratic principles. Many of these accounts focus on questions of delegation (cf. Roth, 1966; Bell, 1977). However, researchers also have to address questions about the extent to which they can successfully work together to integrate multiple sets of data and represent different theoretical positions.

Multiple Theories
Multiple theoretical positions are rarely achieved within one study (Denzin, 1970a). Yet, if researchers seriously took account of problems concerning internal and external validity, then bringing various theories to bear on a particular problem would be a central part of research design and the research process. Westie (1957) has argued that this procedure can be achieved in the following ways:

1 Bringing together all existing and plausible propositions that relate to the area of study.
2 Constructing plausible interpretations for each of the propositions.

3   Conducting the research to discover which of the various empirical relationships actually exist.
4   Rejecting relationships and interpretations that are not found in the empirical work.
5   Conducting further empirical investigation to select the best interpretations.
6   Reassessing the theories from which the initial propositions were derived.
7   Reformulating a theoretical system based on the theoretical work.

Such a procedure, it is argued, minimises the chance of ignoring contradictory propositions outside the theoretical scheme, allows an opportunity to try out alternative interpretations, extends confirmation or doubt to a range of theoretical propositions and may encourage research programmes where alternative explanations can be developed.

However, it is relatively rare for researchers to indicate how theories are developed and generated within their studies (cf. Baldamus, 1972) or to indicate the procedures that are adopted. On examining researchers' accounts of 'doing research' which were reported in Hammond (1964), Baldamus concludes that the word 'theory' is used to refer to continuous speculation without a definitive purpose. Accordingly, he finds that 'theorising' more accurately reflects the activities in which these researchers were engaged as they were concerned with

> an 'integrating principle' (Blanche Geer), 'a new theoretical amalgam' (David Riesman and Jeanne Watson), 'a basic conceptual framework' (Robert N. Bellah), 'an organisation or synthesis which provides the essential structure into which the pieces of analysis fit' (James S. Coleman), 'a crucial insight' (Peter M. Blau), 'a major idea' (James A. Davis), 'a relevant typology' (Stanley H. Udy), and so forth. (Baldamus, 1972, pp. 290–1)

Yet we need to know more about these activities that are involved in 'theorising' as they often go unreported in empirical studies.

Many researchers merely report on one theoretical position that dominates their work. In the study of schools and classrooms, interactionism is used in the studies of Hargreaves, Hester and Mellor (1975) and Delamont (1976), while Sharp and Green (1975), Willis (1977) and Corrigan (1979) utilise a Marxist framework to explain and understand the activities involved. In these terms, there is a danger that theoretical propositions may be imposed on the data rather than arising out of the situations that are studied. For example, studies within an interactionist mode will emphasise the definitions that are established within schools and classrooms, while the Marxist writers focus on the constraints external to the school and classroom that influence the activities therein. Meanwhile, Woods (1979) attempts to bridge the gap between interactionists and structuralists by bringing together substantive and formal theories in the course of his study of a secondary school (see Chapter 8). Yet, as many sociologists have indicated, the problem that confronts the researcher is not merely putting various accounts alongside one another but integrating these accounts (Banks, 1978; Hargreaves, 1979).

From Multiple Strategies to Integration

So far we have considered the way in which different methods, data, investigators and theories can be brought together in a research project. However, some researchers have suggested a further development which involves the *integration* of these various approaches. In a discussion of field studies Zelditch (1962) poses the questions: what kind of methods are relevant? What kinds of information are relevant? How can the 'goodness' of different methods for different purposes be evaluated? In addressing these problems Zelditch compares three types of information and three types of method and summarises his results in table form (see Table 7.1). Here, Zelditch evaluates the methods of investigation according to 'efficiency' and 'informational adequacy' in terms of gathering different kinds of data. While different methods may be used for gathering different kinds of data, they may also be used within a single study. Sieber (1973) has taken the debate a stage further by considering ways in which methods can be integrated by researchers, paying special attention to field research and surveys. On the basis of examining field projects he argues that the contribution that field research can make to the collection of survey data is in assisting in the pre-testing of questionnaires, providing a rationale for a survey and gaining legitimation for it and, finally, assisting the researcher to gain access to respondents. Meanwhile, in terms of the contribution that field research can make to the analysis and interpretation of survey data he lists the following:

> First, the *theoretical structure* that guides the analysis can be derived wholly or largely from qualitative fieldwork. Secondly . . . certain of the survey results can be *validated*, or at least given persuasive plausibility, by recourse to observations and informant interviews . . . Thirdly, statistical relationships can be *interpreted* by reference to field observations. Fourthly, the selection of survey items for the *construction of indices* can be based on field observations. Fifthly, *external validation* of statistical constructs

(indices) is afforded by comparison with observational scales. Sixthly, *case studies* that illustrate statistical and historical types are supplied by field protocols and finally; provocative but puzzling replies to the questionnaires can be *clarified* by resort to field notes. (Sieber, 1973, p. 1345)

Table 7.1   *Methods of Obtaining Information.*

Information types	Enumerations and samples	Participant observation	Interviewing informants
Frequency distributions	Prototype and best form	Usually inadequate and inefficient	Often but not always inadequate; if adequate, it is efficient
Incidents, histories	Not adequate by itself; not efficient	Prototype and best form	Adequate with precautions and efficient
Institutionalised norms and statuses	Adequate but inefficient	Adequate but inefficient except for unverbalized norms	Most efficient and hence best form

Source: Zelditch (1962), p. 576.

Meanwhile, he considers that the contribution which surveys can make to the collection of field data is to identify individuals who could be studied in depth, and to identify representative and unrepresentative cases. In terms of data analysis, he considers that surveys can contribute to field research by:

1   Correcting the holistic fallacy that all aspects of a situation are congruent.
2   Demonstrating the generality of a single observation.
3   Assisting in the verification of observations.
4   Casting light on field observations.

It is this kind of approach that highlights the importance of flexibility on the part of the researcher who in bringing methods of investigation closer together will in turn help to dissolve boundaries between research styles and promote work on common problems. This in turn has the potential to bring about substantive and theoretical developments in field-based studies which will allow research to become genuinely cumulative within particular subfields (cf. Hargreaves, 1980).

Conclusion

In this chapter we have been concerned with bringing together various methods of investigation. Accordingly, such an approach relates to questions concerning the validity of investigations. However, multiple strategies pose a number of problems for the researcher: which methods are to be brought together? What are the advantages and disadvantages of bringing methods, data, investigators and theories together? How can substantive and theoretical developments be made using multiple strategies in field research? But we might ask what criteria can be used in selecting a given method for a particular problem? Zelditch (1962) suggests that researchers might consider the efficiency and adequacy of methods of investigation for particular research problems when evaluating the mixture of methods to be used in multiple strategies of research. However, researchers must always balance such criteria against real constraints in social research such as the time and money that are available. This is not to argue for crass expediency, but it does point to the fact that just as there is no best method so there is no rigid requirement that every project requires researchers using a variety of methods all the time. It has been the purpose of this chapter to consider some of the issues that are relevant to the researcher addressing these questions in relation to the methodological, substantive and theoretical problems that are confronted in the field.

Suggestions for Further Reading

Methodology

Bulmer, M. (1977) (ed.), *Sociological Research Methods* (London: Macmillan); is a basic text that focuses on the *interconnections* between sociological theories and methods and the practice of research. The editor's introduction is particularly helpful (Bulmer, 1977b).

Burgess, R. G. (1982) (ed.), *Field Research: a Sourcebook and Field Manual* (London: Allen & Unwin). Section six focuses on combining strategies in field research. After a general consideration of multiple strategies there are essays by Zelditch (1962) and Sieber (1973) that focus on the integration of methods and methodologies.

Denzin, N. (1970), *The Research Act* (Chicago: Aldine); contains a chapter on triangulation in which the author outlines the main elements involved in multi-method research. A second edition of this text was published by McGraw Hill in 1978.

Denzin, N. (1970) (ed.), *Sociological Methods: a Sourcebook* (London: Butterworths); complements Denzin's textbook and contains papers on methodological triangulation; by Hovland (1959) on experimental and survey methods; by Zelditch (1962) on field studies; and by Vidich and Shapiro (1955) on participant observation and surveys. The second edition of this sourcebook (Denzin, 1978) contains the paper by Sieber (1973) on the *integration* of methods.

Douglas, J. (1976), *Investigative Social Research* (Beverly Hills, Calif.: Sage) discusses the use of various methods in an individual research project drawing on his study *The Nude Beach* (Douglas, Rasmussen and Flanagan, 1977).

McCall, G. J. and Simmons, J. L. (1969) (eds), *Issues in Participant Observation: A Text and Reader* (Reading, Mass.: Addison-Wesley); contains two papers by Becker and Geer (1957, 1958) and a paper by Trow (1957) in which the authors debate the uses of participant observation and interviewing.

Stacey, M. (1969), *Methods of Social Research* (Oxford: Pergamon); contains a chapter on combined operations – a term which the author uses to refer to multi-method research as well as inter-disciplinary and multi-disciplinary studies.

Webb, E. J., Campbell, D. T., Schwartz, R. D. and Sechrest, L. (1966), *Unobtrusive Measures: Nonreactive Research in the Social Sciences* (Chicago: Rand McNally); contains an important basic discussion on the principles of triangulation.

Empirical Studies

This list could contain all the studies that have been recommended at the end of all the other chapters in this book. Indeed, you could examine all the studies that have been recommended with a view to considering the extent to which the principles of multiple strategies have been deployed by the researchers. However, the following studies are especially recommended as they explicitly discuss the use of multiple strategies or 'triangulation' in the conduct of research.

Adelman, C. (1981), 'On first hearing', in C. Adelman (ed.), *Uttering Muttering: Collecting, Using and Reporting Talk for Social and Educational Research* (London: Grant McIntyre), pp. 78–97.

Becker, H. S., Geer, B., Hughes, E. C. and Strauss, A. L. (1961), *Boys in White: Student Culture in Medical School* (Chicago: University of Chicago Press).

Cicourel, A. V., Jennings, K. H., Jennings, S. H. M., Leiter, K. C. W., Mackay, R., Mehan, H. and Roth, D. H. (1974), *Language Use and School Performance* (New York: Academic Press).

Douglas, J. D., Rasmussen, P. K. and Flanagan, C. A. (1977), *The Nude Beach* (Beverly Hills, Calif.: Sage).

Elliott, J. and Adelman, C. (1976), *Innovation at the Classroom Level: A Case Study of the Ford Teaching Project*, Unit 28 of the Curriculum Design and Development Course (Milton Keynes: Open University Press).

Elliott, J. and Partington, D. (1975), *Three Points of View in the Classroom: Generating Hypotheses from Classroom Observations, Recordings and Interviews* (Norwich: Centre for Applied Research in Education).

Gans, H. J. (1962), *The Urban Villagers* (New York: The Free Press).

Gans, H. J. (1967), *The Levittowners* (London: Allen Lane).

Rist, R. (1981), *Earning and Learning: Youth Employment Policies and Programs* (Beverly Hills, Calif.: Sage).

Shipman, M. (1974), *Inside a Curriculum Project* (London: Methuen).
Stacey, M. (1960), *Tradition and Change: A Study of Banbury* (Oxford: OUP).
Stacey, M., Batstone, E., Bell, C. and Murcott, A. (1975), *Power, Persistence and Change: A Second Study of Banbury* (London: Routledge & Kegan Paul).
Stacey, M., Dearden, R., Pill, R. and Robinson, D. (1970), *Hospitals, Children and their Families* (London: Routledge & Kegan Paul).
Woods, P. (1979), *The Divided School* (London: Routledge & Kegan Paul).

8

Recording and Analysing Field Data

Field research involves the simultaneous collection and analysis of data. In collecting data the field researcher develops sets of notes, entries in journals and diaries, and generates sets of interview transcripts, and photographs. There is also a vast range of documentary material on which the researcher can work and out of which data analysis and report writing arise. In these circumstances, a number of questions arise about the way in which researchers record, analyse and report their data. Yet published accounts of field research methods and field studies pay relatively little attention to these processes and to the connections between them. Some of the key questions that need to be addressed in this area include: how are fieldnotes made? When are fieldnotes taken? How are fieldnotes coded, indexed and filed? How are the materials organised for the purpose of data analysis? How are these materials reported? What is the process of report writing? It is to some of these issues that this chapter is devoted, drawing on a variety of research projects, especially where it is possible to highlight the relationship between recording, analysing and reporting data.

Wright Mills (1959) indicated that such issues involved a discussion of the way in which researchers go about their craft. Mills discussed the way in which he conducted his own work and advocated that researchers should keep a journal in which

> there is joined personal experience and professional activities, studies under way and studies planned. In this file, you, as an intellectual craftsman, will try to get together what you are doing intellectually and what you are experiencing as a person. Here, you will not be afraid to use your experience and relate it directly to various work in progress. (Mills, 1959, p.196)

Mills considered that such a journal would generate work of intellectual relevance; it would be a storehouse of ideas on which the social scientist could work. Such a collection of material is essential for the field researcher to acquire. However, the field researcher's notes, journal entries or diary might differ from Mills's file in two respects. First, it would include experiences from everyday life as a central feature. Secondly, these experiences would need to be systematically recorded. Diary entries need to be regularly written and contain details of the date, time, personnel and location in which the notes were made. Here, the researcher needs to constantly address the questions: when (did an event occur)? What (was involved)? Who (was involved)? Where (did it occur)? Such a list of questions involves researchers making notes on places, events, activities, people and conversations. However, it is not possible to record everything that occurs in a situation and therefore researchers will be involved in making a set of decisions about what to include depending on their substantive and theoretical interests. Furthermore, notes have to be maintained not only on the researchers' substantive interests but also on their methodology so that they can reconstruct their involvement in a project from a first-hand account (cf. Burgess, 1984b). Finally, some notes can be made on early theoretical and analytic developments. Accordingly, I have distinguished between substantive, methodological and analytic field notes (cf. Burgess, 1981a, 1982a, pp. 191–4) to which we now turn.

Substantive Fieldnotes

Substantive fieldnotes consist of a continuous record of the situations, events and conversations in which the researcher participates. They are a record of the observations and interviews that are obtained by the researcher and of the content of documents. In some cases, these notes are systematically recorded using pre-set sections and categories for particular events and situations. In other instances, substantive and conceptual issues may influence the selection of materials that are recorded. Just as the researcher focuses the observations that are made and the interviews that are conducted, so some selection and some focusing takes place when recording substantive fieldnotes.

In Laud Humphreys's study of homosexual behaviour in public conveniences in the USA (Humphreys, 1970), a systematic observation sheet was developed as shown in Figure 8.1. Humphreys took a covert role in his study, acting as a 'watch queen' or lookout in a public convenience where homosexual activity occurred. His observations were recorded on the systematic observation sheet after leaving the research site.

This systematic observation sheet was developed on the basis of preliminary observations in public conveniences and was designed by Humphreys to ensure consistency between himself and a fellow observer. I have removed Humphrey's comments and diagrams from the sheet in order that the categories that were to be recorded and the layout of the sheet are given some prominence. In each instance details of the date, time and location were recorded together with a description of the participants (according to age, attire, distinguishing characteristics, car and their role in the encounter). Each record sheet also contains space for a diagram to indicate the movements of the participants, their roles and the progress of the activities. Finally, there is some space to record the action and the reactions of the observer.

Date: Day: _____

O = Observer (1) (2) General Condition: Weather & temp.
X = Principal Aggressor ♯ & type of people in parks:
Y = Principal Passive Participant est. volume of gay activity:
A – N = Other Participants Place:
Z = Law Enforcement Personnel

Time Began: _____

Time Ended: _____

Participants: (include symbol, est. age, attire, other distinguishing characteristics, type of auto driven)

X: _____
   _____

Y: _____
   _____ DIAGRAM

Others: _____
   _____
   _____
   _____

Description of Action: (note: when possible, indicate: delays in autos, etc. before entering tearoom . . . manner of approaches . . . types of sexual roles taken . . . nature of interruptions and reaction to them . . . ANYTHING WHICH MAY BE SPOKEN . . . any masturbation going on . . . actions of lookout(s) . . . REACTION TO TEENAGERS AND ANY PARTICIPATION BY THEM . . . reactions to observer . . . length of time of sexual acts . . . spitting, washing of hands, wiping, etc).

[Area for description of activities observed written up after observation]

Source: Adapted from Humphreys (1970), p. 35.

Figure 8.1 *Systematic Observation Sheet.*

Humphreys indicates that all parts of the form apart from the final descriptive section were completed in his car which was located some distance from the lavatory in which the observations were made. Meanwhile, the descriptive section was written up when he returned to his office. Such a strategy of data recording, Humphreys argues, gives some objective validity to the data that were gathered. It also allows for replication and for comparative studies to be made as a number of variables have been controlled. Indeed, the advantage that this provides in terms of data analysis is demonstrated in the third and fourth chapters of the study (Humphreys, 1970).

In my own work I found that it was essential to keep some systematic substantive notes but I did not develop sheets on which to record these data. My notes were predominantly descriptive and aimed to provide a detailed portrait of the various situations in which I became involved. The fieldnotes included physical descriptions of situations and informants, details of conversations, and accounts of events (cf. Bogdan and Biklen, 1982, pp. 84–6). For each day that I was in the school my notes comprised: a continuous record of the events in which I was involved and the conversations in which I participated. Here, I focused on the words and phrases that were used so as to provide an almost literal account of what had been said. My notes also focused upon details of particular events in each school day and therefore always involved a record of: early morning meetings with the Head of House, morning assembly in the House, break time in the staff room, lunch hour activities and the period in the staff room at the end of the day, as well as detailed observations of lessons in which I participated. In some of these situations I used diagrams to summarise details about particular settings. For example, I used diagrams to show the individuals who sat next to each other in meetings and to summarise interactions and conversations between participants. Often these diagrammatic notes were written shortly after the period of observation and provided a summary that could be used later in the day to write up more detailed notes. In particular, I kept diagrams of who sat with whom in the early morning meetings, in morning assembly and at break times in the staff common room. The result was that I was able to build up a portrait of the relationships in particular settings and of the structure of particular groups. For example, in the staff common room my first set of fieldnotes begin by locating the position of the individuals with whom I sat. Gradually my notes detail a wider group of individuals, their names and their positions in the school until I could subdivide the groups in the staff common room according to their major characteristics, as shown in Figure 8.2. In the staff common room the group that I sat with during most morning breaks was the Heads of Houses corner group. I was especially interested in who sat with them and therefore I kept a record of who sat in the group, their position in the school and who (if anyone) brought individuals into that group. On the basis of these observations and records that I kept in the first half of the summer term I was able to chart the membership of this group, which is shown in Table 8.1. It is such diagrams and records that were used in my analysis of informal relations among teachers at Bishop McGregor School (cf. Burgess, 1983, pp. 72–6).

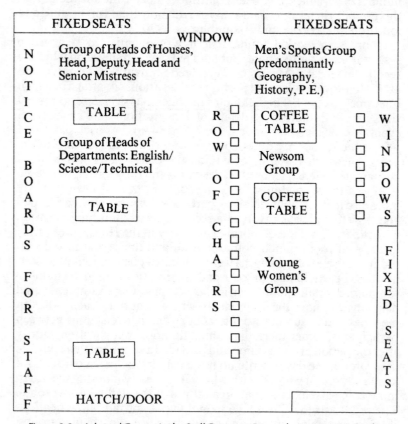

Figure 8.2   *Informal Groups in the Staff Common Room during Morning Breaks.*

In addition, some topics were followed up in conversations that occurred at different times during my research. One topic I was especially interested in was the way in which morning assembly was used to reinforce the norms and values of senior members of the school. After morning assembly I therefore tried to note down as accurately as I could all the announcements that had been made. The kind of note that was produced read as follows:

Once the Senior Mistress had finished talking, Ron Ward stood up and said that he had several notices to give out and various things to talk about. He began by saying that 'in connection with the Lenten

Table 8.1 *Staff who sat in the Heads of Houses Group in the First Half of the Summer Term 1973.*

Staff member	Position in the school	Member of staff who brought individual to the group (if any)
Maggie Rolls	Head of Clifton House	
Roy Carey	Head of Maths	
Jean Chapman	Senior Mistress	
Sylvia Robinson	Head of Careers/Newsom	
Frank Lloyd	Deputy Head	
Robert Burgess	Part-time teacher/ researcher	Maggie Rolls and Sylvia Robinson
Gillian Davies	Head of Hexham House	
Eileen Marsh	Head of Arundel House	
Don Williams	Religious Education teacher	Sylvia Robinson
Keith Dryden	Art/Newsom teacher	
Geoffrey Goddard	Headmaster	
June Harper	Head of Commerce	Sylvia Robinson

charities collection, Lancaster House will be organizing a cake stall on Thursday lunchtime'. However, he followed this with the words 'I'm not sure that this is very important for you' (I think this indicates the competition between House Heads as Ron has been keen for the members of his House to participate in their own activities for the Lenten charities). He told the pupils that there would be a meeting at lunchtime (12.05) to discuss the local authority cruise to the Mediterranean that is to take place. Thirdly, he said there is to be a badminton competition for second and third year pupils who should watch the P.E. department's notice boards as 'we want to do well in this House'. 'Next', he said, 'I would like to remind you about the school Mass that takes place each Wednesday morning at ten minutes past eight. There was a good attendance last week but I did not think there were many people from this House. I hope, therefore, that we shall be well represented in future weeks.' Then he said, 'I haven't mentioned litter for a fortnight' (a point which is not correct according to my notes). He said, 'I came back from Mr. Goddard's (the Headmaster's) office yesterday and I was disgusted (he raises his voice here) when I looked at this House Hall. I thought how bad it looked and realised that this was my House Hall. But it is not just *my* (he emphasises) area it is *our* (emphasis again) House area and it is important to keep it clean and tidy. We need to do better. We need to improve.' Finally, he talked about the mess that was left in the House Hall after lunch yesterday. He said, 'you should all remember not to leave mess around in the Hall. It is important for us all to be tidy in Westminster House.' After this Ron indicated that he wanted pupils to leave the Hall quietly and go to their first lesson. (Fieldnotes: 12 March 1974)

Sets of similar fieldnotes were kept on other announcements that were made in the House assemblies I attended. The result was that I could examine the categories that were used by teachers who took morning assembly, the terminology that was used and the subject areas that were covered. However, before analysis could begin it was essential to code my notes according to the themes that were developed. These code words can be placed either in the margins of the fieldnotes or on separate pages on which the fieldnotes are transcribed so that all the notes relating to a particular topic can be easily retrieved. On the basis of working on such materials I was able subsequently to analyse the ways in which norms and values were established in the school (Burgess, 1983, pp. 41–8).

Methodological Notes

As well as keeping substantive notes about what occurred in the school I also kept a set of methodological fieldnotes. These notes consisted of personal reflections on my activities in the field. Some notes dealt with problems, impressions, feelings and hunches as well as with some of the processes and procedures associated with field research. The main purpose of these notes is reflection. Here, researchers can consider their methods and speculate on ways in which these methods can be adopted, adapted and developed in particular settings (cf. Bogdan and Biklen, 1982, pp. 86–9). The first methodological notes that I produced devoted considerable space to the degree of access that I was given and the way in which my role was perceived by different teachers. This approach followed the strategy adopted by Geer (1964). I began to keep notes on my research role from my first day in the school when I remarked:

In Clifton House I was asked by Maggie Rolls (the Head of House) what I was doing. I replied, 'I am a research student at Warwick University and I'm coming into the school to observe the way in which teachers and pupils are dealing with the raising of the school leaving age. I will be teaching in the school during this term.' (Fieldnotes, 1 May 1973)

At this time, I had only negotiated access for one term in the school, and the focus of my work was more towards 'less able' pupils and the decision that had recently been taken to raise the school leaving age to 16 (Department of Education and Science, 1971). While this was the position on day one, I found that changes occurred throughout the research period as I gained access to further areas in the school, developed and sharpened the focus of my study, and developed my role. Indeed, I found that I was continually having to define my role for different teachers. Often this occurred not in relation to a question, but in relation to situations in which attempts were made to define the role. During my first week in the school I had to handle several queries about what I was doing and what I was prepared to do. Later that week the Head of the Newsom Department asked if I would like to take some of her classes. While this provided a further opportunity for participation, I considered that it might influence my role in a direction which I might not necessarily want, as I recorded in my fieldnotes:

> Sylvia Robinson found me in the staff common room where I was talking to several teachers. After the others had gone she came over and asked 'Haven't you any classes to teach?' I indicated that this was a period when I was working in the common room in order 'to get to know people, to get to know the school and to get the feel of the place'. However, Sylvia was not convinced and asked if I would like to go and observe her classes or to teach her lessons. However, I resisted this as I did not want to be regarded by the pupils as someone who just took other people's lessons – I want to be regarded as a permanent, part-time member of staff. (Fieldnotes, 3 May 1973)

On the basis of these two extracts from my fieldnotes in the first week I spent in the school I was able to reflect on the implications that my role had for data collection and for developing subsequent work, including relationships with individuals. I found that it was important to make regular entries about my role, the way in which it was perceived by different members of the staff and by pupils and the way in which this assisted or impeded the collection of data. Indeed, as Geer (1964) indicates, the researcher must be aware of the way in which field roles may be utilised by the informant for political purposes and in ways which were not originally intended. Keeping a set of methodological fieldnotes will, therefore, allow the researcher to be reflexive and to engage in some form of self analysis during the research process, a procedure that has been followed by some social anthropologists (cf. Malinowski, 1967; Spindler, 1970) and which is to be recommended to all who engage in field research.

Analytic Notes

Another dimension to fieldnotes is the preparation of preliminary analyses that are worked out in the field. These notes may include the preliminary questions that were posed and the hypotheses that are to be developed and tested. This dimension of fieldnotes has been most clearly developed by Geer (1964) who indicates that during the course of field research the researcher develops a set of ideas from the data itself. This is an informal process which Geer identifies as taking place in three stages. First, testing crude yes-or-no propositions. Secondly, working with negatively expressed hypotheses and, thirdly, working eventually with rough models. In these terms, themes do not suddenly emerge in field data but are established on the basis of a series of working hypotheses.

When themes emerge from data, Glaser and Strauss (1967) and Schatzman and Strauss (1973) highlight the importance of analytic memos which they see as separate from the fieldnotes. They encourage researchers to write continually a series of analytic memos which can form the core of the preliminary analysis (cf. Johnson, 1975). Such memos may include summaries that are written at the end of a day in the field in which the researcher indicates themes that have emerged, and concepts that can be developed, together with preliminary thoughts about the analytic framework. If these summaries are regularly maintained throughout the research period it will mean that the researcher will have some themes worked out before a full index is prepared.

Indexing Fieldnotes

Fieldnotes need to be regularly written and recorded so that they can be carefully categorised by the researcher. In these terms it is generally recommended that wide margins are established on pages of fieldnotes so that preliminary categories can be inserted at the time of writing together with further categories at a later date. In turn, it is also recommended that several copies of the fieldnotes should be produced so that the same set of notes that apply to different categories can be inserted into different files. However, when researchers assemble their fieldnotes a technical problem arises through the sheer mass of material that has to be considered. For example, in Becker *et al.*'s study *Boys in White* (1961) they report that by the end of their research they had amassed 5,000 pages of notes. With such a mass of material it would be impractical to have to go through each page every time they wished to check a proposition. To overcome this problem, they indexed their fieldnotes and labelled each item with code numbers that related to major topics. The various entries could then be reassembled under code numbers so that all the material on a particular topic was available in one place. Similarly, Whyte (1955) reports that he had such a mass of material that he could not locate items quickly. Accordingly, he devised

> a rudimentary indexing system: a page in three columns containing, for each interview or observation report, the date, the person or people interviewed or observed, and a brief summary of the interview or observation record. Such an index would cover from three to eight pages. When it came to review the notes or to write from them, a five-to-ten minute perusal of the index was enough to give me a reasonably full picture of what I had and of where any given item could be located. (Whyte, 1955, pp. 308–9)

Clearly, some such system is required if researchers are to use qualitative data efficiently and effectively. A basic strategy for organising fieldnotes is in terms of chronological order. However, it can be taken a stage further by getting

> the material out of the sheer chronological narrative of one's field or interview notes and into a *flexible storage, ordering* and *retrieval* format. (Lofland, 1971, p. 118)

In this sense, Lofland considers that different sets of files may be established that concern such topics as people, places, organisations and documents, while a set of analytic files may embody an emergent sociological-analytic coding scheme. However, Read (1980) has argued that such a system has two major disadvantages. First, it is physically and conceptually disruptive as it is difficult to recognise instances that occur in different analytic files. Secondly, this system with numerous copies of text is very bulky for the researcher to handle. As a result, Read proposes that a system of indirect indexing using a manual system of index cards containing details of page numbers, dates and categories would provide a flexible system for dealing with one set of chronologically ordered notes. However, he suggests that the main disadvantage of this system would be the retrieval process that might involve scanning all the cards.

A strategy for organising fieldnotes using computer facilities has been discussed by Walter (1975) who provides a summary of the key phases associated with this approach. He suggests that researchers should begin by numbering the paragraphs in their fieldnotes. This is followed by the exploratory construction of categories, after which the researcher can index a few pages of fieldnotes to see if these categories can be used. Thirdly, some categories will be rejected and the researcher can then produce a tentative final list of categories. Finally, the researcher can number these categories in some rational order. Essentially, the system involves entering fieldnotes on 80 column punched cards, the notes being subdivided so that particular paragraphs can be identified. While such a system focuses on categories and indexing, Read maintains that it overlooks the emergence of categories which regularly occur in fieldnotes. Accordingly, he argues that if the original text is computerised it will allow for quick retrieval. Among the retrieval operations that he considers could be achieved are:

1   Compiling a list of categories which can be produced as an alphabetic list.
2   Retrieving all instances of a category – cross-relating the category index relations and printing a sorted list of category index relations.
3   Printing the text associated with each category and cross-relating the category index and the text.
4   Retrieving instances which may be categorised in different ways.
5   Printing a dictionary of words contained in text chunks but presenting the retrieved text as a sorted word list where duplicates are removed.

However, Read indicates that research on modes of indexing, the suitability of computer representations and the use of the text is still in its early stages.

Similarly in the USA Drass (1980) has discussed the computer programme LISPQUAL and outlined the way in which this package can assist in the analysis of data collected using participant observation and unstructured interviews. This package replicates many of the tedious, time-consuming, mechanical operations associated with traditional analytic procedures which have had to be done by hand. The advantage of LISPQUAL is that it performs these operations with greater efficiency, greater accuracy and with great speed, thus allowing the researcher more time to spend on the interpretative phase of data analysis.

While these approaches have only recently been developed, they would appear to have great potential. Indeed, data could be stored more easily and archives could be established for field research data (cf. Stenhouse, 1978). This would not only allow field data to become accessible for public inspection but also facilitate more rapid retrieval. However, at the present time data retrieval and data analysis is usually a slow process whereby researchers have continually to comb and recomb their fieldnotes.

From Fieldnotes to Data Analysis: Some Empirical Examples

Sociologists who engage in field research seldom discuss the ways in which they analyse their data. However, Macintyre (1979) indicates the main stages involved in analysing the data for her study *Single and Pregnant* (1977) using a computerised indexing system for data retrieval. She indicates that the computer was not used for analysis as such but was invaluable in indexing a mass of bulky data and retrieving relevant sections of it. She divides her analysis into stages which are identified as having taken place: before the period in the field, during the period of field research and after data collection had occurred. Her seven major stages were:

Stage 1 Constructing a list of research problems, concepts and indices before the period in the field. This stage culminated during the early period of data collection when she had a list of categories that could be used to index the data. These categories were subdivided into: socio-demographic characteristics, events, and conceptual categories which were based on an imaginative rehearsal of the careers of pregnant women, sociological theory, conceptualisation and the inspection of early interviews. In this respect, the categories could be developed, extended, deleted or refined in subsequent work.

Stage 2 Coding took place throughout the research period using a procedure recommended by Glaser (1965). Here, categories were constructed from statements and events with the result that comparisons could be made between the categories. Furthermore, new categories could be devised on the basis of new concepts and themes that arose from the data (cf. Glaser and Strauss, 1967).

Stage 3 The remaining material was coded at the end of the research and all the data were re-read. At this stage, different types of material could be brought together: fieldnotes, interview transcripts and documentary records that could be linked together in terms of conceptual themes and topics. It was this material that she used to write an account about each woman (cf. Macintyre, 1977, pp. 37–52).

Stage 4 Organising the analysis and presenting the materials. Macintyre considered that this could be done in at least four ways. First, using detailed case studies, but as she notes this would prevent comparison and would have created difficulties concerning the integration of data. Secondly, using time periods to compare what happened to the women at different points of time. However, this would have resulted in similar events being utilised in different chapters of her study. Thirdly, comparing the women's accounts, the professionals' accounts and the client/professional interaction, a strategy that she thought would have masked pregnancy careers. Finally, analysing conceptual categories or themes such as 'moral character' and 'bargaining in encounters', a strategy that would mask the individual's career and the relationship between events. The result was that Macintyre decided to compromise by providing an account in which themes and events presented in chronological order were used to present the data (cf. Macintyre, 1977).

Stage 5   The data retrieval system was used to locate data that were relevant for the topics that had been identified.

Stage 6   The preliminary types and inter-relationships were checked using Barton and Lazarsfeld's notion of quasi-statistics to look at frequencies and distributions of themes (cf. Barton and Lazarsfeld, 1955). In particular, this approach was used to give credibility to categories such as 'moral career'.

Stage 7   The relationships between major topics were examined.

In this example, the major stages of Macintyre's research link up with Becker and Geer's major stages of field analysis: selecting and defining the problems, concepts and indices of the study, checking on the frequency, range, distribution and collective character of the data and, finally, the incorporation of the material into a model (cf. Becker and Geer, 1960). A similar range of stages has been identified by Woods (1977) who adds a further stage of linking models to external forms and structures as he aimed to bridge the gap between inter-actionist and structuralist work within his study. He discusses the way in which he engaged in data analysis while conducting a study of a secondary school (Woods, 1979) in the following terms:

> After a term's participant observation in which I talked to over 300 pupils, I listened to all my tapes and read through all my notes. There were regularities in the pupils' conversations with me which provided certain 'themes'. One of their preoccupations was an aversion to being 'shown up' by teachers. Satisfied that this was acutely felt and common enough to warrant further investigation, I engaged in 'theoretical sampling', that is, I purposely began to seek and accumulate material from all sources which bore on the phenomenon.
>
> I constructed a typology, examined the internal structure of the process, considered its functions and results, and who was involved. Much of this was at the level of substantive theory, but

some formal theory entered in relation to functions and who was involved. This is because the functions are connected with general sociological concepts like power, socialisation and status, and could therefore be related to other contexts. 'Who was involved' led to a consideration of other distinctive features they might have in common, and a tentative identification with one of the pedagogical paradigms . . . an elaboration of a paternalist style of control, all within an umbrella of alienation. (Woods, 1977, p. 53)

In this instance, an attempt is made to develop an analysis from face-to-face interaction and to connect it with 'grand theory', an approach that links up with the two major strategies for analysing qualitative data that have been identified in the methodological literature: analytic induction and grounded theory, to which we now turn.

Analytic Induction

It was Znaniecki (1934) who first used this approach in order that field researchers could attempt to come to terms with the problem of causal inference while remaining faithful to their data. The approach involved the researcher being able to generalise from a small number of cases without engaging in pre-categorisation. The main steps involved in analytic induction have been identified as:

1   Defining the phenomenon to be explained.
2   A hypothetical explanation of the phenomenon is formulated.
3   One case is studied to see whether the hypothesis relates to the particular case.
4   If the hypothesis does not fit the case, it is either reformulated or the phenomenon is redefined in order to exclude the particular case.
5   Practical certainty is achieved with a small number of cases, but negative cases disprove the explanation and require a reformulation.
6   The examination of cases, redefinition of the phenomenon and reformulation of hypotheses is continued until a universal relationship is established. (cf. Robinson, 1951, p. 813)

This procedure has been used in studies to develop classifications and explanatory hypotheses. A classic use of analytic induction was in Lindesmith's study of opiate addiction where it provided explanatory hypotheses (Lindesmith, 1947). However, Robinson (1951) and Turner (1953) have criticised this approach by questioning its logic of explanation and whether universal propositions can apply to all case studies. None the less, it is argued that this approach to data analysis does allow concepts and propositions to be derived from data for, as Turner states:

> The operation in practice is one which alternates back and forth between tentative cause and tentative definition, each modifying the other so that in a sense closure is achieved when a complete and integral relation between the two is established. (Turner, 1953, p. 609)

Grounded Theory

A second major approach to data analysis that has been advocated for field research is the use of Glaser and Strauss's model of generating theories from data. This approach gives rise to either substantive grounded theories or formal abstract theories which they distinguish in the following terms:

> By substantive theory, we mean that developed for a substantive, or empirical area of sociological enquiry, such as patient care, race relations, professional education, delinquency, or research organizations. By formal theory, we mean that developed for a formal, or conceptual area of sociological enquiry, such as stigma, deviant behaviour, formal organization, socialization, status congruency, authority and power, reward systems, or social mobility. Both types of theory may be considered as 'middle range'. That is they fall between the 'minor working hypotheses' of everyday life and the 'all-inclusive' grand theories. (Glaser and Strauss, 1967, pp. 32–3)

As far as Glaser and Strauss are concerned, theory can be generated on the basis of comparative analysis between or among groups within a substantive area. In contrast to analytic induction they suggest the constant comparative method which is concerned with generating and developing categories, properties and hypotheses rather than testing them. In contrast to analytic induction, Glaser and Strauss argue that this approach requires the saturation of data rather than the consideration of all data. They identify four stages in the constant comparative method. First, the researcher compares incidents applicable to each category. Here, the data have to be coded (cf. Macintyre, 1979) and compared with previous data which Glaser and Strauss maintain results in the generation of theoretical properties of the category. Secondly, the researcher integrates categories and their properties. Thirdly, the theory is delimited so that the researcher is involved in reducing theory and delimiting the saturation of categories. Here, the researcher needs to keep check of the criteria that are used to select and delimit categories. Finally, Glaser and Strauss identify a writing period when analytic memos are produced which will provide major themes for further publications.

Glaser and Strauss (1967) and more recently Glaser (1978) have discussed ways in which this approach can be used in qualitative social investigations with the result that theory testing is seen as unnecessary, as

> Theory based on data can usually not be completely refuted by more data or replaced by another theory. Since it is too intimately linked to data, it is destined to last despite its inevitable modification and reformulation. (Glaser and Strauss, 1967, p. 4)

However, this view has been considered problematic for as Ford (1975) indicates, it is doubtful whether testing or refining hypotheses can be excluded from the process. Several commentators have also raised further questions about grounded theory. For example, Bulmer (1979) considers that Glaser and Strauss's *tabula rasa* view of inquiry is open to debate. He argues that their suggestion that researchers should ignore the theoretical literature on an area of study and avoid presuppositions or prior conceptualisation in areas that have been well researched is exceedingly difficult for researchers to achieve. Furthermore, he argues, it is difficult to follow the process of category development which appears uncontrolled and prompts the question: when does category development stop?

Further difficulties with grounded theory have been identified by Brown (1973) and Williams (1976) who indicate that there is some doubt about what Glaser and Strauss consider to be 'theory'. Indeed, Brown maintains that Glaser and Strauss are not clear about the nature of grounded theory, nor about the link between theory and data. Similarly, Williams indicates that Glaser and Strauss use the term 'theory' to refer to properties, categories and hypotheses. Finally, Rose (1982) has questioned whether theory construction is intimately linked to field research. As a consequence, any researcher who intends to utilise Glaser and Strauss's approach to data analysis needs critically to evaluate their work and the kinds of strategies that will be of use in analysing data. Indeed, some researchers may not wish their studies to be merely concerned with theory-building but may be more interested in theory-testing or providing detailed ethnographic description which may involve elements of theory that are revealed in the writing.

The Presentation of Field Data

The analysis that is presented by the field researcher will be both descriptive and analytic. However, the presentation that is made will depend upon the theoretical perspective that is used, the goals of the researcher and the audience that the researcher wants to address (cf. Warren, 1980). Indeed, Bruyn (1966) has shown that the research report needs to indicate at which descriptive level the researcher is working; the description of the culture, the themes and concepts of the social scientist, configurations of themes in the cultures studied or at the level of theory. Various writers including Schatzman and Strauss (1973) and Woods (1977) have identified different ways in which studies may be written. First, there are *descriptive accounts* where the emphasis is upon providing detailed description which is informed by theoretical schemes. Secondly, there are accounts that provide *analytic descriptions* whereby the conceptual scheme used is developed on the basis of the data that are obtained. Thirdly, there are *substantive theoretical accounts* that are concerned with substantive theory where the researcher generates theoretical statements that will have applicability beyond the individual case that has been studied. The main difference between a descriptive account and an analytic account is discussed by Ditton (1977) when he indicates that his study is not a full-blown ethnography of the bread salesman, but focuses attention on the general social processes associated with fiddling. In these terms, he argues that his work might be termed a 'theorised ethnography'.

Recent accounts of field research by Bogdan and Taylor (1975) and by Spradley (1980) have provided suggestions about writing style, a point that was clearly articulated by Mills (1959) when he demonstrated how sections of Talcott Parsons's writing in *The Social System* (Parsons, 1951) could be 'translated' into intelligible language. However, even when field studies are clearly written it is essential to provide detailed cases of individuals' lives. For without that, the studies are devoid of material that brings a people to life:

> they are pinned like butterflies in a glass case, with the difference, however, that we often cannot tell what colour these specimens are, and we are never shown them in flight, never see them soar or die except in generalities. (Read, 1965, p. ix)

Read's comment is directed at anthropologists who, he argues, are merely concerned with the particular as a means of understanding the general. If field researchers follow this route their research reports will contain little reference to personal experience and whole worlds will be lost from view. Yet it would be churlish to suggest that all field researchers find difficulty in drawing on personal experience. Indeed, if we turn to Whyte's *Street Corner Society* (1955), Liebow's *Tally's Corner* (1967), and Pons's *Stanleyville* (1969), we can find accounts where the authors have combined the depth, colour and richness of their own experience with explanation and understanding. Such writing skills although difficult to acquire are worthy of our attention. For we should aim to convey our experience as we write our fieldnotes, our analytic memoranda and our research reports. However, field studies do not merely rest upon good writing, for the final report relies upon the researcher blending together personal experience with theories and data in order to make some contribution to our understanding of the social world.

Conclusion

This chapter has attempted to examine the relationship between what is observed, recorded and analysed by the field researcher, paying particular attention to some of the central problems involved. Inevitably, the focus has been upon examples of materials, for no 'rules' can be given about how to record, code, index, analyse and report observations that are made in field settings. However, the processes that have been discussed indicate that organisation, reflection, commitment, thought, and flexibility are as essential to data analysis as they are to data collection.

Suggestions for Further Reading

Methodology

Barton, A. H. and Lazarsfeld, P. F. (1955), 'Some functions of qualitative analysis in social research', *Frankfurter Beiträge Zur Soziologie*, pp. 321–61; reprinted in G. J. McCall and J. L. Simmons (1969) (eds), *Issues in Participant Observation* (Reading, Mass.: Addison-Wesley), pp. 163–96, 239–44; a classic paper on data analysis that provides suggestions for handling data.

Becker, H. S. and Geer, B. (1960), 'Participant observation: the analysis of qualitative field data', in R. N. Adams and J. J. Preiss (eds), *Human Organization Research: Field Relations and Techniques* (Homewood, Ill.: Dorsey Press), pp. 267–89; reprinted in Burgess (1982a). A paper in which the authors outline some major stages in data analysis.

Blaxter, M. (1979), 'The analysis of qualitative data: a symposium', *Sociological Review*, vol. 27, no. 4; the complete issue is devoted to data analysis and includes conceptual papers by Bulmer (1979) and by Halfpenny (1979), as well as examples.

Bogdan, R. and Taylor, S. J. (1975), *Introduction to Qualitative Research Methods* (New York: Wiley); contains particularly useful sections on writing fieldnotes and field reports. It includes examples of both.

Burgess, R. G. (1982) (ed.), *Field Research: a Sourcebook and Field Manual* (London: Allen & Unwin). Sections seven and nine consider questions of recording, analysing and reporting field data. Section nine includes the paper by Becker and Geer (1960).

Geer, B. (1964), 'First days in the field', in P. Hammond (ed.), *Sociologists at Work* (New York: Basic Books); an excellent paper that demonstrates the relationship between data recording and data analysis.

Lofland, J. (1971), *Analyzing Social Settings* (New York: Wadsworth). The first part of this book contains a detailed discussion of different styles of data analysis. The final chapter contains some helpful comments on writing fieldnotes and reports.

Read, M. (1980), 'Ethnographic field notes and interview transcripts: some preliminary observations on the computer management of text', *Sociological Research Unit Working Paper No. 8*, University College, Cardiff; provides a useful discussion and evaluation of the use of computers in the indexing of fieldnotes and field data.

Wolff, K. (1960), 'The collection and organization of field materials: a research report', in R. N. Adams and J. J. Preiss (eds), *Human Organization Research: Field Relations and Techniques* (Homewood, Ill.: Dorsey Press), pp. 240–54; provides a useful discussion of the relationship between fieldnotes and analysis using an empirical example.

Empirical Studies

Inevitably, this chapter has had to be highly selective. Accordingly, these studies have been specifically chosen for the details they give about material from field notebooks that is subsequently incorporated into data analysis. In particular, the studies by Bell (1968) and Burgess (1983) focus on the use of event analysis (cf. Chapter 3), a strategy used by social anthropologists, while the other studies provide examples of analytic induction and grounded theorising.

Bell, C. (1968), *Middle Class Families* (London: Routledge & Kegan Paul).

Burgess, R. G. (1983), *Experiencing Comprehensive Education: A Study of Bishop McGregor School* (London: Methuen).

Ditton, J. (1977), *Part-Time Crime: an Ethnography of Fiddling and Pilferage* (London: Macmillan).

Macintyre, S. (1977), *Single and Pregnant* (London: Croom Helm). (See also her paper (Macintyre, 1979) on the analysis of her field data.)

Rist, R. (1981), *Earning and Learning: Youth Employment Policies and Programs* (Beverly Hills, Calif.: Sage).

Strauss, A. L., Schatzman, L., Bucher, R., Ehrlich, D. and Sabshin, M. (1964), *Psychiatric Ideologies and Institutions* (New York: The Free Press).

Wiseman, J. P. (1979), *Stations of the Lost* (Phoenix edn) (Chicago: University of Chicago Press).

Woods, P. (1979), *The Divided School* (London: Routledge & Kegan Paul) (see also his commentary on the analysis in Woods (1977).)

9

Ethical Problems, Ethical Principles and Field Research Practice

While earlier chapters have focused upon key phases and methods in the conduct of field research, this chapter returns to consider the whole of the research process. A series of common ethical and political problems are involved in research sponsorship, research relations, data collection, data analysis and data dissemination and it is to these that we now turn. The chapter begins by identifying ethical issues that have arisen in empirical research, after which we turn to examine the attempts that have been made to handle these issues by professional associations. Finally, we consider the extent to which ethical problems can be handled in the practice of field research.

Over the last twenty years sociologists and social anthropologists (especially those working in the USA) have examined a series of major questions concerning the ethical conduct of social research: how can research take place without interference from the state? What are the risks and benefits for those individuals who participate in research? What should individuals be told about the conduct of social research? Is secret research justifiable? Is secret research desirable? What data should be collected? How should data be disseminated? What protection can be given to those individuals who co-operate with social scientists? Many of these questions arise out of abstract theoretical debates, reflections on the conduct of research and the internal discussions that have been conducted by the ethics committees of professional associations. However, some of these questions have also arisen out of the conduct of social researchers in what are by now infamous projects. Three projects that have generated furious debate among academics are the Project Camelot study (Horowitz, 1967), the study of homosexuality in public restrooms by Laud Humphreys (1970) and the study of the Springdale community by Vidich and Bensman (1958, 1968). Each of these studies has raised broad issues: sponsorship in the case of Project Camelot, secrecy and deception in the case of Humphreys, and questions concerning the publication of data in Springdale.

Ethical Problems in Field Research: Three Examples

Project Camelot was an Army-sponsored project which was conducted under the Special Operations Research Office of the American University in Washington DC in 1965 before its sudden cancellation. Horowitz (1967) reports that the project proposal was concerned with the following aims and objectives:

> to determine the feasibility of developing a general social systems model which would make it possible to predict and influence politically significant aspects of social change in the developing countries. Somewhat more specifically its objectives are:
> *First*, to devise procedures for assessing the potential for internal war within national societies;
> *Second*, to identify with increased degrees of confidence those actions which a government might take to revert conditions which are assessed as giving rise to a potential for internal war and:
> *Finally*, to assess the feasibility of prescribing the characteristics of a system for obtaining and holding the essential information needed for doing the above two things. (Horowitz, 1967, pp. 47–8)

The project was to involve the collection of data in Latin American countries and if successful was expected to be of use to the Army in its counter-insurgency missions. Project Camelot was exposed when Hugo Nutini attempted to recruit staff for the project in Chile without indicating the source from which funds had been derived. This project raised questions about the extent to which social science research would be jeopardised by military intervention and the ethics of using social scientific skills in the service of government. In reviewing this study Oppenheim (1969) considers the implications of Project Camelot for British research. He summarises the main objections that have been made to direct government sponsorship of research: the violation of free exchange of information, the dangers of academic freedom, and the influence that particular forms of sponsorship can have upon the direction of research. In addition, he indicates that such projects can create divisions in the academic community, violate supra-national ideology and present dangers to peace. In turn he points towards some lessons that can be learned from such debates. First, he argues that public debates will help to arouse watchfulness on the part of social scientists who may find it easier to refuse to do secret policy-oriented research. Secondly, he recommends the use of 'buffer institutions' in research funding in order to avoid direct government intervention. Finally, he suggests that some consideration needs to be given to the risks and benefits for individuals who have participated in the project.

It is this question of the risks and benefits involved in social research that has surrounded the publication of Laud Humphreys's study on impersonal sexual activity between male homosexuals. Humphreys located several public rest-rooms where homosexual activities took place. Here, he found that the role of watch queen (a third man who serves as a look-out for those engaged in homosexual acts and who obtains voyeuristic pleasure from his observations) could be used to conduct his research. By taking this role he could conduct covert research. In addition to making covert observations, he also kept records of each participant's car and recorded its state and licence numbers. Having obtained these data he then approached the police in order to gain access to licence registers which helped him to establish details of 100 names and addresses of individuals whom he had observed engaging in homosexual activities. With this information he located each individual's house and neighbourhood before the final stage of the project. By this time Humphreys was engaged on a health survey on another project. With the permission of the survey director, he added the names of fifty individuals he had observed engaging in homosexual acts, but, fearing that he might be recognised he waited at least a year from the initial contact and changed his car, dress and hairstyle before calling on them.

Humphreys's research has been reviewed in numerous articles, texts and readers on social research methodology and social research ethics (cf. Bulmer, 1982). One of the most comprehensive reviews is provided by Warwick (1973) who considers that Humphreys's work involved deception, for he passed as a deviant, misrepresented himself when acting as a 'watch queen', disguised the fact that he was making a record of the activities that he observed by hiding a tape-recorder in his car, deceived the police by referring to his work as 'market research' to gain access to car registration numbers, and deceived his respondents in the survey he conducted by including them in a 'health survey' and by changing his personal appearance to avoid recognition. The second major consideration arising from this study concerns freedom and privacy. Whose freedom should be considered; that of the researcher or the researched? Those individuals who support Humphreys's work, justify it on the basis that social scientists and citizens have a right to know about the activities that Humphreys observed. However, against this is the argument that such research constitutes an invasion of personal privacy, for Humphreys intruded into the lives of others without them having any knowledge of his real intentions. Finally, Donald Warwick raises questions concerning the misuse of data. While it could be argued that the data were collected for social science research, they could also be used for blackmail or criminal prosecution. Furthermore, this work could create anxiety among the participants who did not ask to be studied and who might wonder whether their reputations would be destroyed if they were identified.

The key question is whether the methods used were ethically justifiable, for Warwick goes on to ask: 'should every social scientist who feels that he has a laudable cause have the right to deceive respondents about the nature of surveys, engage in covert observation, and resort to other kinds of trickery?' (Warwick, 1973, p. 37). In addressing this and related questions, Warwick finds three objections to these research tactics. First, that the researcher took advantage of a relatively powerless group. Secondly, that Humphreys's activities make it more difficult for social scientists to engage in research as they will be suspected of trickery. Finally, that deception, misrepresentation and manipulation cannot and should not be used by social scientists.

While covert activities represent an extreme form of social research, they do nevertheless raise questions about privacy that have been identified in other field studies. In the 1950s Vidich was involved in a study of the Springdale 'community' where the residents were concerned about whether they would be identified in the final report. To gain permission to study this area, the researcher promised that no individual would be identified in any report with the result that the residents felt they were to be the subjects of a social survey. However, when the study was published it was evident that the authors had failed to maintain anonymity. Although pseudonyms were used, individuals could be identified by means of the problems being analysed. Vidich and Bensman (1958, 1968) indicate that their book caused considerable disturbance in the locality, as a local newspaper reported:

> The people of the Village [Springdale] waited quite awhile to get even with Art Vidich, who wrote a *Peyton Place*-type book about their town recently. The featured float of the annual Fourth of July parade followed an authentic copy of the jacket of the book, *Small Town in Mass Society*, done large-scale by Mrs. Beverly Robinson. Following the book cover came residents of [Springdale] riding masked in cars labeled with the fictitious names given them in the book.
>
> But the pay-off was the final scene, a manure spreader filled with a very rich barnyard fertilizer, over which was bending an effigy of 'The Author'. (Quoted by Vidich and Bensman, 1968, p. 397)

While this may seem an elaborate ceremonial, it does raise crucial questions about the obligations that researchers have to those who are researched, whether they should be identified and what steps, if any, should be taken to avoid harming those individuals who are identified or identifiable. As Vidich had published this study with Joseph Bensman who had no previous connection with the project, this work also raised questions about the right that individual investigators have to use data: should writers use data that they have not personally collected? Who owns project data? What are the responsibilities of the researcher?

These three American research projects have generated much public debate, for they illustrate some of the major ethical dilemmas that confront social scientists. While each case illustrates major ethical issues at different phases of the research process, they also raise questions about the way in which ethical problems can be handled in the field. As a consequence, some attempts have been made to control the conduct of research in the USA through federal regulations (Wax and Cassell, 1979) and Institutional Review Boards (Olesen, 1979). In addition, professional associations for anthropologists and sociologists have established statements of ethical principles which are considered fundamental to the ethical pursuit of the profession. The key areas of discussion have been: relationships with 'subjects', responsibility to the public, to the discipline, to students, to sponsors, to one's own government and to host governments (cf. American Anthropological Association, 1971). Meanwhile, in Britain there is, as yet, no legislation governing the conduct of social research. Nevertheless, learned societies have established statements of ethical principles (cf. British Sociological Association, 1982) and codes of ethics (cf. Market Research Society, 1976). While the latter can be enforced and may lead to expulsion from the Market Research Society, the former merely provides a framework within which it is suggested sociologists might work.

Enter the Professional Association

The British Sociological Association (BSA) which was founded in 1950 did not formally deal with professional ethics until 1967 when, in response to a request by members at the Annual General Meeting of that year, the Executive Committee appointed a sub-committee

> to explore ethical problems concerning the professional practice of sociologists and to consider what action, if any, the B.S.A. should take in this regard. (British Sociological Association, 1968a, p. 1)

This sub-committee collected case histories of ethical problems which were of concern to sociologists. In addition, data were collected about procedures used by BSA members to ensure the maintenance of ethical standards in professional practice. On the basis of these data, together with information about 'codes' and statements from anthropological and sociological associations overseas, and information from other professions, the BSA Executive Committee called upon the Association to 'affirm its determination to institute and maintain the highest standards of ethical practice among sociologists' (British Sociological Association, 1968a, p. 1). In turn, a preliminary statement was issued on the general principles upon which such practice should be based, together with illustrations of the way in which these principles could be applied. The BSA went on to comment that:

> The presentation of the statement is an interim measure which the Committee hope will have the effect of acting as an informal sanction among professional sociologists in Great Britain and also serve an educative purpose, sensitizing members to areas where particular care is needed. At this stage it is not implied that the applications of the general principles should have any more weight than suggestions or illustrations. (British Sociological Association, 1968a, p. 1)

This statement of ethical principles (British Sociological Association, 1968b) was circulated to all members with a view to achieving a more considered statement or 'code' of ethics. At the Association's Annual General Meeting in 1968 members took the view that a set of principles and recommendations would give general and specific guidance on particular issues. However, doubts were expressed about the desirability of having a set of principles which were vacuous and vague as it was considered that sociologists were covered by general ethics and the law. The record indicates that the Executive Committee were not asking the Association to commit itself to a code, to the principle of having a code or to any particular set of principles and their application. However, the Association did establish a Standing Sub-Committee on professional ethics to receive comments from members about the statement of ethical principles (British Sociological Association, 1968b) and related comments on professional ethics.

It is this 'preliminary statement' on ethical principles that was published in 1970, revised in 1973 and amended in 1982 (British Sociological Association, 1970, 1973, 1982) that is still in use today. This statement considers the duties of sociologists to the discipline and to the 'subjects' of their studies and maintains that it is the duty of sociologists:

> to maintain the independence and integrity of sociology as a discipline, the freedom to research and to study, publish and disseminate the results of sociological research, saving that in the

pursuit of these ends they should remember at all times their responsibility to safeguard the proper interests of those studied or affected. (British Sociological Association, 1982, p. 1)

In particular, the statement considers the implication of these general principles in relation to the maintenance of professional integrity, safeguarding the interests of 'subjects' (both individuals and collectivities), relations with colleagues, employers, employees, sponsoring and other bodies and teaching. Under each of these headings suggestions are provided about the detailed application of the general principles.

Professional integrity This area includes the competence of sociologists to conduct research using appropriate techniques. Sociologists are advised to state the limitations on their involvement and detachment in areas of study and to 'recognise and state any way in which their presence may have affected the subjects of their studies' (British Sociological Association, 1982, p. 2). Sociologists should, it is argued, explain their work fully to sponsors, facilitators and 'subjects' and should not give guarantees of confidentiality that cannot be fulfilled.

As far as covert research is concerned, the statement recommends that this is 'a form of research enquiry which should be resorted to only where it is not possible to use other methods to obtain essential data' (BSA, 1982, p. 2) and that 'these methods should only be used when it is possible to safeguard completely the interests and anonymity of the subjects' (BSA, 1982, p. 2). There is also advice on publication and on communications with the mass media. In particular, sociologists are reminded that they have some responsibility over the use to which their research may be put, the effects of their work on further research and the application of their research evidence including 'the prevention of the *misuse* of research results' (BSA, 1982, p. 3).

The interests of subjects.   This section begins by defining 'subjects' to include 'Individuals and collectivities of all kinds; for example formal organisations and geographical areas' (BSA, 1982, p. 3). In particular, attention is drawn to the doctrine of informed consent and the necessity of explaining the object and implication of research to potential 'subjects'. Good practice with regard to the conduct of inquiry, to confidentiality, and publication is also discussed.

Relations with sponsoring bodies, colleagues, employers, employees and members of other professions.   Here, advice is given on contracts, the rights and duties of individuals who are employers and employees in social research, and the implications of research for formal organisations in which sociologists work. In particular, attention is drawn to the writing of research reports and the problems involved in the dissemination of data when one group can use information to the detriment of others.

Teaching   In this instance, the statement reminds sociologists to take care in presenting research results in the course of their teaching and discusses the implications of the principles contained in earlier sections for the conduct and supervision of student projects.

This statement is part of the debate within the British Sociological Association on methodological competence which in turn is linked to the effort that has been made to professionalise British sociology (Abrams, 1981; Barnes, 1981). However, as Barnes (1981) has noted, the statement cannot be enforced since the BSA, in common with other professional associations, has no effective sanctions that can be used. Furthermore, not all British sociologists belong to the BSA or subscribe to its views.

This statement of ethical principles, in common with the federal regulations and codes of ethics that have been developed in the USA, contains a language and a model which is more closely associated with the experimenter and the subject in biomedical research than with field research (Cassell, 1978, 1980; Olesen, 1979). Furthermore, this model does not take into account all the parties involved in social research: clients, subjects, respondents, informants, research organisations, funding agencies, academic communities, students, colleagues, professional groups and local, national and international political communities (Sjoberg, 1967), all of whom may influence research relations and result in the relationship between researcher and researched varying with the research context, the research problem and the research methodology. Cassell (1980) has compared the relationships that exist between investigators and those who are researched in biomedical experimentation, psychological experimentation, survey research and field research involving participant observation. She argues that it is important to compare the differences between these forms of research along four dimensions: the power of the investigator as perceived by those who are researched, the control of the research setting, the control of the research context and the way in which research interaction is designed and defined. As far as field research is concerned she argues that informants are free to come and go as they wish, have power over the researcher, can control the research setting and exert control over the research interaction as both the researcher and the informants influence interaction. However, she indicates that the relationships between the researcher and the researched do vary depending on the model of field research that is utilised: the veranda model, the *noblesse oblige* model, the going native model or the advocate model (see Chapter 1). She summarises the basic relations between researchers and informants as shown in Table 9.1.

Table 9.1   *Relations between Researchers and Informants.*

| | Type of Field Research | | | |
	Veranda model	*Noblesse oblige*	*Going native*	*Advocate*
Fieldworkers' power as perceived by subjects	High	High–Medium	Low–None	High–Medium
Fieldworkers' control over research setting	High	Medium	Low–None	Low
Fieldworkers' control over context of research	?	Low	Low–None	Medium–Low
Direction of research interaction	Limited two-way	two-way	two-way	variable

Source: Adapted from Cassell (1980), p. 33.

For Cassell different types of field research result in different forms of risk and harm that cannot be universally taken account of by codes, regulations and statements of ethical principles. Indeed, she concludes that

> irrelevant regulations . . . may have symbolic value but little effect upon the ethical adequacy of research, and indeed may distract attention from real moral problems. (Cassell, 1980, p. 37)

This analysis in common with that of Galliher (1980), Burgess (1981b, 1984c) and Barnes (1982) points to several weaknesses in statements of ethical principles. For as Barnes (1982) indicates, statements are prescriptive and contain universalistic and ahistorical phraseology that fails to take account of the conflicts and inequalities in field situations with respect to racial, sexual and economic stratification (Galliher, 1980) and they do not come to terms with the relations between researcher and researched (Burgess, 1981b, 1984c). As a consequence, several commentators (Olesen, 1979; Cassell and Wax, 1980; Dingwall, 1980) have recognised that if we are to understand ethical problems and the way in which they have been handled, it is essential to focus on day-to-day interaction between researchers and informants in a variety of field situations rather than focusing on ethical statements and dramatic instances of ethical violation. Accordingly, we now turn to ethical problems that confront social scientists, sponsors, informants and those who read and use field research.

Ethical Dilemmas in Field Research Practice

Although sociologists have established statements of ethical principles, we need to consider the extent to which these statements can successfully address ethical questions that arise in field research. Accordingly, we return to examine ethical dilemmas that researchers face on a day-by-day basis, drawing on some problems and procedures that have been discussed by British sociologists working in social settings such as schools, hospitals and factories.

Sponsorship

As we noted earlier, questions of sponsorship have been widely debated in the American literature in relation to Project Camelot and the involvement of the government in social science research. Further debates along these lines have also taken place in the USA over the sponsorship of social research by the CIA (cf. Stephenson, 1978). In Britain, there are no documented cases of direct government involvement in social research although some sociologists have questioned the action of the Home Office in connection with their sponsorship of research on prisons (Cohen and Taylor, 1972). Further questions have been raised by sociologists about the sponsorship of social research in general (Payne, Dingwall, Payne and Carter, 1981) and in field research in particular by the SSRC (Ditton and Williams, 1981). One case that has been carefully documented is the events surrounding the problems of getting funds for a major project on North Sea oil (Moore, 1978).

On the basis of documenting the case, Moore attempts to explain why the SSRC had not been able to finance one major research programme nor develop a research strategy on oil and its impact on social life in North East Scotland. In terms of research ethics, the final section of Moore's paper highlights several points that have significance for other projects. Moore indicates that there is relatively little publicly available knowledge on research funding (cf. Ditton and Williams, 1981; Stenhouse, 1984; Wakeford, 1984) and therefore he attempts to indicate the areas in which we need to ask questions. In particular, he points to the power of the SSRC as the main funding body for sociological research and to the role of the committee secretary within the SSRC who is in effect a gatekeeper to funds, being able to mystify communications between applicants and the committee by selecting referees, manipulating the flow of information and editing referees' comments. In short, he indicates that the treatment of applications by the SSRC and the judgements that are made on proposals are protected from scrutiny. The funding of social research and the reasons for success and failure are therefore surrounded by secrecy which sociologists have continued to challenge as they press for open access over the deliberations of the SSRC (cf. Burgess, 1981c).

Just as a gatekeeper holds an essential role in the funding of social research, so many researchers have highlighted the role of other gate-keepers in sponsoring field research. Dingwall (1980) has indicated that in a stratified research setting there is a hierarchy of consent which has implications for the researcher. He argues that it is usual for senior personnel to act as gatekeepers, as they consider they have the right to grant permission for research to be done on individuals lower down the hierarchy (see Chapter 2). Dingwall indicates that he encountered this issue in his study of health visitor training (Dingwall, 1977) where it was problematic for individuals low down the hierarchy to refuse research access. He concludes that any subordinate who refuses to participate in research that has been approved by a superior is taking a risk as they may incur official disfavour. Such issues need active consideration by sociologists. Indeed, Dingwall discusses how he attempted to resolve this issue in home visits with health visitors and social workers by indicating to the clients that he was present for research purposes. However, he found that it was more appropriate for the health visitor or social worker to request permission for him to be present with the result that control of what was said about the research passed out of his hands.

Commenting on another piece of research on the sociology of health and illness, Atkinson (1981) discusses his entry to Edinburgh teaching hospitals to observe the first year of clinical studies. While he indicates that this was not in itself problematic it did take him through a chain of command far removed from the students whom he actually wished to observe on the hospital wards. His negotiations began with the Professor of the Medical Faculty, without whom Atkinson believes his research would not have started. However, it was the members of the Faculty Board who initially allowed him to associate with students. The members of this Board indicated that permission to participate in medical work would be dependent upon the relevant Head of Department and the individual doctors involved. In turn, day-to-day negotiations took place with doctors, with the result that the students who were being taught and the patients who were being used for teaching purposes were not party to the negotiations. It was, therefore, those in the higher reaches of the medical hierarchy who granted permission for research to be conducted. Such situations result in the tendency for sociologists to study down rather than up so that the institutionally powerful are under-researched (cf. Nader, 1969; Warren, 1980).

A similar point can be made with regard to field studies of schools and schooling. Numerous studies (Hargreaves, 1967; Lacey, 1970; King, 1978) discuss negotiating access to schools and to teachers' classrooms through the headteacher, but within these studies we have little or no ethnographic detail on the headteachers themselves. In some studies, the head is but one of many sponsors including education officers and school advisers who provide access to the school, while in other studies such as my own it was the Head who was the principal sponsor. At Bishop McGregor it was the Head who gave me permission to use the school as a research site, to join a House and a department in order to observe social situations and to read documentary materials that were located in the school secretary's office (Burgess, 1979, 1981b, 1984c). However, he insisted that before interviewing pupils I should seek their permission, as no children were to be interviewed without their agreement. Similarly, access to documentary materials held in Houses and departments was to be negotiated with individual teachers as was access to teachers' classrooms (cf. Burgess, 1982b).

The Headmaster was, therefore, the principal sponsor, but other sponsors were required throughout the research if I was to gain access to a number of social situations in the school. Once again, permission to conduct research was granted by senior personnel and by teachers rather than pupils. Indeed, I raised this matter in a meeting with the Headmaster when I inquired if I or both he and I should approach the pupils' parents for permission to do research with their children. In this instance I recorded in my fieldnotes:

> Mr. Goddard (the Headmaster) indicated that if I was to contact the families it was unlikely that I would get their full co-operation. Indeed, he indicated that because many of their children had behavioural problems, members of the school had often written to them. The product of these contacts was considerable hostility towards the school and school activities. In this sense, he thought it would be best if the families were not contacted. 'Anyway', he remarked, 'the school will co-operate as much as possible'. (Fieldnotes, 10 July 1973)

Here, the Head spoke not only for himself but also on behalf of parents, teachers and pupils all of whom were involved directly or indirectly in my research. Similarly, I was given access to letters, notes and documents within and beyond the school. No questions were raised about the use that I might make of this material other than by the school secretary (Burgess, 1982b). The Head assumed that these could be released for research purposes without checking with individual authors. Secondly, when I asked if the research could continue in the school the Head indicated that as he had received no objections *from teachers* the research could proceed. In these circumstances, the power of the Head is shown by the ways in which he gave me permission to conduct research with *other* people in the school.

In this example, together with those from the work of Dingwall and Atkinson, it is evident that research sponsorship and access to situations is defined by the institutionally powerful who not only grant access to research sites but also to individuals and to research materials. But how might such situations be handled? Often, as I found, even when individuals are given the option to refuse to be observed or interviewed it is seldom taken up. In sixteen months in the field I only came across one teacher who restricted research access as he refused to allow me to sit in on a meeting that was held with the Headmaster. Similarly, Atkinson found only one doctor who refused to allow him to observe teaching on the hospital ward – perhaps in these instances Dingwall is correct in concluding that most individuals respond to the structural situations in which they are located.

Open and Closed Research

In considering the relationships between researcher and researched, statements of ethical principles and commentaries on the ethics of social research consider the distinctions between open and closed research which, it is argued, are at opposite ends of the research continuum. This debate together with research examples has been taken up in Britain by Homan (1980) and by Bulmer (1980), although it has a long history (Bulmer, 1982). In the USA researchers such as Erikson (1967, 1968) and Denzin (1968) have debated the points for and against covert research. Erikson's attack on covert methods rests on four particular points. First that sociologists have responsibilities to those whom they research. Secondly, that sociologists have responsibilities to their colleagues, as covert work will jeopardise the reputation of sociology and future research. Thirdly, that much covert research is done by graduate students who will suffer personal stress by involvement in this work and, finally, that covert investigation is bad science. In short, Erikson's position is that

(1) it is unethical for a sociologist to deliberately misrepresent his identity for the purpose of entering a private domain to which he is not eligible; and (2) it is unethical for a sociologist to deliberately

misrepresent the character of the research upon which he is engaged. (Erikson, 1967, p. 373)

Meanwhile, Denzin responds to Erikson by taking each of his major points. First, on the invasion of privacy Denzin indicates that this assumes some distinction can be made between private and public settings (cf. Roth, 1962). Secondly, as far as jeopardy to the professional community is concerned, Denzin maintains that any method poses a potential threat to colleagues. Thirdly, he questions whether disguised roles are more uncomfortable than open roles and fourthly, that sociologists should assess the disruption which they bring to social situations. In his reply, Erikson (1968) responds to each of Denzin's points but indicates that he disagrees with the basic value position that 'what is good for sociology is inherently ethical' (Erikson, 1968, p. 506).

Since this debate took place the whole question of covert research has been more widely discussed. However, much of the debate in the USA over the last two decades has focused on dramatic instances and celebrated studies of sectarian groups (Festinger et al., 1956) of deviants (Lofland and Lejeune, 1960; Humphreys, 1970) and pseudo-patient studies (Caudill et al., 1952; Rosenhan, 1973). Similarly, in Britain the focus is upon classic cases, and research with extreme groups: Homan on old-time Pentecostal fellowships (1978) and Fielding on the National Front (1981). One of the major debates has taken place around Homan's work as Dingwall (1979) and Barbour (1979) generated a correspondence through the pages of *Network* (the newsletter of the British Sociological Association) about whether this work should have ever been published by the *Sociological Review*. The debate has continued through an article by Homan (1980) and a reply by Bulmer (1980), followed by a further article from Dingwall (1980) and a published discussion between Homan and Bulmer (1982).

Homan (1980) indicates that he initially decided to do covert research with old-time Pentecostalists because he thought that there were particular problems in doing overt research with this group. He argues that their view of the world, of universities and their stance towards sociology and towards himself persuaded him to do covert research. He therefore took a covert role in order to observe the actual language behaviour of old-time Pentecostalists. He concludes that these methods do not damage those who are studied and do not harm the standing of sociology. Rather, he argues that some account must be taken of the effect that these methods have on those who practise them. In Bulmer's (1980) response to this article he objects to Homan's position which, he considers, disregards the principle of informed consent, constitutes a betrayal of trust and a gross invasion of personal privacy. In the subsequent dialogue (Homan and Bulmer, 1982) many of these points are repeated with Homan arguing that he decided to use covert methods given the kind of study that he wished to conduct. He also considers that it is doubtful that privacy is threatened more by covert than overt methods. However, Bulmer's response is in terms of the harm that can be done to those who are researched and to the discipline. Finally, Homan responds by indicating that he believes that it is not simply a matter of covert researchers being wholly guilty and overt researchers being innocent, for he shows that the problems which Bulmer has raised are not exclusive to covert research.

Such a statement suggests that researchers need to examine the relationship between covert and overt research. Many discussions on this issue tend to oversimplify the situation by posing secret research against non-secret research in order to assess the advantages and disadvantages of each, for as Roth (1962) argues, the ends of this continuum probably do not exist. All research is to some extent secret, as researchers do not know everything they wish to investigate at the beginning of a study, a situation which makes informed consent difficult. Secondly, in some studies, researchers do not want to influence the behaviour of those researched by saying what it is they are particularly interested in. Furthermore, even if researchers do provide precise details about an investigation, it will have different meanings for different individuals since their experiential contexts differ and their conceptions of the goals of a study will be different (cf. Roth, 1962).

In my research at Bishop McGregor School I found that there was some difficulty in distinguishing between 'open' and 'closed' research. My work with teachers was 'open' while the work with pupils was 'closed' for one-and-a-half terms (cf. Burgess, 1984c). However, for some teachers, my work may have been publicly 'open', but was 'closed' to them. Indeed, some individuals were unclear about what activities constituted 'doing research'. In these terms, there were situations in which I was present where individuals were either uncertain or unaware of my research role. In particular, I realised that this was the case in public gatherings such as school assembly. Secondly, in social situations, over drinks and at staff parties I was still gathering data yet I never interrupted conversations to indicate that anything that was said or done would be included in my field notebook. Finally, even among those who frequently talked to me about research, surprise has been expressed about the kinds of experiences which I discussed in my study. A central part of the analysis of school structure included a discussion of critical situations (Burgess, 1983, pp. 84–119) among which was an examination of the events surrounding bomb scares in the school. Some time after I had written this up and discussed it with the Headmaster I was party to a conversation between the Head and his Deputy. The Head expressed surprise that while they had been handling this critical situation I had been studying it. In these terms, there are several areas of grey involved in the conduct of field research. I would, therefore, agree with Roth who concludes:

> Social science research cannot be divided into the 'secret' and the 'non-secret'. The question is rather how much secrecy shall there be with which people in which circumstances? Or, to state the question in a more positive (in more researchable) manner: when we are carrying out a piece of social science research involving the behaviour of other people, what do we tell whom under what circumstances? (Roth, 1962, p. 284)

This question of what is discussed with individuals in the field raises two further aspects of field relations: informed consent and truth-telling and lying.

Informed Consent
The principle of informed consent arises out of the Nuremberg war trials in the aftermath of the Second World War when it was argued that:

> The voluntary consent of the human subject is absolutely essential. This means that the person involved should have legal capacity to give consent; should be so situated as to exercise free power of choice, without the intervention of any element of force, fraud, deceit, duress, over-reaching or any other ulterior form of constraint or coercion; and should have sufficient knowledge and comprehension of the elements of the subject matter involved as to enable him to make an understanding and enlightened decision. (Nuremberg Code, 1949, reprinted in Reiser *et al.*, 1977, pp. 272–3)

As with many of the ethical principles involved in social research, the concept of 'informed consent' is derived from biomedical research and as such creates problems when attempts are made to apply it to social research. In the USA some Institutional Review Boards not only call for informed consent but require written consent forms to be signed before research begins. However, this presupposes that designs can be successfully explained to informants (cf. Coser, 1978; Gray, 1978). Furthermore, where written consent is required, problems arise over confidentiality and anonymity as the risk of identification is increased. Indeed, similar objections could be made to the BSA's injunction in the statement of ethical principles about fully informing all parties. For even in research that is nominally 'open', it is difficult to uphold the principle of informed consent. Although I told teachers at Bishop McGregor School about my study, it was seen by different teachers to involve different research experiences. Furthermore, there is the issue of what individuals perceive as being 'research'. In this respect, the problems have much in common with those that have already been discussed under the heading of covert research. However, the key issue is what to tell individuals and what information to withhold, a problem that over-laps considerably with the question of truth-telling and lying.

Truth-telling and Lying

The problem here is the extent to which questions of truth and lying pervade all that is said or left unspoken in research situations as well as in social life generally. There are numerous choices: to lie, equivocate, be silent, or tell the truth, are decisions that have to be taken (Bok, 1978). Among the lies that Bok distinguishes are white lies that are considered harmless, lies that are told in crises, lies that are told to liars, lies that are told to enemies and lies that are told to protect peers and clients. During the course of conducting my study of Bishop McGregor School I told lies to protect colleagues who themselves were telling lies in the course of rationalising their work. I also told lies in order to maintain confidentiality and to protect friends in a crisis situation (cf. Burgess, 1984c). Yet I would agree with Bok that 'truthful statements are preferable to lies in the absence of special considerations' (Bok, 1978, p. 30). However, in field research there are situations where white lies are told not with a view to harming others but merely to gain authentic data in a situation. Such an exchange is clearly reported by Paul Atkinson in his study of medical education. A student is in the process of describing a medical examination of the central nervous system which Atkinson denies he has ever seen done. On the basis of Atkinson's lie the student proceeds to explain how humour can arise in bedside teaching:

Student   It'll all come with practice anyway; in the summer when we start clerkships, probably within a week we'll be so good – so used to doing it – that it'll only take a couple of hours. Whereas I can only do the central nervous system in a couple of hours now. Ever seen anybody doing that?
P.A.   (Untruthfully) No.
Student   You have to try and work out the field of vision, so you hold their head down and get them to look straight into your eye and cover one eye – they have to cover one eye – and then you say 'Tell me when you see my finger', and

> you move like that with your finger till they see it moving
> ... (he demonstrated the tangle that a student can get into).
> It's not unusual for a patient to burst out laughing ...
> taking the piss out of the poor student. I think that
> happened to Loraine Beckett, you know her. Of course she
> giggles so much anyway. I think when they both got
> started, the examination ended. Poor Loraine. (Atkinson,
> 1981, p. 50)

In these circumstances, Atkinson's untruthful statement helped
him to get further data on bedside teaching including a detailed
demonstration of the way in which the student conducts an
examination of the central nervous system, the humour that can arise
in the situation and the comedy surrounding a particular
examination by another student. While this untruthful statement
appears to have caused no harm, it has generated data that could be
followed up in further interviews and observations.

In my own research I also told white lies in similar circumstances.
On one occasion I had read a document that was supposedly 'secret'
but that I knew was being shown by House Heads to many of their
teachers. The document contained a plan to get all the pupils away
from the school site with minimum disruption at the end of a term. I
was interested in finding out the circumstances in which teachers
were shown the document and their conception of the plan. In this
instance, I denied any knowledge of the plan when questioned
about it by another teacher. This yielded further data as shown in the
following exchange:

> In the early part of the afternoon I was in the common room when
> Don Williams came in. He came over and asked if I had heard
> anything about the arrangements for the end of term. I replied that I
> did not know what was happening as everything was in a state of
> flux during the last week. He laughed as he told me that there was to
> be a special system for dismissing the pupils this term with many of
> the staff travelling on the buses. Don said he was surprised I did not
> know about these arrangements as he had heard that Eileen Marsh
> had read out a whole list of instructions to Arundel House staff and
> his head of house, Maggie Rolls, had told him that he was 'riding
> shot gun on the number twenty-one bus'. He explained that this
> was only a small part of the plan which he understood was designed
> to overcome the problems associated with the end of term.
> (Burgess, 1983, pp. 110–11)

Once again, a white lie told in order to gather more field data
generates further material, confirms points that I had been told by

others and gives another teacher's perspective of the situation. Yet it could be argued that although no direct harm has been caused, deception has taken place and that this will create problems for me if my informants discover the deception involved. This raises the question of openness and secrecy, not only in field relations but also in the dissemination of data.

Data Dissemination

There is now a considerable literature on ethical issues that makes reference to the publication of research data (Fichter and Kolb, 1953; Becker, 1964; Barnes, 1979; Bulmer, 1982). However, to deal merely with publication is to overlook other means of communicating data. In these terms, I discuss data dissemination which includes the communication of research data orally, visually and in writing. Many of the issues that have arisen in other phases of the research process come into view: confidentiality, privacy, deception and harm. These issues have always been present. For example, Barnes (1979) has noted that early anthropologists who treated many of the people they worked among as 'subjects', appeared to give little thought to the data they published. Yet these data could be subsequently used by colonial powers (cf. Asad, 1973). Indeed, many classical anthropological studies (cf. Evans-Pritchard, 1940) contain maps, diagrams and photographs, all of which helped to locate precisely villages and individuals who were clearly named in the text. It would appear that data dissemination was regarded as unproblematic. However, when anthropologists turned to the study of their own societies, and sociologists engaged in detailed field studies, some protection had to be given to those who were studied and in some cases to those who conducted the research (Patrick, 1973). Here, the law of libel put a brake on the dissemination of data.

However, as Barnes (1982) indicates, the demand is for researchers to disseminate their findings as widely and as quickly as possible. While this may be the situation endorsed by the funding body, by the researcher and in some cases by the informants, other individuals who co-operate in an investigation may want anonymity and confidentiality. In these terms, researchers have to consider what to do with their research findings, what to include and what to exclude, what to disguise and what to make public. The researcher cannot just do nothing, for this in itself is a decision and is a political act (cf. Barnes, 1982).

The problem for the researcher is well put by Platt (1976) who remarks:

> People often told me things that they would not have been prepared to see published in ways that could identify them, or that

could have embarrassed them or other people. (Platt, 1976, pp. 201–2)

A similar situation is illustrated in David Morgan's paper on the British Association Scandal (Morgan, 1972). Morgan had been conducting research in a factory in a northern city and during the course of his study had an opportunity to give a paper at the conference of the British Association for the Advancement of Science. In the course of the paper, Morgan gave illustrations from his data which included responses that women working in the factory had made to the broadcast of the wedding of Princess Alexandra and Angus Ogilvie. This was quickly picked up by the 'popular' press who discovered the name of the factory in which Morgan had conducted his work and reported the details together with the illustrative material under such headings as: 'A factory girl's dream of romance' and 'What a giggle! When a man tells the secrets of life among the girls' (Morgan, 1972). This account is a timely warning to researchers about the use of pseudonyms and the degree of protection that can be given to informants.

In another instance of field research 'at home', Nancy Scheper-Hughes reports on the reception of her study of 'Ballybran' County Kerry (Scheper-Hughes, 1979). When she returned to 'Ballybran' five years after data collection and three years after the publication of her study she found that the study had challenged the local people's interpretations of the meanings of events and of their lives. In her study, Scheper-Hughes had reported on a woman giving up a disapproved love match to care for her widowed father and unmarried brothers. Before publication this had been locally regarded as a moral 'Christian' thing to do but was now openly challenged. There were alternative views of pity and of questioning her attachment to her family. The local people also questioned the accessibility she had given to their lives. They were annoyed that she had written the book in terms that they could understand (which ironically was the reason the Society for Applied Anthropology had honoured her with the Margaret Mead Award for interpreting anthropological data that made them meaningful to a wide audience). In response, Scheper-Hughes argues that she had not disseminated personal secrets but had only discussed commonly known and widely shared community secrets. However, she was told:

There is quite a difference between whispering something beside a fire or across a counter and seeing it printed for the world to see. It becomes *public* shame. (An informant quoted by Scheper-Hughes, 1981, p. 371, emphasis in original)

In turn, further questions were raised: did she have the right to discuss their lives even though she had reported situations truthfully and accurately? Did they not have the right to lead unexamined lives? However, there were also benefits to her study. Hitherto unspoken issues were now discussed: problems of the aged, problems of family and marriage and new insights about their lives. Such an account clearly raises the question posed in Scheper-Hughes's title: for whose good is field research conducted?

For researchers working in Britain there are problems of publication, given the British libel laws. In the 1970s Bell and Newby (1977) outlined the difficulties that they encountered in attempting to discuss the actions and activities of fellow researchers, let alone those activities of individuals whom they had studied. Some of these difficulties are highlighted by Cavendish (1982) in her study of women working in a factory. She explains that when she first wrote her account she changed all the names of individuals so that they could not be identified, but

> I deliberately left in the name of the firm; there is very little direct information available about working conditions and production processes in particular industries and companies in Britain, and next to nothing about how these affect women workers . . . I wasn't attempting an exposé of the factory . . . nor was my aim to point a finger at any particular company. (Cavendish, 1982, p. vii)

However, she was told that the firm could bring a libel action against her and the publisher and under the British libel laws the burden of proof would be with the author. Lawyers were agreed that pseudonyms had to be used to make the firm unidentifiable. She indicates that she has invented names for the firm, the union, the products produced and changed the location of the factory in order to include as much detail on the work process and the events that she reports. However, she believes that such changes limit freedom of speech and protect the institutionally powerful.

The use of pseudonyms and the modification of situations and events is now common practice in reporting field studies (Gibbons, 1975) as it is regularly argued that this facilitates access to institutions when individuals learn that anonymity and confidentiality will be maintained. In some classic studies such as Whyte's *Street Corner Society* (Whyte, 1955, 1981) the pseudonyms for his informants are as well known as the study. However, it is only in the latest edition that one of his informants has 'come out' (some forty years after the study was conducted) and reported on his relationship with Whyte during the research and in subsequent years. Some researchers have invented pseudonyms for themselves as well as for their informants so as to offer protection to themselves and to make it more difficult to locate the research (cf. West, 1945; Patrick, 1973; Cavendish, 1982). However, inventing pseudonyms is no easy task. Names give meaning to people's actions and activities. Names of institutions have in some cases a symbolic value. In my study of Bishop McGregor School, I found that the House system was an important element in my analysis (Burgess, 1983, pp. 52–83). The real names had symbolic meaning for Catholics and therefore I considered it was essential to use pseudonyms that would continue to have some meaning.

Yet it could be argued that an easy way out would have been to name the six Houses after colours: red, blue, green, yellow, grey, and orange, but these would have no specific meaning in a Catholic school. Accordingly I acquired a copy of the *Catholic Directory* (1976) which I used to find names with symbolic value. My search resulted in the Houses in my study being named after a number of dioceses: Arundel, Westminster, Hexham, Southwark, Clifton and Lancaster. Similarly, in the case of towns, cities, local authorities and names of individuals all have been replaced by pseudonyms. However, when this exercise is done a careful record needs to be kept of real names and pseudonyms.

Even in these circumstances individuals and locations are not completely disguised. Individuals will in some instances be identifiable to themselves and to others. For example, individual office holders such as the Head or small groups of teachers working within a particular department. Some researchers such as Tomlinson (1982) have attempted to overcome this problem by changing the sex of the individuals concerned. However, I would argue that this results in distortion of the data and deception in relation to the reader of the completed study.

In addition to using pseudonyms and modifying situations and events, some researchers have engaged in repondent validation of their studies. Whyte (1955) reports how his key informant Doc reviewed the complete manuscript prior to publication. Similarly, Ball (1983) indicates how he discussed draft chapters of his study (Ball, 1981) with groups of teachers. In the course of my research I discussed some of my findings with teachers in the school and I also asked the Head to read a complete draft of the study. This allowed evidence to be checked and further data to be added. However, in two instances when his analysis was different from my own, footnotes have been added to provide an alternative view for the reader.

None of these 'solutions' are foolproof. As Morgan's paper (1972) indicates, locations can be discovered and as I have found, guesses can be made about the real names of locations, institutions and individuals. I have never confirmed or refuted the guesses that have been made by the Headmaster about the real identity of individuals in my study as I am aware that data about teachers' work could be used in assessing their professional practice. However, this will still not prevent politicians and pundits from utilising my evidence to support or attack comprehensive schools.

There is evidently no 'answer' to these problems. Much depends upon the researcher and the researched and the kinds of research bargain which they make. In some cases pseudonyms will be used. In some investigations informants will be invited to comment on drafts of the study while in others they will not. None of these approaches either used together or alone will ever satisfy all of those who participate in or receive field studies. The task is to continue to reflect on the issues involved so that we are sensitive to the problems and to the wishes of our informants.

Conclusion

The focus of this chapter has been upon the ethical problems involved in the research process. Having identified some major problems associated with classic studies, some consideration has been given to the attempts that have been made to come to terms with such problems and to control the actions and activities of researchers. While statements of ethical principles can provide a framework within which individuals can work, they cannot provide 'answers' to problems that vary with the researcher, the researched and the research context. Accordingly, we need to examine ethical problems in field practice if we are to understand the 'solutions' that have been adopted by researchers. However, if the activities of researchers were to be considered in relation to a statement of ethical principles or a code of ethics, they would be found wanting and considered unethical. This highlights the central issue that all field researchers must constantly address, namely the extent to which their activities are unethical. For it is only by constant self-evaluation and reflection on our research experiences that we are most likely to understand moral dilemmas and the compromises that we are required to make in the conduct of field research. At this point we should recall Bronfenbrenner's remark that:

> The only safe way to avoid violating principles of professional ethics is to refrain from doing social research altogether. (Bronfenbrenner, 1952, p. 453)

Suggestions for Further Reading

Methodology
There is a large literature on ethical issues in social research in general and

field research in particular. The following texts provide the main components of the British and American debate and contain detailed bibliographies in order that particular topics can be followed up.

Barnes, J. A. (1979), *Who Should Know What? Social Science, Privacy and Ethics* (Harmondsworth: Penguin); provides a detailed discussion of the main debates on the ethics of social research drawing examples from a range of social science research.
Bok, S. (1978), *Lying: Moral Choice in Public and Private Life* (London: Quartet); is a challenging book that raises a variety of questions which will be invaluable to those engaged in field research.
British Sociological Association (1982), *Statement of Ethical Principles and their Application to Sociological Practice* (London: BSA) (mimeo); contains broad general principles for consideration by sociologists. (Copies available from: British Sociological Association, 10 Portugal Street, London WC2A 2HU.)
Bulmer, M. (1982) (ed.), *Social Research Ethics* (London: Macmillan); is a collection of papers that include classic debates about the merits and demerits of covert participant observation. The papers include discussions of American and British research.
Cassell, J. and Wax, M. L. (1980) (eds), 'Ethical problems of fieldwork', *Social Problems* (special issue), vol. 27, no. 3, pp. 259–378; contains a range of American papers that focus on federal regulations, the research process, and informed consent.
Filstead, W. J. (1970) (ed.), *Qualitative Methodology: First-hand Involvement with the Social World* (New York: Markham). Section six contains a set of papers that summarise the key areas of debate on ethical issues in social research in the 1960s (especially in the USA).

Empirical Studies

The empirical studies that are usually recommended when discussing ethical issues are classic cases of covert research, deception and harm. Yet ethical problems are present in *all* forms of social research. The following studies that involve research in everyday settings should also be examined to consider the ethical problems which have confronted researchers in hospitals (Atkinson), schools (Ball and Burgess), factories (Cavendish and Pollert) and churches (Pryce).

Atkinson, P. (1981), *The Clinical Experience* (Aldershot: Gower).
Ball, S. J. (1981), *Beachside Comprehensive: A Case Study of Secondary Schooling* (Cambridge: CUP).
Burgess, R. G. (1983), *Experiencing Comprehensive Education: A Study of Bishop McGregor School* (London: Methuen).
Cavendish, R. (1982), *Women on the Line* (London: Routledge & Kegan Paul).
Pollert, A. (1981), *Girls, Wives, Factory Lives* (London: Macmillan).
Pryce, K. (1979), *Endless Pressure* (Harmondsworth: Penguin).

10

Evaluating Field Studies

This book has focused on the conduct of field research. In particular, attention has been devoted to discussing the processes and principles of field research together with field methods. In each chapter, examples have been taken from field studies in order to sensitise researchers to the potential problems involved in conducting research and to provide some indication of the ways in which these problems may be handled. For it is essential to be acquainted with what researchers do and how they go about doing it in order to understand the practice of field research. In turn, this not only provides an introduction to field research for those who wish to conduct their own investigations, but also gives social scientists who are the recipients of field studies some indication of the kinds of methodological issues that need to be considered when evaluating a research report.

But what evidence can be used to evaluate research reports? In some cases, researchers have not only published their empirical studies but also a range of theoretical and methodological papers. Among the latter are autobiographical accounts or reflections on the research process in which researchers discuss the natural history of their research projects (cf. Hammond, 1964; Shipman, 1976; Bell and Newby, 1977; Shaffir, Stebbins and Turowetz, 1980; Roberts, 1981; Burgess, 1984a). Such accounts have been likened to confessions in which researchers 'come clean' about their methodology. However, as some sociologists have warned, they are selective reconstructions of the research process that give us some insights on methodology, but they do not tell us how the research was actually conducted (Burgess, 1978; Burgess and Bulmer, 1981).

On many occasions the evidence within the studies themselves is overlooked. Many studies contain introductory chapters with brief sections devoted to 'field work' (cf. Lacey, 1970; Ball, 1981; Burgess, 1983), while others contain appendices that outline particular aspects of the researcher's role (cf. Hargreaves, 1967; Woods, 1979). In turn, there are prefaces which carry details about the conduct of research (cf. Shipman, 1974) as well as comments about the background of the researcher, details of the researcher's aims and objectives, and acknowledgements to funding bodies. Many studies also contain acknowledgements to individuals which give an indication of the researcher's academic social network and provide some clues about the theoretical and methodological perspectives that are deployed within the study. Finally, in the study itself, extracts may be provided from tape-recorded interviews, from field note-books, from diaries and from documentary evidence that allow judgements to be made about the way in which the study has been conducted and the account structured. In this sense, an under-standing of the methodology used in any field study may demand some sociological detective work through a careful reading of the study itself.

In evaluating social research methodology three inter-related areas need to be considered. First, general methodology, that is the general principles that guide the investigation. Secondly, research strategy; that is the principles of research design and the ways in which these principles are utilised within a study. Finally, research methods or techniques of investigation. As each of these elements of research methodology are involved to a greater or lesser degree in any field study, they will need to be examined when evaluating a research report. However, some consideration has to be given to the kinds of questions that need to be addressed in evaluating field studies and it is to these that we now turn.

How Did the Research Begin?

This question relates to the formal and informal aspects of the research process, to the researcher and the researcher's motives for doing research. In some cases, it may appear that sociological problems directly influenced the generation of a research project. While some sociologists become interested in an area of study through reading other people's work, this is only one part of the story, for the biography of the individual researcher has a part to play (cf. Corrigan, 1979; Stacey, 1982; Burgess, 1984c). Indeed, this could be extended further to see the way the institutional and intellectual location of the researcher influences the topic of investigation (cf. Hudson, 1977). Certainly, particular centres and departments have been associated with particular kinds of work. For example, ethnography in education at Edinburgh (cf. Delamont, 1984) and ethnographies of British society at Manchester (cf. Frankenberg, 1982). Lacey's study of *Hightown Grammar* arose partly out of the interests of the Manchester Department of Social Anthropology and Sociology where Max Gluckman was concerned to apply field methods that were used in the study of small-scale societies to the study of institutions in urban–industrial societies (cf. Frankenberg, 1982). Meanwhile, if we turn to Ruth Cavendish's study of women factory workers we find that personal political motives have influenced the generation of the research project. Cavendish indicates that she was looking for a new way of being politically involved and having daily contact with working-class women. Accordingly, she took a job in a factory that resulted in her writing about the lives of women working on an assembly line.

In this sense, looking at the origins of the project may tell us something about the values of the researcher and the way in which this has influenced the direction of the study and the presentation of the findings. For example, if we look at Cohen and Taylor's *Psychological Survival* (1972) a number of elements come together, for the study arose out of an extra-mural class and was designed to challenge the orthodox position that had been established in criminology. The last point is not without significance, as a few years earlier Cohen and Taylor had both been involved in establishing the National Deviancy Conference, a group of young radical academics who were out to challenge the prevailing orthodoxy which was represented by academic criminology and by the Home Office (cf. Cohen, 1980). In this respect, the origins of the study are not merely related to the values of the investigators but also to wider structural influences at a particular point in time.

Some studies are part of a research programme either within a particular institution or within an intellectual social network. In the area of field research, Frankenberg (1982) has charted the influence that Max Gluckman has had upon field-based studies in central Africa and in the United Kingdom in such divergent fields as factory workshops, villages, political groups, prisons and schools. Indeed, if we take the school studies by Lacey (1970) and Hargreaves (1967) we find that they owe much of their inspiration to Gluckman and to Ronald Frankenberg and Valdo Pons who had conducted urban studies and were responsible for the supervision of this work (cf. Hargreaves, 1967, p. viii; Lacey, 1970, p. ix). Indeed, the influence of the Manchester School's approach to social investigation can be seen in these writers' subsequent educational studies (Hargreaves, Hester and Mellor, 1975; Lacey, 1977). Furthermore, a third generation of such studies within the Manchester tradition have been produced by Ball (1981) who was supervised by Colin Lacey, and by Burgess (1983) who was originally supervised by Valdo Pons. Each of these studies reports something of their origins and their indebtedness to individuals and intellectual traditions which have shaped their work and influenced the perspectives that have been adopted.

What Theoretical Perspective Is Employed?

In empirical studies the theoretical perspective will have some influence upon the questions that are posed, the data that are collected and the evidence that is produced. In short, if a functionalist, interactionist, Marxist and feminist were to be involved in studying social relations in the same factory, prison, school or hospital the questions addressed and the focus of interest would be different. The functionalist might concentrate upon the needs of individuals within an institution, while the interactionist would be more concerned with interactions and meanings that are attached to social situations and explain interaction from the actor's point of view. Meanwhile, the Marxist might relate micro studies to macroscopic analysis based upon relations to the production process, while the feminist would be concerned with a critical appraisal of the ways in which sex and gender were used to generate social categories and divisions within the institution. While these perspectives have been simply drawn they do alert us to the need to consider the way in which theoretical perspectives influence questions, concepts and analyses.

If we turn to the study of school classrooms we find that an inter-actionist perspective which informs the work of Peter Woods (1979) results in a set of questions that focus on the *meanings* individuals attach to social situations. In turn, the concepts that are used to address these issues include negotiation, bargain and strategy. In particular, Woods is able to identify eight different survival strategies in his analysis of teacher–pupil interaction in classrooms which are based upon socialisation, domination, negotiation, fraternisation, absence or removal, ritual and routine, occupational therapy and morale boosting. In turn, each of these conceptual categories is illustrated by Woods who makes reference to empirical materials drawn from his study. It is this use of conceptual materials that is at the heart of the analysis. To begin with the concept is developed, after which particular categories of the concept are utilised. Finally, the concepts are linked to a series of examples drawn from the observations made and the interviews that were conducted.

As well as using sociological concepts in field studies, writers also draw on participants' concepts, that is the organising terminology which is used by the participants to distinguish categories for themselves. In Willis's study of working-class boys, for example, the concept of the 'laff' and 'having a laff' is used by the boys in their daily lives and is also used by Willis to organise empirical evidence and to examine the ways in which boys win space from the school and school rules by 'having a laff' (Willis, 1977). In contrast, the sociological concepts that are used in Woods's study fulfil a similar purpose for the researcher, but are different in so far as they would not be used by members of the institution to organise their activities.

Within individual field studies it will be found that both

participants' concepts and sociological concepts will be used to organise the material. For example, in Woods's study both sets of concepts are utilised. Like Willis, he uses the pupils' concept of 'having a laugh' before moving on to use the sociologist's concept of 'subversive laughter' in order to analyse data on classroom humour. The detailed descriptions that are provided in field studies are therefore organised around the concepts and categories, which in some cases sociologists impose on their data, while in other instances concepts and categories are derived from the data itself; a form of presentation that is discussed by Glaser and Strauss (1967) and which has been considered in Chapter 8.

In these terms, the evaluation of theories and the theoretical perspective needs to take several factors into account. First, the particular perspective that is used. Secondly, the relationship between the perspective and the concepts that are used. Thirdly, the relationship between the concepts and the categories used by the sociologist and the implications that this holds for data collection and analysis. However, the main purpose behind such an evaluation is to assess the validity of the argument that is advanced in the research report (cf. Shipman, 1981; Rose, 1982).

What Principles of Selection Are Involved?

Selection is involved in various phases of a field study. First, there is the selection of an area of study and particular units of study. Secondly, there is the selection of events, groups and individuals for study. Such issues involve an assessment of theoretical and technical procedures as various sampling strategies are used within field studies and demand evaluation (see Chapter 3). The main distinction that has been identified is the difference between statistical sampling and theoretical sampling (cf. Burgess, 1982a, pp. 75–8); that is the difference between samples that are selected in advance and those that are used to develop particular categories. Yet in both instances it is essential to consider questions of representativeness and the extent to which it is possible to generalise from the sample that is used.

However, the nature of field research is such that in very few instances will statistical samples be used other than on occasions when sample surveys are conducted before or alongside intensive studies (cf. Pons, 1969; Stacey *et al.*, 1975). In many cases researchers have used what Honigmann (1973) has called a judgement or accidental sample. Certainly, this is the most familiar form of sampling used in studies when the researcher gets to know a small group as in the work of Whyte (1955), Patrick (1973) and Willis (1977). However, in these circumstances we would need to know how the researcher monitored the group and the control that was exercised over the use of the group.

There is, therefore, a need to consider the criteria that were used to select the situations, events, groups and individuals within a study. Furthermore, some consideration needs to be given to the evidence that is obtained from these groups, the use to which it is put and the extent to which it is possible to generalise from the material presented. Such an exercise focuses attention upon the units of study and in turn the methods of investigation that are used.

What Methods of Investigation Are Used?

At first sight this may appear to be a relatively straightforward question to address. However, research processes as well as research techniques need to be examined as the research process may modify the research techniques used. Furthermore, the particular techniques need to be scrutinised as the same technique may be used in different ways in different studies depending on the problem at hand.

Among the processes that need to be considered are those concerning access to and exit from the field (see Chapter 2), together with issues concerning the ethics and politics of doing research (see Chapter 9). For these elements of the research process will influence the data that are collected and the ways in which they are used in the research report. Accordingly, questions need to be addressed about how access was achieved and the extent to which the individuals through whom access was achieved influenced the researcher and the research roles that were taken. In turn, this may lead on to questions about research relations, especially at the points of entry to and exit from the research site. As far as ethical issues are concerned, it would be far too easy to pass critical judgements upon the conduct of any investigator. In these terms, attention should be focused on the particular problems that arose in the investigation and the ways in which these were handled by the researcher.

Having reviewed the research process some assessment can then be made of the way in which the researcher has used particular techniques of social investigation. In the conduct of field research the principal techniques are: participant observation, unstructured interviews and conversations and the use of documentary evidence. However, these techniques cannot be used in a uniform way and therefore some assessment needs to be made about the actual approach that was taken. When a researcher does participant observation we might ask: what kind of observations were made? What field roles were taken? How did the roles vary throughout the research process? Many of these questions can be addressed by referring to the fieldnotes that are provided in the final research report.

As I have indicated in Chapter 8, fieldnotes are the basis upon which research reports are produced. It is therefore essential to inspect the extracts from fieldnotes to see what theoretical, methodological and substantive perspectives were taken by the researcher. If there are very few extracts from fieldnotes and interview transcripts, there is little evidence to assess the report. In these terms, some commentators have called for a second record; a case record to be developed alongside the case study so that the reader may go back to the source material (cf. Stenhouse, 1978, 1979, 1982, 1984).

When unstructured interviews and conversations are used, it is rare to find a complete list of the questions that were posed, as they may vary according to the situation investigated. Yet it is important to establish the circumstances in which interviews took place, the kinds of questions that were posed and the ways in which the data were recorded. In this sense, there is a need to examine the transcripts that are provided from tape-recorded interviews in order to consider the relationship between the questions that were posed, the data obtained and the analysis provided.

Finally, in relation to documentary evidence, similar criteria are again used. The range of materials that are used needs to be considered, along with extracts that are provided from those materials. At this point four particular questions need to be addressed: when were the materials produced? Where were they produced? Who produced the materials and for what purpose? What do the materials contain? In this sense, it is possible to review the context in which documents were written in order to shed some light on their content and use within an investigation.

Having examined each method in detail it is also appropriate to review the ways in which these methods have been used alongside one another, or in combination with each other. In turn, some researchers may have integrated different methods of investigation within one study (see Chapter 7). Once again, validity becomes a key concern in the assessment of the sociological evidence.

Although I have indicated the kinds of issues and questions that need to be considered in examining the methods of investigation that are used in a field study they are not always easy to identify, as there are relatively few standard procedures that are adopted by those engaged in field research. Accordingly, a detailed reading of the research report is essential so that the research process and the research methods can be examined by the reader. In particular, attention also needs to be given to the relationship between data collection and data analysis.

What Form Does Data Analysis Take?

In some respects, the analyses that are presented in the final research report are only partial, as much analysis that has occurred in the field will not have been incorporated into the final report. In field research, analysis includes the way fieldnotes are assembled, questions are posed and categories constructed. It is, therefore, essential to look at extracts from fieldnotes and at the questions that are posed to see the way in which they relate to the findings. In addition, it is important to examine chapters that deal with the early days of field research to see how questions were developed and preliminary analyses were made in the field (cf. Geer, 1964; Pons, 1969, pp. 133–46; Burgess, 1983, especially pp. 123–46).

In turn, consideration has to be given to the theoretical and conceptual approach that has been adopted. Questions need to be addressed about the purpose of the study regarding theory construction, the generation of theory from data or the production of a detailed ethnographic description. In particular some attention needs to be given to the links that are made between theory and data, the theoretical perspective that has been used and the influence this has had upon the data that are selected for inclusion in the research report.

What Is the Impact of the Study?

This question may be considered at different levels. First, in terms of the use of research findings to participants and practitioners in a field of study. Secondly, the contribution that research makes to our cumulative knowledge in a particular field and, finally, the implications that it has for social policy.

At this point, we need to consider not only the content of the study but the way in which it is written. Many social researchers inhabit a world where theories and concepts count and where credibility rests upon the successful use of those concepts. Accordingly, the language of research reports is often inpenetrable for participants and practitioners. In some instances, researchers have attempted to overcome this by producing separate research reports for participants and for sociologists (cf. Oakley, 1979, 1980). Yet such a move may suggest that a distinction is being made between members of the social scientific community and lay persons. However, it is essential for social scientists to communicate with a wide audience if their evidence is to be taken into account. In this respect, the style of writing and the language of research reports needs to be evaluated. For if the language that is used is not as clear and plain as glass, the research results will only reach a limited audience.

In turn, this puts an added responsibility upon the researcher. For if the researcher is to engage with practitioners and policy-makers who may utilise the evidence in the course of their work, some consideration has to be given to questions of accuracy, reliability and validity (cf. Shipman, 1984). Furthermore, a judgement has to be made concerning whether the researcher has adequately protected those who have participated in the study (see Chapter 9). In short, an assessment needs to be made of the risks and benefits that surround the study.

As well as evaluating the use that can be made of the study by practitioners, some consideration needs to be given to the contribution that the research makes to social science. This especially applies to field research, as much of the evidence has failed to provide cumulative accounts (cf. Hargreaves, 1980). Instead, we have simply repeated many research findings in slightly different contexts. Research reports should, therefore, be considered for the contribution they make to advancing our knowledge in a particular field of study and to the way in which they relate to previous knowledge.

What Kinds of Research Questions Remain Unanswered?

Once an assessment has been made of the contribution that a particular study makes to knowledge, some of the gaps that still exist become identifiable. In turn, these gaps may give rise to further questions that will generate further investigations. Some consideration can then be given to the design of further investigations and the ways in which the problems encountered in the study under review might be overcome.

Reviewing a Field Study

So far we have focused on the key questions that could be addressed in conducting a methodological evaluation of a field study. In turn, we now consider the way in which the issues that have been discussed could be used in writing a methodological review of a field study. The main sections that could be covered include:

1   A brief survey of the context of the study: the subfield to which it belongs, its origins, and the way in which it relates to previous work.
2   The methodology: relationships between problems, theories and methods within the investigation.
3   Research processes and research methods: the major elements of data collection, the problems encountered and the ways in which

these problems were handled. The major elements of data analysis.

4   The presentation of evidence: questions of reliability and validity together with an assessment of the way in which the author communicates with an audience/audiences.

5   Areas for further research: the gaps in the study and an assessment of how these gaps might be filled.

Such an assessment brings us back not only to the questions that we have raised about evaluating field studies but also to the characteristics of field research and field research reports.

Characteristics of Field Studies

A review of any set of research reports that are considered to be 'field studies' reveals great diversity in terms of their research aims, objectives, processes, problems and methods. However, they also have much in common. Accordingly, it is important to outline some of the common characteristics of studies based on field research. There is no single attribute that is represented equally in all reports. However, many of the following attributes might be expected to be found to a greater or lesser degree in many field studies:

1   The focus is on the observed present, but the findings are contextualised within a social, cultural and historical framework.

2   The research is conducted within a theoretical framework. While there may only be a small number of questions to orientate a study, further questions may arise during the course of research.

3   The research involves close, detailed, intensive work. The researcher participates in the social situation under study.

4   The major research instrument is the researcher who attempts to obtain a participant's account of the social setting.

5   Unstructured interviews in the form of extended conversations may complement the observational account.

6   Personal documents may give depth and background to the contemporary account.

7   Different methods of investigation may be used to complement field methods with the result that different methodologies may be integrated by the researcher.

8   The decisions regarding the collection and analysis of data take place in the field and are products of the inquiry.

9   The researcher attempts to disturb the process of social life as little as possible.

10 Research reports disseminate the knowledge which informants have provided without rendering harm to them, taking into account ethical problems that confront the researcher and the researched.

A field study with some of these characteristics would provide in-depth knowledge of a social setting, group, or event. However, the reception that we give to such studies needs to be informed by healthy scepticism and critical evaluation in order to advance our understanding of social situations and the future practice of field research.

Suggestions for Further Reading
Methodology
There are relatively few methodology books that deal with the reception and evaluation of evidence. However, three books that merit careful study are:

M. Riley (1963), *Sociological Research: A Case Approach* (New York: Harcourt Brace Jovanovich); contains research reports and a commentary by Riley on the evaluation of the reports.
G. Rose (1982), *Deciphering Sociological Research* (London: Macmillan). Chapters 7 and 8 deal with field research. At times the processes suggested for deciphering reports appear to be mechanical.
M. Shipman (1981), *The Limitations of Social Research* (2nd edn) (London: Longman). A useful book especially for those concerned with educational studies.

Empirical Studies
Consider the way in which you would review any of the field studies that have been recommended in earlier chapters. Examine how these studies have been reviewed by social scientists in professional journals. The journals you might consult are:

From Britain:
  British Journal of Sociology
  Man
  Oral History
  Sociology: the Journal of the British Sociological Association
  Sociological Review

From America:
  American Anthropologist
  American Ethnologist
  American Journal of Sociology
  Human Organization
  Qualitative Sociology
  Symbolic Interaction
  Urban Anthropology
  Urban Life

These journals, together with specialist journals in substantive subfields such as criminology, education, health and illness, industrial relations and social administration, should be regularly consulted for their reviews of new field studies and contributions to field research.

References

Abrams, P. (1981), 'Visionaries and virtuosi: competence and purpose in the education of sociologists', *Sociology*, vol. 15, no. 4, pp. 530–8.

Adelman, C. (1981), 'On first hearing', in C. Adelman (ed.), *Uttering, Muttering: Collecting, Using and Reporting Talk for Social and Educational Research* (London: Grant McIntyre), pp. 78–97.

Agar, M. H. (1973), *Ripping and Running: A Formal Ethnography of Urban Heroin Addicts* (New York: Seminar Press).

Agar, M. H. (1981), *The Professional Stranger: An Informal Introduction to Ethnography* (New York: Academic Press).

Aguilar, J. L. (1981), 'Insider research: an ethnography of a debate', in D. A. Messerschmidt (ed.), *Anthropologists at Home in North America: Methods and Issues in the Study of One's Own Society* (Cambridge: CUP), pp. 15–26.

Allport, G. W. (1942), *The Use of Personal Documents in Psychological Science*, Bulletin No. 49 (New York: Social Science Research Council).

American Anthropological Association (1971), 'Statements on ethics: principles of professional responsibility'; reprinted in T. Weaver (1973) (ed.), *To See Ourselves: Anthropology and Modern Social Issues* (Chicago: Scott, Foresman), pp. 46–8.

Anderson, I. G. and Lee, J. R. E. (1982) 'Taking Professor Gluckman seriously: the case of participant observation', in R. Frankenberg (ed.), *Custom and Conflict in British Society* (Manchester: Manchester University Press), pp. 286–312.

Anderson, N. (1923), *The Hobo: The Sociology of the Homeless Man* (Chicago: University of Chicago Press).

Argyris, C. (1952), 'Diagnosing defences against the outsider', *Journal of Social Issues*, vol. 8, no. 3, pp. 24–34.

Asad, T. (1973) (ed.), *Anthropology and the Colonial Encounter* (London: Ithaca Press).

Askham, J. (1982), 'Telling stories', *Sociological Review*, vol. 30, no. 4, pp. 555–73.

Atkinson, J. M. (1978), *Discovering Suicide: Studies in the Social Organization of Sudden Death* (London: Macmillan).

Atkinson. P. (1981), *The Clinical Experience: The Construction and Reconstruction of Medical Reality* (Aldershot: Gower).

Bailey, K. D. (1978), *Methods of Social Research* (New York: The Free Press).

Baldamus, W. (1972), 'The role of discoveries in social science', in T. Shanin (ed.), *The Rules of the Game* (London: Tavistock), pp. 276–302; reprinted in R. G. Burgess (1982) (ed.) *Field Research: a Sourcebook and Field Manual* (London: Allen & Unwin), pp. 213–24.

Ball, S. J. (1980), 'Initial encounters in the classroom and the process of establishment', in P. Woods (ed.), *Pupil Strategies: Explorations in the Sociology of the School* (London: Croom Helm), pp. 143–61.

Ball, S. J. (1981), *Beachside Comprehensive: A Case Study of Secondary Schooling* (Cambridge: CUP).

Ball, S. J. (1984), 'Beachside reconsidered: reflections on a methodological apprenticeship', in R. G. Burgess (ed.), *The Research Process in Educational Settings: Ten Case Studies* (Lewes: Falmer Press), pp. 69–96.

Banks, O. (1978), 'School and society', in L. Barton and R. Meighan (eds), *Sociological Interpretations of Schooling and Classrooms: A Reappraisal* (Driffield: Nafferton Books), pp. 37–46.

Barbour, R. (1979), 'The ethics of covert research', *Network*, no. 15, p. 9.

Barnes, J. A. (1979), *Who Should Know What? Social Science, Privacy and Ethics* (Harmondsworth: Penguin).

Barnes, J. A. (1981), 'Professionalism in British sociology', in P. Abrams, R. Deem, J. Finch and P. Rock (eds), *Practice and Progress: British Sociology 1950–1980* (London: Allen & Unwin), pp. 13–24.

Barnes, J. A. (1982), 'Ethische en politieke compromissen in sociaal onderzoek', in C. Bouw, F. Bovenkerk, K. Bruin and L. Brunt (eds), *Hoe weet de jat? Wegen van sociaal onderzoek* (Amsterdam: Vitgererij), pp. 27–37 (English version: 'Ethical and political compromises in social research').

Barton, A. H. and Lazarsfeld, P. F. (1955), 'Some functions of qualitative analysis in social research', *Frankfurter Beiträge Zur Soziologie*, pp. 321–61; reprinted in G. J. McCall and J. L. Simmons (1969) (eds), *Issues in Participant Observation: A Text and Reader* (Reading, Mass.: Addison-Wesley), pp. 163–96.

Basham, R. and De Groot, D. (1977), 'Current approaches to the anthropology of urban and complex societies', *American Anthropologist*, vol. 79, no. 2, pp. 414–40.

Beattie, J. (1964), *Other Cultures* (London: Routledge & Kegan Paul).

Becker, H. S. (1958), 'Problems of inference and proof in participant observation', *American Sociological Review*, vol. 23, no. 6, pp. 652–60.

Becker, H. S. (1963), *The Outsiders* (New York: The Free Press).

Becker, H. S. (1964), 'Problems in the publication of field studies', in A. J. Vidich, J. Bensman and M. Stein (eds), *Reflections on Community Studies* (New York: Harper and Row), pp. 267–84.

Becker, H. S. (1970a) (ed.), *Sociological Work* (Chicago: Aldine).

Becker, H. S. (1970b), 'On methodology', in H. S. Becker (ed.), *Sociological Work* (Chicago: Aldine), pp. 3–24.

Becker, H. S. (1970c), 'Practitioners of vice and crime', in R. W. Habenstein (ed.), *Pathways to Data* (Chicago: Aldine), pp. 30–49.

Becker, H. S. (1971), 'Comment', in M. Wax, S. Diamond and F. O. Gearing (eds), *Anthropological Perspectives on Education* (New York: Basic Books), p. 10.

Becker, H. S. and Geer, B. (1957), 'Participant observation and interviewing: a comparison', *Human Organization*, vol. 16, no. 3, pp. 28–32.

Becker, H. S. and Geer, B. (1958), 'Participant observation and interviewing: a rejoinder', *Human Organization*, vol. 17, no. 2, pp. 39–40.

Becker, H. S. and Geer, B. (1960), 'Participant observation: the analysis of qualitative field data', in R. N. Adams and J. J. Preiss (eds), *Human Organization Research* (Homewood, Ill.: Dorsey Press), pp. 267–89;

reprinted in R. G. Burgess (1982) (ed.), *Field Research: a Sourcebook and Field Manual* (London: Allen & Unwin), pp. 239–50.

Becker, H. S. Geer, B. Hughes, E. C. and Strauss, A. L. (1961), *Boys in White: Student Culture in Medical School* (Chicago: University of Chicago Press).

Bell, C. (1968), *Middle Class Families* (London: Routledge & Kegan Paul).

Bell, C. (1977), 'Reflections on the Banbury restudy', in C. Bell and H. Newby (eds), *Doing Sociological Research* (London: Allen & Unwin), pp. 47–62.

Bell, C. and Encel, S. (1978) (eds), *Inside the Whale* (Oxford: Pergamon Press).

Bell, C. and Newby, H. (1972), *Community Studies* (London: Allen & Unwin).

Bell, C. and Newby, H. (1977) (eds), *Doing Sociological Research* (London: Allen & Unwin).

Bennett, J. (1981), *Oral History and Delinquency* (Chicago: University of Chicago Press).

Bennett, N. and McNamara, D. (1979) (eds), *Focus on Teaching* (London: Longman).

Benney, M. and Hughes, E. C. (1956), 'Of sociology and the interview', *American Journal of Sociology*, vol. 62, no. 2, pp. 137–42.

Berger, J. and Mohr, J. (1967), *A Fortunate Man: The Story of a Country Doctor* (London: Allen Lane).

Berger, J. and Mohr, J. (1975), *A Seventh Man: A Book of Images and Words about the Experiences of Migrant Workers in Europe* (Harmondsworth: Penguin).

Berger, P. and Luckmann, T. (1967), *The Social Construction of Reality* (London: Allen Lane).

Bernstein, B., Elvin, L. and Peters, R. S. (1966), 'Ritual in education', *Philosophical Transactions of the Royal Society of London B*, vol. 251, pp. 429–36.

Bertaux, D. (1981) (ed.), *Biography and Society: The Life History Approach in the Social Sciences* (Beverly Hills, Calif.: Sage).

Beynon, H. (1973), *Working for Ford* (Harmondsworth: Penguin).

Birksted, I. K. (1976), 'School performance viewed from the boys', *Sociological Review*, vol. 24, no. 1, pp. 63–77.

Blau, P. M. (1964), 'The research process in the study of *The Dynamics of Bureaucracy*', in P. Hammond (ed.), *Sociologists at Work* (New York: Basic Books), pp. 16–49.

Blaxter, M. (1979) (ed.), 'The analysis of qualitative data: a symposium', Special issue of *Sociological Review*, vol. 27, no. 4, pp. 649–827.

Blumer, H. (1939), *Critiques of Research in the Social Sciences: An Appraisal of Thomas and Znaniecki's The Polish Peasant in Europe and America*, Social Science Research Council Bulletin 44.

Blumer, H. (1966), 'Sociological implications of the thought of George Herbert Mead', *American Journal of Sociology*, vol. 71, no. 5, pp. 535–44.

Blumer, H. (1969), *Symbolic Interactionism: Perspective and Method* (Englewood Cliffs, NJ: Prentice-Hall).

Boehm, A. and Weinberg, R. A. (1977), *The Classroom Observer: A Guide for Developing Observational Skills* (New York: Teachers College Press).

Bogdan, R. (1972), *Participant Observation in Organizational Settings* (Syracuse: Syracuse University Press).

Bogdan, R. (1974), *Being Different: The Autobiography of Jane Fry* (New York: Wiley).

Bogdan, R. and Biklen, S. K. (1982), *Qualitative Research for Education: An Introduction to Theory and Methods* (Boston: Allyn & Bacon).

Bogdan, R. and Taylor, S. J. (1975), *Introduction to Qualitative Research Methods* (New York: Wiley).

Boissevain, J. (1969), *Hal-Farrug: A Village in Malta* (New York: Holt, Rinehart & Winston).

Boissevain, J. (1975), 'Introduction: towards a social anthropology of Europe', in J. Boissevain and J. Friedl (eds), *Beyond the Community: Social Process in Europe* (The Hague: European–Mediterranean Study Group, University of Amsterdam).

Bok, S. (1978), *Lying: Moral Choice in Public and Private Life* (London: Quartet).

Bott, E. (1957), *Family and Social Network* (London: Tavistock).

Bott, E. (1971), *Family and Social Network* (2nd edn) (London: Tavistock).

British Sociological Association (1968a), 'Professional ethics' (London: BSA) (mimeo).

British Sociological Association (1968b), *Statement of Ethical Principles and their Application to Sociological Practice* (London: BSA) (mimeo).

British Sociological Association (1970), 'Statement of ethical principles and their application to sociological practice', *Sociology*, vol. 4, no. 1, pp. 114–17.

British Sociological Association (1973), *Statement of Ethical Principles and their Application to Sociological Practice* (London: BSA) (mimeo).

British Sociological Association (1982), *Statement of Ethical Principles and their Application to Sociological Practice* (London: BSA) (mimeo).

Bronfenbrenner, U. (1952), 'Principles of professional ethics: Cornell studies in social growth', *American Psychologist*, vol. 7, no. 8, pp. 452–5.

Brookover Bourque, L. and Back, K. W. (1966), 'Time sampling as a field technique', *Human Organization*, vol. 25, no. 1, pp. 64–70; reprinted in R. G. Burgess (1982) (ed.), *Field Research: a Sourcebook and Field Manual* (London: Allen & Unwin), pp. 91–7.

Brown, C., Guillet De Monthoux, P. and McCullough, A. (1976), *The Access Casebook* (Stockholm: THS).

Brown, G. W. (1973), 'Some thoughts on grounded theory', *Sociology*, vol. 7, no. 1, pp. 1–16.

Bruyn, S. T. (1966), *The Human Perspective in Sociology: The Methodology of Participant Observation* (Englewood Cliffs, NJ: Prentice-Hall).

Bucher, R., Fritz, C. E. and Quarantelli, E. L. (1956), 'Tape-recorded interviews in social research', *American Sociological Review*, vol. 21, no. 3, pp. 359–64.

Bulmer, M. (1977a) (ed.), *Sociological Research Methods* (London: Macmillan).

Bulmer, M. (1977b), 'Problems, theories and methods in sociology – (how) do they interrelate?', in M. Bulmer (ed.), *Sociological Research Methods* (London: Macmillan), pp. 1–33.

Bulmer, M. (1979), 'Concepts in the analysis of qualitative data', *Sociological Review*, vol. 27, no. 4, pp. 651–77.

Bulmer, M. (1980), 'Comment on "The ethics of covert methods"', *British Journal of Sociology*, vol. 31, no. 1, pp. 59–65.

Bulmer, M. (1982) (ed.), *Social Research Ethics* (London: Macmillan).

Burgess, R. G. (1978), 'Researchers come clean' (review of C. Bell and H. Newby (eds), *Doing Sociological Research*) *The Times Higher Education Supplement*, no. 325, (27 January).

Burgess, R. G. (1979), 'Gaining access: some problems and implications for the participant observer', paper presented at SSRC Workshop on Participant Observation, University of Birmingham (September, 1979).

Burgess, R. G. (1980), 'Some fieldwork problems in teacher-based research', *British Educational Research Journal*, vol. 6, no. 2, pp. 165–73.

Burgess, R. G. (1981a), 'Keeping a research diary', *Cambridge Journal of Education*, vol. 11, no. 1, pp. 75–83.

Burgess, R. G. (1981b), 'Ethical "codes" and field relations', paper prepared for 41st annual meeting of the Society for Applied Anthropology at the University of Edinburgh (April).

Burgess, R. G. (1981c), 'Review of J. Ditton and R. Williams (1981), *The Fundable vs. the Doable: Sweet Gripes, Sour Grapes and the SSRC* (Glasgow: University of Glasgow, Background Papers, 1)', *Network*, no. 21, pp. 16–17.

Burgess, R. G. (1982a) (ed.), *Field Research: a Sourcebook and Field Manual* (London: Allen & Unwin).

Burgess, R. G . (1982b), 'The practice of sociological research: some issues in school ethnography', in R. G. Burgess (ed.), *Exploring Society* (London: British Sociological Association), pp. 115–35.

Burgess, R. G. (1983), *Experiencing Comprehensive Education: A Study of Bishop McGregor School* (London: Methuen).

Burgess, R. G. (1984a) (ed.), *The Research Process in Educational Settings: Ten Case Studies* (Lewes: Falmer Press).

Burgess, R. G. (1984b), 'Autobiographical accounts and research experience', in R. G. Burgess (ed.), *The Research Process in Educational Settings: Ten Case Studies* (Lewes: Falmer Press), pp. 251–70.

Burgess, R. G. (1984c), 'The whole truth? Some ethical problems in the study of a comprehensive school', in R. G. Burgess (ed.), *Field Methods in the Study of Education* (Lewes: Falmer Press).

Burgess, R. G. and Bulmer, M. (1981), 'Research methodology teaching: trends and developments', *Sociology*, vol. 15, no. 4, pp. 477–89.

Campbell, D. T. and Fiske, D. W. (1959), 'Convergent and discriminant validation by the multitrait–multimethod matrix', *Psychological Bulletin*, vol. 56, no. 2, pp. 81–105.

Cane, B. and Schroeder, C. (1970), *The Teacher and Research* (Slough: National Foundation for Educational Research).

Casagrande, J. (1960) (ed.), *In the Company of Man* (New York: Harper & Row).

Cassell, J. (1977a), 'The relationship of observer to observed in peer group research', *Human Organization*, vol. 36, no. 4, pp. 412–16.

Cassell, J. (1977b), *A Group Called Women: Sisterhood and Symbolism in the American Feminist Movement* (New York: David McKay).

Cassell, J. (1978), 'Risk and benefit to subjects of fieldwork', *American Sociologist*, vol. 13, no. 3, pp. 134–43.

Cassell, J. (1980), 'Ethical principles for conducting fieldwork', *American Anthropologist*, vol. 82, no. 1, pp. 28–41.

Cassell, J. and Wax, M. L. (1980) (eds), 'Ethical problems of fieldwork', *Social Problems*, vol. 27, no. 3, pp. 259–378.

Catholic Directory of England and Wales (1976) (London: The Universe–Associated Catholic Publications).

Caudill, W., Redlich, F., Gilmore, H. and Brody, E. (1952), 'Social structure and interaction processes on a psychiatric ward', *American Journal of Orthopsychiatry*, vol. 22, (April), pp. 314–34.

Cavan, S. (1966), *Liquor License* (Chicago: Aldine).

Cavendish, R. (1982), *Women on the Line* (London: Routledge & Kegan Paul).

Cicourel, A. V. (1973), *Cognitive Sociology* (Harmondsworth: Penguin).

Cicourel, A. V., Jennings, K. H., Jennings, S. H. M., Leiter, K. C. W., MacKay, R., Mehan, H. and Roth, D. H. (1974), *Language Use and School Performance* (New York: Academic Press).

Cleary, J. (1979), 'Demands and responses: the effects of the style of work allocation on the distribution of nursing attention', in D. Hall and M. Stacey (eds), *Beyond Separation: Further Studies of Children in Hospital* (London: Routledge & Kegan Paul), pp. 109–27.

Coffield, F., Robinson, P. and Sarsby, J. (1980), *A Cycle of Deprivation? A Case Study of Four Families* (London: Heinemann).

Cohen, A. (1982), 'Drama and politics in the development of a London carnival', in R. Frankenberg (ed.), *Custom and Conflict in British Society* (Manchester: Manchester University Press), pp. 313–43.

Cohen, A. P. (1982) (ed.), *Belonging: Identity and Social Organisation in British Rural Cultures* (Manchester: Manchester University Press).

Cohen, S. (1972), *Folk Devils and Moral Panics: the Creation of the Mods and Rockers* (London: MacGibbon & Kee).

Cohen, S. (1980), *Folk Devils and Moral Panics: The Creation of the Mods and Rockers* (2nd edn) (Oxford: Martin Robertson).

Cohen, S. and Taylor, L. (1972), *Psychological Survival* (Harmondsworth: Penguin).

Coleman, J. S. (1958), 'Relational analysis: the study of social organizations with survey methods', *Human Organization*, vol. 16, no. 4, pp. 28–36.

Collier, K. G. (1978), 'School focused INSET: questions posed by a three month consultancy', *British Journal of In-Service Education*, vol. 5, no. 1, pp. 43–9.

Conklin, H. C. (1968), 'Ethnography', in D. L. Sills (ed.), *International Encyclopaedia of the Social Sciences*, Vol. 5 (New York: Macmillan and The Free Press), pp. 172–8.

Corbin, M. (1971), 'Problems and procedures of interviewing', in J. M. and R. E. Pahl, *Managers and Their Wives* (London: Allen Lane), pp. 286–306.

Corrigan, P. (1979), *Schooling the Smash Street Kids* (London: Macmillan).

Coser, R. L. (1978), 'Comments on ethics symposium', *American Sociologist*, vol. 13, no. 3, pp. 156–7.

Crossman, R. (1975), *The Diaries of a Cabinet Minister: Volume One Minister of Housing 1964–66* (London: Hamish Hamilton and Jonathan Cape).

Cunnison, S. (1966), *Wages and Work Allocation* (London: Tavistock).

Cunnison, S. (1982), 'The Manchester factory studies, the social context, bureaucratic organisation, sexual divisions and their influence on patterns of accommodation between workers and management', in R. Frankenberg (ed.), *Custom and Conflict in British Society* (Manchester: Manchester University Press), pp. 94–139.

Dalton, M. (1959), *Men Who Manage* (New York: Wiley).

Dalton, M. (1964), 'Preconceptions and methods in *Men Who Manage*', in P. Hammond (ed.), *Sociologists at Work* (New York: Basic Books), pp. 50–95.

Davies, L. (1984), 'Ethnography and status: focusing on gender in educational research', in R. G. Burgess (ed.), *Field Methods in the Study of Education* (Lewes: Falmer Press).

Davis, A., Gardner, B. B. and Gardner, M. R. (1941), *Deep South* (Chicago: University of Chicago Press).

Dawe, A. (1973), 'The role of experience in the construction of social theory: an essay in reflexive sociology', *Sociological Review*, vol. 21, no. 1, pp. 25–55.

Delamont, S. (1976), *Interaction in the Classroom* (London: Methuen).

Delamont, S. (1980), *Sex Roles and the School* (London: Methuen).

Delamont, S. (1981), 'All too familiar? A decade of classroom research', *Educational Analysis*, vol. 3, no. 1, pp. 69–83.

Delamont, S. (1984), 'The old girl network: recollections on the fieldwork at St. Luke's', in R. G. Burgess (ed.), *The Research Process in Educational Settings: Ten Case Studies* (Lewes: Falmer Press), pp. 15–38.

Delamont, S., and Hamilton, D. (1976), 'Classroom research: a critique and a new approach', in M. Stubbs and D. Hamilton (eds), *Explorations in Classroom Observation* (London: Wiley), pp. 3–20.

Delph, E. W. (1978), *The Silent Community: Public Homosexual Encounters* (Beverly Hills, Calif.: Sage).

Denzin, N. (1968), 'On the ethics of disguised observation', *Social Problems*, vol. 15, no. 4, pp. 502–4.

Denzin, N. (1970a), *The Research Act* (Chicago: Aldine).

Denzin, N. (1970b) (ed.), *Sociological Methods: a Sourcebook* (London: Butterworths).

Denzin, N. (1978) (ed.), *Sociological Methods: a Sourcebook* (2nd edn), (London: McGraw Hill).

Department of Education and Science (1971), *Raising the School Leaving Age to 16*, Circular 8/71 (London: HMSO).

Devons, E. and Gluckman, M. (1964), 'Modes and consequences of limiting a field of study', in M. Gluckman (ed.), *Closed Systems and Open Minds: The Limits of Naïvety in Social Anthropology* (Edinburgh: Oliver & Boyd), pp. 158–261.

Diamond, S. (1964), 'Nigerian discovery: the politics of field work', in A. J. Vidich, J. Bensman and M. R. Stein (eds), *Reflections on Community Studies* (New York: Harper & Row), pp. 119–54.

Dingwall, R. (1977), *The Social Organisation of Health Visitor Training* (London: Croom Helm).

Dingwall, R. (1979), 'Correspondence on ethics', *Network*, no. 14, p. 7.

Dingwall, R. (1980), 'Ethics and ethnography', *Sociological Review*, vol. 28, no. 4, pp. 871–91.

Ditton, J. (1977), *Part-Time Crime: an Ethnography of Fiddling and Pilferage* (London: Macmillan).

Ditton, J. and Williams, R. (1981), *The Fundable vs. the Doable: Sweet Gripes, Sour Grapes and the SSRC* (Glasgow: University of Glasgow, Background Papers, 1).

Douglas, J. (1976), *Investigative Social Research* (Beverly Hills, Calif.: Sage).

Douglas, J. D., Rasmussen, P. K. and Flanagan, C. A. (1977), *The Nude Beach* (Beverly Hills, Calif.: Sage).

Drass, K. A. (1980), 'The analysis of qualitative data: a computer program', *Urban Life*, vol. 9, no. 3, pp. 332–53.

Dua, V. (1979), 'A woman's encounter with Arya Samaj and untouchables: a slum in Jullindur', in M. N. Srinivas, A. M. Shah and E. A. Ramaswamy (eds), *The Fieldworker and the Field: Problems and Challenges in Sociological Investigation* (Delhi: OUP), pp. 115–26.

Dymond, D. (1981), *Writing Local History* (London: Bedford Square Press).

Easterday, L., Papademas, D., Schorr, L. and Valentine, C. (1977), 'The making of a female researcher: role problems in field work', *Urban Life*, vol. 6, no. 3, pp. 333–48; reprinted in R. G. Burgess (1982) (ed.), *Field Research: a Sourcebook and Field Manual* (London: Allen & Unwin), pp. 62–7.

Eggleston, J. (1980), 'The perspectives of the educational research project', *British Educational Research Journal*, vol. 6, no. 1, pp. 85–9.

Elliott, J. and Adelman, C. (1976), *Innovation at the Classroom Level: A Case Study of the Ford Teaching Project*, Unit 28 of the Curriculum Design and Development Course (Milton Keynes: Open University Press).

Elliott, J. and Partington, D. (1975), *Three Points of View in the Classroom: Generating Hypotheses from Classroom Observations, Recordings and Interviews* (Norwich: Centre for Applied Research in Education).

Emmett, I. and Morgan, D. H. J. (1982), 'Max Gluckman and the Manchester shop-floor ethnographies', in R. Frankenberg (ed.), *Custom and Conflict in British Society* (Manchester: Manchester University Press), pp. 140–65.

Epstein, A. L. (1967) (ed.), *The Craft of Social Anthropology* (London: Tavistock).

Erikson, K. T. (1967), 'A comment on disguised observation in sociology', *Social Problems*, vol. 14, no. 4, pp. 366–73.

Erikson, K. T. (1968), 'On the ethics of disguised observation: a reply to Denzin', *Social Problems*, vol. 15, no. 4, pp. 505–6.

Evans-Pritchard, E. E. (1940), *The Nuer: A Description of the Modes of Livelihood and Political Institutions of a Nilotic People* (Oxford: OUP).

Fairhurst, E. (1981), 'A Sociological Study of the Rehabilitation of Elderly Patients in an Urban Hospital', unpublished Ph.D thesis, (Leeds: University of Leeds).

Festinger, L., Riecken, H. W. and Schachter, S. (1956), *When Prophecy Fails* (New York: Harper & Row).

Fichter, J. H. and Kolb, W. L. (1953), 'Ethical limitations on sociological reporting', *American Sociological Review*, vol. 18, no. 5, pp. 544–50.

Fielding, N. (1981), *The National Front* (London: Routledge & Kegan Paul).

Filstead, W. J. (1970) (ed.), *Qualitative Methodology: Firsthand Involvement with the Social World* (Chicago: Markham).

Finch, J. (1983), *Married to the Job: Wives' Incorporation in Men's Work* (London: Allen & Unwin).

Finch, J. (1984), ' "It's great to have someone to talk to": the ethics and politics of interviewing women', in C. Bell and H. Roberts (eds), *Social Researching: Policies, Problems and Practice* (London: Routledge & Kegan Paul), pp. 70–87.

Fine, G. A. and Glassner, B. (1979), 'Participant observation with children: promise and problems', *Urban Life*, vol. 8, no. 2, pp. 153–74.

Firth, R. (1981), 'Engagement and detachment: reflections on applying social anthropology to social affairs', *Human Organization*, vol. 40, no. 3, pp. 193–201.

Flanders, N. (1970), *Analyzing Teacher Behavior* (Reading, Mass.: Addison-Wesley).

Fletcher, C. (1974), *Beneath the Surface* (London: Routledge & Kegan Paul).

Ford, J. (1975), *Paradigms and Fairy Tales* (London: Routledge & Kegan Paul).

Frankenberg, R. (1957), *Village on the Border* (London: Cohen & West).

Frankenberg, R. (1963), 'Participant observers', *New Society*, vol. 1, no. 23, pp. 22–3; reprinted in R. G. Burgess (1982) (ed.), *Field Research: a Sourcebook and Field Manual* (London: Allen & Unwin), pp. 50–2.

Frankenberg, R. (1976), 'In the production of their lives, men (?) . . . sex and gender in British community studies', in D. L. Barker and S. Allen (eds), *Sexual Divisions and Society: Process and Change* (London: Tavistock), pp. 25–51.

Frankenberg, R. (1982) (ed.), *Custom and Conflict in British Society* (Manchester: Manchester University Press).

Fried, M. H. (1968) (ed.), *Readings in Anthropology: Cultural Anthropology* (2nd edn) (New York: Thomas Y. Crowell).

Fujisaka, S. and Grayzel, J. (1978), 'Partnership research: a case of divergent ethnographic styles in prison research', *Human Organization*, vol. 37, no. 2, pp. 172–9.

Galliher, J. F. (1980), 'Social scientists' ethical responsibilities to super-ordinates: looking upward meekly', *Social Problems*, vol. 27, no. 3, pp. 298–308.

Galton, M. and Delamont, S. (1984), 'Speaking with forked tongue? Two styles of observation in the Oracle project', in R. G. Burgess (ed.), *Field Methods in the Study of Education* (Lewes: Falmer Press).

Galton, M. and Simon, B. (1980) (eds), *Progress and Performance in the Primary Classroom* (London: Routledge & Kegan Paul).

Galton, M., Simon, B. and Croll, P. (1980), *Inside the Primary Classroom* (London: Routledge & Kegan Paul).

Galton, M. and Willcocks, J. (1983), *Moving from the Primary Classroom* (London: Routledge & Kegan Paul).

Gans, H. J. (1962), *The Urban Villagers* (New York: The Free Press).

Gans, H. J. (1967), *The Levittowners* (London: Allen Lane).

Gans, H. J. (1968), 'The participant-observer as a human being: observations on the personal aspects of field work', in H. S. Becker, B. Geer, D. Riesman and R. S. Weiss (eds), *Institutions and the Person: Papers Presented to Everett C. Hughes* (Chicago: Aldine), pp. 300–17; reprinted in R. G. Burgess (1982) (ed.), *Field Research: a Sourcebook and Field Manual* (London: Allen & Unwin), pp. 53–61.

Geddes, D. (1954) (ed.), *An Analysis of the Kinsey Reports on Sexual Behaviour* (London: Frederick Muller).

Geer, B. (1964), 'First days in the field', in P. Hammond (ed.), *Sociologists at Work* (New York: Basic Books), pp. 322–44.

Geer, B. (1970), 'Studying a college', in R. Habenstein (ed.), *Pathways to Data* (Chicago: Aldine), pp. 81–98.

Gibbons, D. C. (1975), 'Unidentified research sites and fictitious names', *American Sociologist*, vol. 10, no. 1, pp. 32–6.

Gittins, D. (1982), *Fair Sex: Family Size and Structure, 1900–1939* (London: Hutchinson).

Gittus, E. (1972), *Key Variables in Social Research* (London: Heinemann for the British Sociological Association).

Glaser, B. G. (1965), 'The constant comparative method of qualitative analysis', *Social Problems*, vol. 12, no. 4, pp. 436–45.

Glaser, B. G. (1978), *Theoretical Sensitivity* (Mill Valley, Calif.: The Sociology Press).

Glaser, B. G. and Strauss, A. L. (1967), *The Discovery of Grounded Theory: Strategies for Qualitative Research* (Chicago: Aldine).

Gluckman, M. (1961), 'Ethnographic data in British social anthropology', *Sociological Review*, vol. 9, no. 1, pp. 5–17.

Gluckman, M. (1964) (ed.), *Closed Systems and Open Minds: The Limits of Naïvety in Social Anthropology* (Edinburgh: Oliver & Boyd).

Gluckman, M. (1967), 'Introduction', in A. L. Epstein (ed.), *The Craft of Social Anthropology* (London: Tavistock), pp. xi–xx.

Gold, R. (1958), 'Roles in sociological field observation', *Social Forces*, vol. 36, no. 3, pp. 217–23.

Golde, P. (1970) (ed.), *Women in the Field: Anthropological Experiences* (Chicago: Aldine).

Goode, W. J. and Hatt, P. K. (1952), *Methods in Social Research* (New York: McGraw-Hill).

Goodson, I. F. (1982), *School Subjects and Curriculum Change* (London: Croom Helm).

Gorden, R. L. (1980), *Interviewing: Strategy, Techniques and Tactics* (3rd edn) (Homewood, Ill.: Dorsey Press).

Gottschalk, L. (1945), 'The historian and the historical document', in L. Gottschalk, C. Kluckhohn and R. Angell (eds), *The Use of Personal Documents in History, Anthropology and Sociology*, Bulletin 53 (New York: Social Science Research Council), pp. 3–75.

Gottschalk, L., Kluckhohn, C. and Angell, R. (1945) (eds), *The Use of Personal Documents in History, Anthropology and Sociology*, Bulletin 53 (New York: Social Science Research Council).

Graef, R. (1980), 'The case study as Pandora's box', in H. Simons (ed.), *Towards a Science of the Singular* (Norwich: Centre for Applied Research in Education, Occasional Publication No. 10), pp. 162–78.

Gravel, P. B. (1976), ' "And sometimes all for nought" or reflections of an anthropologist upon his return from the field', *Western Canadian Journal of Anthropology*, vol. 6, no. 4, pp. 103–123.

Gray, B. H. (1978), 'Comments on ethics symposium', *American Sociologist*, vol. 13, no. 3, pp. 160–4.

Gupta, K. A. (1979), 'Travails of a woman fieldworker: a small town in Uttar

Pradesh', in M. N. Srinivas, A. M. Shah and E. A. Ramaswamy (eds), *The Fieldworker and the Field: Problems and Challenges in Sociological Investigation* (Delhi: OUP), pp. 103–14.

Habenstein, R. W. (1970) (ed.), *Pathways to Data* (Chicago: Aldine).

Halfpenny, P. (1979), 'The analysis of qualitative data', *Sociological Review*, vol. 27, no. 4, pp. 799–825.

Hall, D. and Stacey, M. (1979) (eds), *Beyond Separation: Further Studies of Children in Hospital* (London: Routledge & Kegan Paul).

Hammersley, M. (1980), 'Classroom ethnography', *Educational Analysis*, vol. 2, no. 2, pp. 47–74.

Hammersley, M. (1981), 'Ideology in the staffroom? A critique of false consciousness', in L. Barton and S. Walker (eds), *Schools, Teachers and Teaching* (Lewes: Falmer Press), pp. 331–42.

Hammersley, M. (1982), 'The sociology of classrooms', in A. Hartnett (ed.), *The Social Sciences in Educational Studies: A Selective Guide to the Literature* (London: Heinemann), pp. 227–42.

Hammersley, M. (1984), 'The researcher exposed: a natural history', in R. G. Burgess (ed.), *The Research Process in Educational Settings: Ten Case Studies* (Lewes: Falmer Press), pp. 39–67.

Hammond, P. (1964) (ed.), *Sociologists at Work* (New York: Basic Books).

Hannan, A. (1975), 'The problem of the "unmotivated" in an open school: a participant observation study', in G. Chanan and S. Delamont (eds), *Frontiers of Classroom Research* (Slough: National Foundation for Educational Research), pp. 146–62.

Hannerz, U. (1980), *Exploring the City: Inquiries Toward an Urban Anthropology* (New York: Columbia University Press).

Hargreaves, A. (1979), 'Synthesis and the study of strategies: a project for the sociological imagination', in P. Woods (ed.), *Pupil Strategies: Explorations in the Sociology of the School* (London: Croom Helm), pp. 162–97.

Hargreaves, D. H. (1967), *Social Relations in a Secondary School* (London: Routledge & Kegan Paul).

Hargreaves, D. H. (1972), *Interpersonal Relations in Education* (London: Routledge & Kegan Paul).

Hargreaves, D. H. (1980), 'Classrooms, schools and juvenile delinquency', *Educational Analysis*, vol. 2, no. 2, pp. 75–87.

Hargreaves, D. H., Hester, S. K. and Mellor, F. J. (1975), *Deviance in Classrooms* (London: Routledge & Kegan Paul).

Hayano, D. M. (1979), 'Auto-ethnography: paradigms, problems and prospects', *Human Organization*, vol. 38, no. 1, pp. 99–104.

Hilton, K. (1967) (ed.), *The Lower Swansea Valley Project* (London: Longman).

Hite, S. (1977), *The Hite Report: A Nationwide Study of Female Sexuality* (New York: Summit Books).

Hoffman, J. E. (1980), 'Problems of access in the study of social elites and boards of directors', in W. B. Shaffir, R. A. Stebbins and A. Turowetz (eds), *Fieldwork Experience: Qualitative Approaches to Social Research* (New York: St Martin's Press), pp. 45–56.

Holdaway, S. (1982), ' "An inside job": a case study of covert research on the police', in M. Bulmer (ed.), *Social Research Ethics* (London: Macmillan), pp. 59–79.

Homan, R. (1978), 'Interpersonal communication in Pentecostal meetings', *Sociological Review*, vol. 26, no. 3, pp. 499–518.

Homan, R. (1980), 'The ethics of covert methods', *British Journal of Sociology*, vol. 31, no. 1, pp. 46–59.

Homan, R. and Bulmer, M. (1982), 'On the merits of covert methods: a dialogue', in M. Bulmer (ed.), *Social Research Ethics* (London: Macmillan), pp. 105–21.

Honigmann, J. J. (1973), 'Sampling in ethnographic fieldwork', in R. Naroll and R. Cohen (eds), *A Handbook of Method in Cultural Anthropology* (Columbia: Columbia University Press), pp. 266–81; reprinted in R. G. Burgess (1982) (ed.), *Field Research: a Sourcebook and Field Manual* (London: Allen & Unwin), pp. 79–90.

Horowitz, I. L. (1967) (ed.), *The Rise and Fall of Project Camelot* (Cambridge, Mass.: MIT Press).

Horland, C. I. (1959), 'Reconciling conflicting results derived from experimental and survey studies of attitude change', *American Psychologist*, vol. 14, no. 1, pp. 8–17.

Hudson, L. (1977), 'Picking winners: a case study of the recruitment of research students', *New Universities Quarterly*, vol. 32, no. 1, pp. 88–106.

Hughes, E. C. (1971), *The Sociological Eye* (Chicago: Aldine).

Humphreys, L. (1970), *Tearoom Trade* (London: Duckworth).

Humphries, S. (1981), *Hooligans or Rebels? An Oral History of Working Class Childhood and Youth 1889–1939* (Oxford: Blackwell).

Ives, E. D. (1980), *The Tape-Recorded Interview* (2nd edn) (Knoxville: University of Tennessee Press).

Janes, R. W. (1961), 'A note on the phases of the community role of the participant observer', *American Sociological Review*, vol. 26, no. 3, pp. 446–50.

Jarvie, I. C. (1969), 'The problem of ethical integrity in participant observation', *Current Anthropology*, vol. 10, no. 5, pp. 505–8; reprinted in R. G. Burgess (1982) (ed.), *Field Research: a Sourcebook and Field Manual* (London: Allen & Unwin), pp. 68–72.

Johnson, J. M. (1975), *Doing Field Research* (New York: The Free Press).

Junker, B. H. (1960), *Field Work: An Introduction to the Social Sciences* (Chicago: University of Chicago Press).

Kaplan, D. and Manners, R. A. (1971), 'Anthropology: some old themes and new directions', *Southwestern Journal of Anthropology*, vol. 27, pp. 19–40.

King, R. (1978), *All Things Bright and Beautiful? A Sociological Study of Infants' Classrooms* (Chichester: Wiley).

Kinsey, A. C., Pomeroy, W. B. and Martin, C. E. (1948), *Sexual Behavior in the Human Male* (Philadelphia and London: W. B. Saunders).

Kinsey, A. C., Pomeroy, W. B., Martin, C. E. and Gebhard, P. H. (1953), *Sexual Behavior in the Human Female* (Philadelphia and London: W. B. Saunders).

Kleinman, S. (1980), 'Learning the ropes as fieldwork analysis', in W. B. Shaffir, R. A. Stebbins and A. Turowetz (eds), *Fieldwork Experience: Qualitative Approaches to Social Research* (New York: St Martin's Press), pp. 171–83.

Klockars, C. B. (1975), *The Professional Fence* (London: Tavistock).

Klockars, C. B. (1977), 'Field ethics for the life history', in R. S. Weppner (ed.), *Street Ethnography* (Beverly Hills, Calif.: Sage), pp. 201–26.

Kluckhohn, C. (1945), 'The personal document in anthropological science' in L. Gottschalk, C. Kluckhohn and R. Angell (eds), *The Use of Personal Documents in History, Anthropology and Sociology*, Bulletin 53 (New York: Social Science Research Council), pp. 79–173.

Kuper, A. (1973), *Anthropology and Anthropologists: The British School 1922–1972* (London: Allen Lane).

Lacey, C. (1966), 'Some sociological concomitants of academic streaming in a grammar school', *British Journal of Sociology*, vol. 17, no. 3, pp. 245–62.

Lacey, C. (1970), *Hightown Grammar: The School as a Social System* (Manchester: Manchester University Press).

Lacey, C. (1974), 'Destreaming in a "pressured" academic environment', in J. Eggleston (ed.), *Contemporary Research in the Sociology of Education* (London: Methuen), pp. 148–66.

Lacey, C. (1976), 'Problems of sociological fieldwork: a review of the methodology of "Hightown Grammar"', in M. Shipman (ed.), *The Organization and Impact of Social Research* (London: Routledge & Kegan Paul), pp. 63–88.

Lacey, C. (1977), *The Socialization of Teachers* (London: Methuen).

Lacey, C. (1981), 'Foreword', in S. J. Ball, *Beachside Comprehensive: A Case-Study of Secondary Schooling* (Cambridge: CUP), pp. xi–xiv.

Lacey, C. (1982), 'Freedom and constraints in British education', in R. Frankenberg (ed.), *Custom and Conflict in British Society* (Manchester: Manchester University Press), pp. 166–87.

Lambart, A. M. (1970), 'The sociology of an unstreamed urban grammar school for girls', unpublished MA thesis (Manchester: University of Manchester).

Lambart, A. M. (1976), 'The sisterhood', in M. Hammersley and P. Woods (eds), *The Process of Schooling* (London: Routledge & Kegan Paul in association with the Open University), pp. 152–7.

Lambart, A. M. (1982), 'Expulsion in context: a school as a system in action', in R. Frankenberg (ed.), *Custom and Conflict in British Society* (Manchester: Manchester University Press), pp. 188–208.

Langlois, C. V. and Seignobos, C. (1898), transl. by C. G. Berry, *Introduction to the Study of History* (London: Duckworth).

Leach, E. (1963), Review of M. N. Srinivas, *Caste in Modern India and Other Essays* (Bombay: Asia Publishing House, 1962), *British Journal of Sociology*, vol. 14, no. 4, pp. 377–8.

Leach, E. (1966), 'Introduction', in B. Malinowski, *Coral Gardens and their Magic Volume 1* (2nd edn), (London: Allen & Unwin), pp. vii–xvii.

Liebow, E. (1967), *Tally's Corner: A Study of Negro Street Corner Men* (Boston, Mass.: Little, Brown).

Lindesmith, A. (1947), *Opiate Addiction* (Bloomington, Ind.: Principia Press).

Littlejohn, J. (1963), *Westrigg* (London: Routledge & Kegan Paul).

Lofland, J. (1971), *Analyzing Social Settings* (New York: Wadsworth).

Lofland, J. F. and Lejeune, R. A. (1960), 'Initial interaction of newcomers in Alcoholics Anonymous: a field experiment in class symbols and socialization', *Social Problems*, vol. 8, no. 2, pp. 102–11.

Lupton, T. (1963), *On the Shop Floor* (Oxford: Pergamon).

Lynd, R. S. and Lynd, H. M. (1929), *Middletown: A Study in Contemporary American Culture* (New York: Harcourt, Brace Jovanovich).

Lynd, R. S. and Lynd, H. M. (1937), *Middletown in Transition* (New York: Harcourt Brace Jovanovich).

Maas, S. and Kuypers, J. A. (1974), *From Thirty to Seventy: a Forty Year Longitudinal Study of Adult Life Styles and Personality* (London: Jossey-Bass).

Macintyre, S. (1977), *Single and Pregnant* (London: Croom Helm).

Macintyre, S. (1979), 'Some issues in the study of pregnancy careers', *Sociological Review*, vol. 27, no. 4, pp. 755–71.

Malinowski, B. (1922), *Argonauts of the Western Pacific* (London: Routledge & Kegan Paul).

Malinowski, B. (1926), *Crime and Custom in Savage Society* (London: Routledge & Kegan Paul).

Malinowski, B. (1929), *The Sexual Life of Savages* (London: Routledge & Kegan Paul).

Malinowski, B. (1935a), *Coral Gardens and their Magic Volume 1* (London: Allen & Unwin).

Malinowski, B. (1935b), *Coral Gardens and their Magic Volume 2* (London: Allen & Unwin).

Malinowski, B. (1948), *Magic, Science and Religion* (New York: The Free Press).

Malinowski, B. (1967), *A Diary in the Strict Sense of the Term* (London: Routledge & Kegan Paul).

Mandelbaum, D. G. (1973), 'The study of life history: Gandhi', *Current Anthropology*, vol. 14, no. 3, pp. 177–96; reprinted in R. G. Burgess (1982) (ed.), *Field Research: a Sourcebook and Field Manual* (London: Allen & Unwin), pp. 146–51.

Manis, J. G. and Meltzer, B. N. (1967) (eds), *Symbolic Interactionism: A Reader in Social Psychology* (Boston: Allyn & Bacon).

Market Research Society (1976), *Code of Conduct* (London: Market Research Society).

Mars, G. (1982), *Cheats at Work* (London: Allen & Unwin).

Marsden, D. and Duff, E. (1975), *Workless: Some Unemployed Men and their Families* (Harmondsworth: Penguin).

Mayer, P. and I. (1971), *Townsmen or Tribesmen* (2nd edn) (Oxford: OUP).

Mayhew, H. (1851), *London Labour and the London Poor* (London: Griffin Bohn).

McCall, G.J. and Simmons, J. L. (1969) (eds), *Issues in Participant Observation: A Text and Reader* (Reading, Mass.: Addison-Wesley).

McNally, F. (1979), *Women for Hire: A Study of the Female Office Worker* (London: Macmillan).

Mead, M. (1953), 'National character', in A. L. Kroeber (ed.), *Anthropology To-day* (Chicago: University of Chicago Press), pp. 642–67.

Mead, M. (1970), 'Field work in the Pacific Islands', in P. Golde (ed.), *Women in the Field: Anthropological Experiences* (Chicago: Aldine), pp. 293–331.

Mead, M. (1977), *Letters from the Field, 1925–1975* (New York: Harper & Row).

Merton, R. (1972), 'Insiders and outsiders: a chapter in the sociology of knowledge', *American Journal of Sociology*, vol. 78, no. 1, pp. 9–47.

Messerschmidt, D. A. (1981) (ed.), *Anthropologists at Home in North America: Methods and Issues in the Study of One's Own Society* (Cambridge: CUP).

Middleton, H. (1978), 'A marxist at Wattie Creek: fieldwork among Australian Aborigines', in C. Bell and S. Encel (eds), *Inside the Whale* (Oxford: Pergamon), pp. 238–69.

Mills, C. W. (1959), *The Sociological Imagination* (New York: OUP).

Ministry of Health (1959), *The Welfare of Children in Hospital* (Platt Report) (London: HMSO).

Minocha, A. A. (1979), 'Varied roles in the field: a hospital in Delhi', in M. N. Srinivas, A. M. Shah and E. A. Ramaswamy (eds), *The Fieldworker and the Field: Problems and Challenges in Sociological Investigation* (Delhi: OUP), pp. 201–15.

Mitchell, J. C. (1956), *The Kalela Dance*, Rhodes-Livingstone Paper No. 27.

Moore, R. (1977), 'Becoming a sociologist in Sparkbrook', in C. Bell and H. Newby (eds), *Doing Sociological Research* (London: Allen & Unwin), pp. 87–107.

Moore, R. (1978), 'Sociologists not at work – institutionalised inability: a case of research funding', in G. Littlejohn, B. Smart, J. Wakeford and N. Yuval-Davies (eds), *Power and the State* (London: Croom Helm), pp. 267–302.

Morgan, D. H. J. (1969), 'Theoretical and conceptual problems in the study of social relations at work: an analysis of the differing definitions of women's roles in a northern factory', unpublished Ph.D thesis (Manchester: University of Manchester).

Morgan, D. H. J. (1972), 'The British Association scandal: the effect of publicity on a sociological investigation', *Sociological Review*, vol. 20, no. 2, pp. 185–206; reprinted in R. G. Burgess (1982) (ed.), *Field Research: a Sourcebook and Field Manual* (London: Allen & Unwin), pp. 254–63.

Morgan, D. H. J. (1975), 'Autonomy and negotiation in an industrial setting', *Sociology of Work and Occupations*, vol. 2, pp. 203–26.

Morgan, D. H. J. (1981), 'Men, masculinity and the process of sociological enquiry', in H. Roberts (ed.), *Doing Feminist Research* (London: Routledge & Kegan Paul), pp. 83–113.

Moser, C. (1958), *Survey Methods in Social Investigation* (London: Heinemann).

Moser, C. and Kalton, G. (1971), *Survey Methods in Social Investigation* (2nd edn) (London: Heinemann).

Nadel, S. F. (1951), *The Foundations of Social Anthropology* (London: Cohen & West).

Nader, L. (1969), 'Up the anthropologist – perspectives gained from studying up', in D. Hymes (ed.), *Reinventing Anthropology* (New York: Random House), pp. 284–311.

Naroll, R. and Cohen, R. (1973) (eds), *A Handbook of Method in Cultural Anthropology* (Columbia: Columbia University Press).

Nash, D. (1963), 'The ethnologist as stranger: an essay in the sociology of knowledge', *Southwestern Journal of Anthropology*, vol. 13, pp. 527–33.

Nash, R. (1973), *Classrooms Observed* (London: Routledge & Kegan Paul).

Newby, H. (1977a), *The Deferential Worker* (London: Allen Lane).

Newby, H. (1977b), 'In the field: reflections on the study of Suffolk farmers', in C. Bell and H. Newby (eds), *Doing Sociological Research* (London: Allen & Unwin), pp. 108–29.

Newby, H., Bell, C., Rose, D. and Saunders, P. (1978), *Property, Paternalism and Power: Class and Control in Rural England* (London: Hutchinson).

Newman, O. (1973), *Gambling: Hazard and Reward* (London: Athlone Press).

Nichols, T. and Beynon, H. (1977), *Living with Capitalism* (London: Routledge & Kegan Paul).

Nixon, J. (1981) (ed.), *A Teachers' Guide to Action Research* (London: Grant McIntyre).

Nukunya, G. K. (1969), *Kinship and Marriage among the Anlo Ewe* (London: Athlone Press).

Oakley, A. (1979), *Becoming a Mother* (Oxford: Martin Robertson).

Oakley, A. (1980), *Women Confined: Towards a Sociology of Childbirth* (Oxford: Martin Robertson).

Oakley, A. (1981), 'Interviewing women: a contradiction in terms', in H. Roberts (ed.), *Doing Feminist Research* (London: Routledge & Kegan Paul), pp. 30–61.

Olesen, V. (1979), 'Federal regulations, qualitative social science and institutional review boards: comments on a problematic era', in M. L. Wax and J. Cassell (eds), *Federal Regulations: Ethical Issues and Social Research* (Boulder, Colorado: Westview Press), pp. 103–18.

Olesen, V. and Whittaker, E. (1967), 'Role-making in participant observation: processes the researcher–actor relationship', *Human Organization*, vol. 26, no. 4, pp. 273–81; reprinted in N. K. Denzin (1970) (ed.), *Sociological Methods: A Sourcebook* (London: Butterworths), pp. 381–97.

Olesen, V. and Whittaker, E. (1968), *The Silent Dialogue* (San Francisco: Jossey-Bass).

Oppenheim, A. N. (1969), 'Knowledge for what? the Camelot legacy: the dangers of sponsored research in the social sciences', *British Journal of Sociology*, vol. 20, no. 3, pp. 330–6.

Park, R. E. (1952), 'The city: suggestions for the investigation of human behavior in the urban environment', in R. E. Park, *Human Communities* (New York: The Free Press), pp. 13–51.

Parker, H. (1974), *View from the Boys* (Newton Abbot: David & Charles).

Parker, T. (1962), *The Courage of his Convictions* (London: Hutchinson).

Parker, T. (1963), *The Unknown Citizen* (London: Hutchinson).

Parker, T. (1967), *A Man of Good Abilities* (London: Hutchinson).

Parsons, T. (1951), *The Social System* (London: Routledge & Kegan Paul).

Patrick, J. (1973), *A Glasgow Gang Observed* (London: Eyre–Methuen).

Payne, G., Dingwall, R., Payne, J. and Carter, M. (1981), *Sociology and Social Research* (London: Routledge & Kegan Paul).

Plant, M. (1975), *Drugtakers in an English Town* (London: Tavistock).

Platt, J. (1976), *Realities of Social Research* (London: Chatto & Windus for Sussex University Press).

Platt, J. (1981a), 'Evidence and proof in documentary research: some specific problems of documentary research', *Sociological Review*, vol. 29, no. 1, pp. 31–52.

Platt, J. (1981b), 'Evidence and proof in documentary research: some shared problems of documentary research', *Sociological Review*, vol. 29, no. 1, pp. 53–66.

Platt, J. (1981c), 'On interviewing one's peers', *British Journal of Sociology*, vol. 32, no. 1, pp. 75–91.

Plummer, K. (1983), *Documents of Life: An Introduction to the Problems and Literature of a Humanistic Method* (London: Allen & Unwin).

Pollert, A. (1981), *Girls, Wives, Factory Lives* (London: Macmillan).

Polsky, N. (1969), *Hustlers, Beats and Others* (Harmondsworth: Penguin).

Pons, V. (1961), 'Two small groups in Avenue 21: some aspects of the system of social relations in a remote corner of Stanleyville, Belgium Congo', in A. Southall (ed.), *Social Change in Modern Africa* (London: OUP for the International African Institute), pp. 205–16.

Pons, V. (1969), *Stanleyville: an African Urban Community under Belgian Administration* (London: OUP for the International African Institute).

Porter, M. (1984), 'The modification of method in researching postgraduate education', in R. G. Burgess (ed.), *The Research Process in Educational Settings: Ten Case Studies* (Lewes: Falmer Press), pp. 139–61.

Porter, M. and Scott, S. (1981), 'Women postgraduates and liberal academics: a new dimension to disadvantage', paper presented to Society for Research in Higher Education.

Powdermaker, H. (1966), *Stranger and Friend: The Way of an Anthropologist* (New York: Norton).

Pryce, K. (1979), *Endless Pressure* (Harmondsworth: Penguin).

Purcell, K. (1982), 'Female manual workers, fatalism and the reinforcement of inequalities', in D. Robbins with L. Caldwell, G. Day, K. Jones and H. Rose (eds), *Rethinking Social Inequality* (Aldershot: Gower), pp. 43–64.

Radcliffe-Brown, A. R. (1952), 'Foreword', in M. N. Srinivas, *Religion and Society Among the Coorgs of South India* (Oxford: Clarendon Press).

Rainwater, L. (1970), *Behind Ghetto Walls* (Chicago: Aldine).

Read, K. E. (1965), *The High Valley* (New York: Scribner's).

Read, M. (1980), 'Ethnographic field notes and interview transcripts: some preliminary observations on the computer management of text', *Sociological Research Unit Working Paper No. 8* (Cardiff: University College).

Reiser, S. J., Dyck, A. and Curran, W. (1977), *Ethics in Medicine* (Cambridge, Mass.: MIT Press).

Richardson, E. (1973), *The Teacher, the School and the Task of Management* (London: Heinemann).

Richardson, E. (1975), *Authority and Organization in the Secondary School* (London: Macmillan).

Riley, M. (1963), *Sociological Research, Vol. I: a Case Approach* (New York: Harcourt Brace Jovanovich).

Rist, R. (1981), *Earning and Learning: Youth Employment Policies and Programs* (Beverly Hills, Calif.: Sage).

Roberts, H. (1981) (ed.), *Doing Feminist Research* (London: Routledge & Kegan Paul).

Robinson, W. S. (1951), 'The logical structure of analytic induction', *American Sociological Review*, vol. 16, no. 6, pp. 812–18; reprinted in G. J. McCall and J. L. Simmons (1969) (eds), *Issues in Participant*

Observation: a Text and Reader (Reading, Mass.: Addison-Wesley), pp. 196–204.

Rock, P. (1979), *The Making of Symbolic Interactionism* (London: Macmillan).

Rose, A. (1962) (ed.), *Human Behaviour and Social Processes: an Interactionist Approach* (London: Routledge & Kegan Paul).

Rose, G. (1982), *Deciphering Sociological Research* (London: Macmillan).

Rosenhan, D. L. (1973), 'On being sane in insane places', *Science*, vol. 179, no. 4070, pp. 250–8.

Roth, J. A. (1962), 'Comments on "secret observation" ', *Social Problems*, vol. 9, no. 3, pp. 283–4; reprinted in W. J. Filstead (1970) (ed.), *Qualitative Methodology: Firsthand Involvement with the Social World* (Chicago: Markham), pp. 278–80.

Roth, J. A. (1963), *Timetables* (New York: Bobbs-Merrill).

Roth, J. A. (1966), 'Hired-hand research', *American Sociologist*, vol. 1, no. 4, pp. 190–6.

Roth, J. A. (1974), 'Turning adversity to account', *Urban Life and Culture*, vol. 3, no. 3, pp. 347–59.

Roy, D. (1970), 'The study of Southern Labor Union organizing campaigns', in R. Habenstein (ed.), *Pathways to Data* (Chicago: Aldine), pp. 216–44.

Rubington, E. and Weinberg, M. S. (1968) (eds), *Deviance: the Interactionist Perspective* (New York: Collier-Macmillan).

Samuel, R. (1976), 'Local history and oral history', *History Workshop Journal*, no. 1, pp. 191–208; reprinted in R. G. Burgess (1982) (ed.), *Field Research: a Sourcebook and Field Manual* (London: Allen & Unwin), pp. 136–45.

Schatzman, L. and Strauss, A. L. (1973), *Field Research: Strategies for a Natural Sociology* (Englewood Cliffs, NJ: Prentice-Hall).

Scheper-Hughes, N. (1979), *Saints, Scholars and Schizophrenics: Mental Illness in Rural Ireland* (Berkeley, Calif.: University of California Press).

Scheper-Hughes, N. (1981), 'Cui bonum – For whose good?: A dialogue with Sir Raymond Firth', *Human Organization*, vol. 40, no. 4, pp. 371–2.

Schuman, H. and Converse, J. (1971), 'Effects of black and white interviewers on black responses in 1968', *Public Opinion Quarterly*, vol. 35, no. 1, pp. 44–68.

Schutz, A. (1954), 'Concept and theory formation in the social sciences', *Journal of Philosophy*, vol. 51, no. 9, pp. 257–73.

Schwartz, H. and Jacobs, J. (1979), *Qualitative Sociology: A Method to the Madness* (New York: The Free Press).

Schwartz, M. (1964), 'The mental hospital: the research person in the disturbed ward', in A. J. Vidich, J. Bensman and M. Stein (eds), *Reflections on Community Studies* (New York: Harper & Row), pp. 85–117.

Schwartz, M. S. and Schwartz, C. G. (1955), 'Problems in participant observation', *American Journal of Sociology*, vol. 60, no. 4, pp. 343–53.

Seabrook, J. (1967), *The Unprivileged* (London: Longman).

Seabrook, J. (1971), *City Close Up* (London: Allen Lane).

Seabrook, J. (1973), *Loneliness* (London: Temple Smith).

Selltiz, C., Wrightsman, L. S. and Cook, S. W. (1976), *Research Methods in Social Relations* (3rd edn) (New York: Holt, Rinehart & Winston).

Serbin, L. (1978), 'Teachers, peers and play preferences', in B. Sprung (ed.),

Perspectives on Non-Sexist Early Childhood Education (New York: Teachers College Press).

Shaffir, W. B., Stebbins, R. A. and Turowetz, A. (1980) (eds), *Fieldwork Experience: Qualitative Approaches to Social Research* (New York: St Martin's Press).

Sharp, R. (1981), 'Marxism, the concept of ideology, and its implications for fieldwork', in T. S. Popkewitz and B. R. Tabachnick (eds), *The Study of Schooling: Field Based Methodologies in Educational Research and Evaluation* (New York: Praeger), pp. 112–54.

Sharp, R. and Green, A. (1975), *Education and Social Control: A Study in Progressive Primary Education* (London: Routledge & Kegan Paul).

Shaw, C. (1930), *The Jack Roller: A Delinquent Boy's Own Story* (Chicago: University of Chicago Press).

Shaw, K. E. (1969), 'Why no sociology of schools?', *Education for Teaching*, no. 69, pp. 61–7.

Shipman, M. (1967), 'Environmental influences on response to questionnaires', *British Journal of Educational Psychology*, vol. 37, no. 1, pp. 54–7.

Shipman, M. (1974), *Inside a Curriculum Project* (London: Methuen).

Shipman, M. (1976) (ed.), *The Organization and Impact of Social Research* (London: Routledge & Kegan Paul).

Shipman, M. (1981), *The Limitations of Social Research* (2nd edn) (London: Longman).

Shipman, M. (1984), 'Ethnography and educational policy-making', in R. G. Burgess (ed.), *Field Methods in the Study of Education* (Lewes: Falmer Press).

Sieber, S. D. (1973), 'The integration of fieldwork and survey methods', *American Journal of Sociology*, vol. 78, no. 6, pp. 1335–59; reprinted in R. G. Burgess (1982) (ed.), *Field Research: a Sourcebook and Field Manual* (London: Allen & Unwin), pp. 167–88.

Simmel, G. (1950), 'The stranger', in K. Wolff (ed.), *The Sociology of Georg Simmel* (New York: The Free Press), pp. 402–8.

Simon, A. and Boyer, E. G. (1967) (eds), *Mirrors for Behavior: An Anthology of Classroom Observation Instruments* (Philadelphia: Research for Better Schools).

Simon, A. and Boyer, E. G. (1970) (eds), *Mirrors for Behavior: An Anthology of Classroom Observation Instruments* (Philadelphia: Research for Better Schools).

Simon, B. and Willcocks, J. (1981) (eds), *Research and Practice in the Primary Classroom* (London: Routledge & Kegan Paul).

Simons, H. (1981), 'Conversation piece: the practice of interviewing in case study research', in C. Adelman (ed.), *Uttering, Muttering: Collecting, Using and Reporting Talk for Social and Educational Research* (London: Grant McIntyre), pp. 27–50.

Sjoberg, G. (1967) (ed.), *Ethics, Politics and Social Research* (London: Routledge & Kegan Paul).

Smith, L. and Keith, P. M. (1971), *Anatomy of Educational Innovation: An Organizational Analysis of an Elementary School* (New York: Wiley).

Smith, L. and Pohland, P. A. (1976), 'Grounded theory and educational ethnography: a methodological analysis and critique', in J. I. Roberts and

S. K. Akinsanya (eds), *Educational Patterns and Cultural Configurations* (New York: David McKay), pp. 264–79.

Spencer, G. (1973), 'Methodological issues in the study of bureaucratic elites: a case study of West Point', *Social Problems*, vol. 21, no. 1, pp. 90–103; reprinted in R. G. Burgess (1982) (ed.), *Field Research: a Sourcebook and Field Manual* (London: Allen & Unwin), pp. 23–30.

Spindler, G. (1970) (ed.), *Being an Anthropologist: Fieldwork in Eleven Cultures* (New York: Holt, Rinehart & Winston).

Spindler, G. (1974) (ed.), *Education and Cultural Process: Toward an Anthropology of Education* (New York: Holt, Rinehart & Winston).

Spindler, G. D. and Spindler, L. (1982), 'Roger Harker and Schönhausen: From the Familiar to the Strange and Back Again', in G. D. Spindler (ed.), *Doing the Ethnography of Schooling: Educational Anthropology in Action* (New York: Holt, Rinehart & Winston), pp. 20–46.

Spradley, J. P. (1979), *The Ethnographic Interview* (New York: Holt, Rinehart & Winston).

Spradley, J. P. (1980), *Participant Observation* (New York: Holt, Rinehart & Winston).

Spradley, J. P. and Mann, B. J. (1975), *The Cocktail Waitress* (New York: Wiley).

Srinivas, M. N. (1952), *Religion and Society among the Coorgs of South India* (Oxford: Clarendon Press).

Srinivas, M. N. (1962), *Caste in Modern India and Other Essays* (Bombay: Asia Publishing House).

Srinivas, M. N. (1966), 'Some thoughts on the study of one's own society', in M. N. Srinivas (ed.), *Social Change in Modern India* (Berkeley, Calif.: University of California Press), pp. 147–63.

Stacey, M. (1960), *Tradition and Change: A Study of Banbury* (Oxford: OUP).

Stacey, M. (1969a), *Methods of Social Research* (Oxford: Pergamon).

Stacey, M. (1969b), 'The myth of community studies', *British Journal of Sociology*, vol. 20, no. 2, pp. 134–47.

Stacey, M. (1969c) (ed.), *Comparability in Social Research* (London: Heinemann for the British Sociological Association and the Social Science Research Council).

Stacey, M. (1982), 'The sociology of health, illness and healing', in R. G. Burgess (ed.), *Exploring Society* (London: British Sociological Association), pp. 49–67.

Stacey, M., Batstone, E., Bell, C. and Murcott, A. (1975), *Power, Persistence and Change: A Second Study of Banbury* (London: Routledge & Kegan Paul).

Stacey, M., Dearden, R., Pill, R. and Robinson, D. (1970), *Hospitals, Children and their Families* (London: Routledge & Kegan Paul).

Stebbins, R. A. (1967), 'A theory of the definition of the situation', *Canadian Review of Sociology and Anthropology*, no. 4, pp. 148–64.

Stenhouse, L. (1978), 'Case study and case records: towards a contemporary history of education', *British Educational Research Journal*, vol. 4, no. 2, pp. 21–39.

Stenhouse, L. (1979), 'The problem of standards in illuminative research', *Scottish Educational Review*, vol. 11, no. 1, pp. 5–10.

Stenhouse, L. (1982), 'The conduct, analysis and reporting of case study in educational research and evaluation', in R. McCormick (ed.), *Calling Education to Account* (London: Heinemann), pp. 261–73.

Stenhouse, L. (1984), 'Library access, library use and user education in academic sixth forms: an autobiographical account', in R. G. Burgess (ed.), *The Research Process in Educational Settings: Ten Case Studies* (Lewes: Falmer Press), pp. 211–33.

Stenhouse, L., Verma, G. K., Wild, R. D. and Nixon, J. (1982), *Teaching about Race Relations* (London: Routledge & Kegan Paul).

Stephenson, J. B. and Greer, L. S. (1981), 'Ethnographers in their own cultures: two Appalachian cases', *Human Organization*, vol. 40, no. 2, pp. 123–30.

Stephenson, R. M. (1978), 'The CIA and the professor: a personal account', *American Sociologist*, vol. 13, no. 3, pp. 128–33.

Stimpson, G. and Webb, B. (1975), *Going to See the Doctor: The Consultation Process in General Practice* (London: Routledge & Kegan Paul).

Stocking, G. W. (1971), 'What's in a name? The origins of the Royal Anthropological Institute (1837–71)', *Man*, New Series, vol. 6, pp. 369–90.

Strauss, A. L., Schatzman, L., Bucher, R., Ehrlich, D. and Sabshin, M. (1964), *Psychiatric Ideologies and Institutions* (New York: The Free Press).

Sudnow, D. (1967), *Passing On: The Social Organization of Dying* (Englewood Cliffs, NJ: Prentice-Hall).

Sutherland, E. (1937), *The Professional Thief* (Chicago: University of Chicago Press).

Suttles, G. D. (1968), *The Social Order of the Slum* (Chicago: University of Chicago Press).

Terkel, S. (1967), *Hard Times* (New York: Pantheon).

Terkel, S. (1970), *Division Street* (New York: Pantheon).

Terkel, S. (1977), *Working* (Harmondsworth: Penguin).

Thomas, W. I. and Znaniecki, F. (1918–20), *The Polish Peasant in Europe and America* (Chicago: University of Chicago Press).

Thompson, E. P. (1972), 'Anthropology and the discipline of historical context', *Midland History*, vol. 1, no. 3, pp. 41–55; reprinted in R. G. Burgess (1982) (ed.), *Field Research: a Sourcebook and Field Manual* (London: Allen & Unwin), pp. 152–60.

Thompson, P. (1978), *The Voice of the Past: Oral History* (Oxford: OUP).

Thompson, T. (1981), *Edwardian Childhoods* (London: Routledge & Kegan Paul).

Time (1974), 'Studying the American tribe', *Time (Europe)*, 23 December, p. 48.

Times Literary Supplement (1952), 'Review of M. N. Srinivas (1952), *Religion and Society among the Coorgs of South India*' (Oxford: Clarendon Press) (6 September).

Tomlinson, S. (1982), *The Sociology of Special Education* (London: Routledge & Kegan Paul).

Tremblay, M. A. (1957), 'The key informant technique: a non-ethnographic application', *American Anthropologist*, vol. 59, no. 4, pp. 688–701;

reprinted in R. G. Burgess (1982) (ed.), *Field Research: a Sourcebook and Field Manual* (London: Allen & Unwin), pp. 98–104.

Trow, M. (1957), 'Comment on "participant observation and interviewing: a comparison" ', *Human Organization*, vol. 16, no. 3, pp. 33–5.

Turner, R. H. (1953), 'The quest for universals in sociological research;, *American Sociological Review*, vol. 18, no. 6, pp. 604–11; reprinted in G. J. McCall and J. L. Simmons (1969) (eds), *Issues in Participant Observation: A Text and Reader* (Reading, Mass.: Addison-Wesley), pp. 205–16.

Turner, V. W. (1957), *Schism and Continuity in an African Society: a Study of Ndembu Village Life* (Manchester: University of Manchester Press on behalf of the Institute of African Studies University of Zambia).

Turner, V. W. (1964), 'Symbols in Ndembu ritual', in M. Gluckman (ed.), *Closed Systems and Open Minds: The Limits of Naïvety in Social Anthropology* (Edinburgh: Oliver & Boyd), pp. 20–51.

Turner, V. W. (1971), 'An anthropological approach to the Icelandic saga', in T. O. Beidelman (ed.), *The Translation of Culture: Essays to E. E. Evans-Pritchard* (London: Tavistock), pp. 349–74.

Turner, V. W. (1974), *Dramas, Fields and Metaphors: Symbolic Action in Human Society* (Ithaca, NY: Cornell University Press).

Urry, J. (1972), 'Notes and queries on anthropology and the development of field methods in British anthropology, 1870–1920', *Proceedings of the Royal Anthropological Institute of Great Britain and Ireland, 1972*, pp. 45–57.

Van Gennep, A. (1960), *The Rites of Passage* (Chicago: University of Chicago Press).

Van Maanen, J. (1981), 'The informant game: selected aspects of ethnographic research in police organizations', *Urban Life*, vol. 9, no. 4, pp. 469–94.

Van Velsen, J. (1967), 'The extended-case method and situational analysis', in A. L. Epstein (ed.), *The Craft of Social Anthropology* (London: Tavistock), pp. 129–49.

Vidich, A. J. and Bensman, J. (1958), *Small Town in Mass Society* (Princeton, NJ: Princeton University Press).

Vidich, A. J. and Bensman, J. (1968), *Small Town in Mass Society* (2nd edn) (Princeton, NJ: Princeton University Press).

Vidich, A. J., Bensman, J. and Stein, M. R. (1964) (eds), *Reflections on Community Studies* (New York: Harper & Row).

Vidich, A. J. and Shapiro, G. (1955), 'A comparison of participant observation and survey data', *American Sociological Review*, vol. 20, no. 1, pp. 28–33.

Voss, H. L. (1966), 'Pitfalls in social research: a case study', *American Sociologist*, vol. 1, no. 3, pp. 136–40.

Wakeford, J. (1969), *The Cloistered Elite* (London: Macmillan).

Wakeford, J. (1981), 'From methods to practice: a critical note on the teaching of research practice to undergraduates', *Sociology*, vol. 15, no. 4, pp. 505–12.

Wakeford, J. (1984), 'The director's dilemma' in R. G. Burgess (ed.), *Field Methods in the Study of Education* (Lewes: Falmer Press).

Walker, R. (1980), 'The conduct of educational case studies: ethics, theory and procedure', in W. B. Dockrell and D. Hamilton (eds), *Rethinking Educational Research* (London: Hodder & Stoughton), pp. 30–63.

Walker, R. (1981), *The Observational Work of LEA Inspectors and Advisers* (Norwich: Centre for Applied Research in Education).

Walker, R. (1984), 'Using pictures in a discipline of words', in R. G. Burgess (ed.), *Field Methods in the Study of Education* (Lewes: Falmer Press).

Walker, R. and Adelman, C. (1975), *A Guide to Classroom Observation* (London: Methuen).

Wallis, R. (1976), *The Road to Total Freedom: A Sociological Analysis of Scientology* (London: Heinemann).

Wallis, R. (1977), 'The moral career of a research project', in C. Bell and H. Newby (eds), *Doing Sociological Research* (London: Allen & Unwin), pp. 149–67.

Walter, J. A. (1975), ' "Delinquents" in a treatment situation – the processing of boys in a list D school', unpublished Ph.D. thesis (Aberdeen: University of Aberdeen).

Warner, W. L. (1959), *The Living and the Dead. A Study of the Symbolic Life of Americans* (New Haven, Conn.: Yale University Press).

Warner, W. L. and Low, J. O. (1947), *The Social System of the Modern Factory. The Strike: A Social Analysis* (New Haven, Conn.: Yale University Press).

Warner, W. L. and Lunt, P. S. (1941), *The Social Life of a Modern Community* (New Haven, Conn.: Yale University Press).

Warner, W. L. and Lunt, P. S. (1942), *The Status System of a Modern Community* (New Haven, Conn.: Yale University Press).

Warner, W. L. and Srole, L. (1945), *The Social Systems of American Ethnic Groups* (New Haven, Conn.: Yale University Press).

Warren, C. A. B. (1980), 'Data presentation and the audience: responses, ethics and effects', *Urban Life*, vol. 9, no. 3, pp. 282–308.

Warren, C. A. B. and Rasmussen, P. K. (1977), 'Sex and gender in field research', *Urban Life*, vol. 6, no. 3, pp. 349–69.

Warwick, D. P. (1973), 'Tearoom trade: means and ends in social research', *Hastings Center Studies*, vol. 1, pp. 27–38.

Wax, M. L. and Cassell, J. (1979), 'Fieldwork ethics and politics: the wider context', in *Federal Regulations: Ethical Issues and Social Research* (Boulder, Colorado: Westview Press), pp. 85–102.

Wax, M. L. and Wax, R. (1971), 'Great tradition, little tradition and formal education', in M. L. Wax, S. Diamond and F. O. Gearing (eds), *Anthropological Perspectives on Education* (New York: Basic Books), pp. 3–18.

Wax, R. H. (1971), *Doing Field Work: Warnings and Advice* (Chicago: University of Chicago Press).

Wax, R. H. (1979), 'Gender and age in fieldwork and fieldwork education: no good thing is done by any man alone', *Social Problems*, vol. 26, no. 5, pp. 509–22.

Webb, E. J., Campbell, D. T., Schwartz, R. D. and Sechrest, L. (1966), *Unobtrusive Measures: Nonreactive Research in the Social Sciences* (Chicago: Rand McNally).

Webb, S. and Webb, B. (1932), *Methods of Social Study* (London: Longman, Green).

Werner, O. and Campbell, D. T. (1973), 'Translating, working through interpreters, and the problem of decentreing', in R. Naroll and R. Cohen (eds), *A Handbook of Method in Cultural Anthropology* (New York: Columbia University Press), pp. 398–420.

West, J. (1945), *Plainville, U.S.A.* (New York: Columbia University Press).

West, W. G. (1980), 'Access to adolescent deviants and deviance', in W. B. Shaffir, R. A. Stebbins and A. Turowetz (eds), *Fieldwork Experience: Qualitative Approaches to Social Research* (New York: St Martin's Press), pp. 31–44.

Westie, F. R. (1957), 'Toward closer relations between theory and research: a procedure and an example', *American Sociological Review*, vol. 22, no. 2, pp. 149–54.

Whyte, W. F. (1955), *Street Corner Society* (2nd edn) (Chicago: University of Chicago Press).

Whyte, W. F. (1964), 'The slum: on the evolution of Street Corner Society', in A. J. Vidich, J. Bensman and M. R. Stein (eds), *Reflections on Community Studies* (New York: Harper & Row), pp. 3–69.

Whyte, W. F. (1981), *Street Corner Society* (3rd edn) (Chicago: University of Chicago Press).

Williams, R. (1976), 'Symbolic interactionism: the fusion of theory and research?' in D. C. Thorns (ed.), *New Directions in Sociology* (Newton Abbot: David & Charles), pp. 115–38.

Williams, R. (1981), 'Learning to do field research: intimacy and inquiry in social life', *Sociology*, vol. 15, no. 4, pp. 557–64.

Williams, W. M. (1956), *The Sociology of an English Village: Gosforth* (London: Routledge & Kegan Paul).

Willis, P. (1977), *Learning to Labour* (Farnborough: Saxon House).

Willmott, P. (1969), *Adolescent Boys of East London* (Harmondsworth: Penguin).

Wiseman, J. P. (1979), *Stations of the Lost* (Phoenix edn) (Chicago: University of Chicago Press).

Wolcott, H. (1971), 'Handle with care: necessary precautions in the anthropology of schools', in M. Wax, S. Diamond and F. O. Gearing (eds), *Anthropological Perspectives on Education* (New York: Basic Books), pp. 98–117.

Wolcott, H. (1973), *The Man in the Principal's Office: An Ethnography* (New York: Holt, Rinehart & Winston).

Wolcott, H. (1975), 'Criteria for an ethnographic approach to research in schools', *Human Organization*, vol. 34, no. 2, pp. 111–27.

Wolcott, H. F. (1982), 'Mirrors, models and monitors: educator adaptations of the ethnographic innovation', in G. Spindler (ed.), *Doing the Ethnography of Schooling: Educational Anthropology in Action* (New York: Holt, Rinehart & Winston), pp. 68–95.

Wolff, K. (1960), 'The collection and organization of field materials: a research report', in R. N. Adams and J. J. Preiss (eds), *Human Organization Research: Field Relations and Techniques* (Homewood, Ill.: Dorsey Press), pp. 240–54.

Woods, P. (1977), *The Ethnography of the School*, Units 7–8 of Open University course E202: Schooling and Society (Milton Keynes: Open University Press).

Woods, P. (1979), *The Divided School* (London: Routledge & Kegan Paul).

Woods, P. (1984), 'Teacher self and curriculum' in I. F. Goodson and S. J. Ball (eds), *Defining the Curriculum* (Lewes: Falmer Press).

Xiaotong, F. (1980), 'Towards a people's anthropology', *Human Organization*, vol. 39, no. 2, pp. 115–20.

Young, J. (1971), *The Drugtakers: the Social Meaning of Drug Use* (London: Paladin).

Zelditch, M. (1962), 'Some methodological problems of field studies', *American Journal of Sociology*, vol. 67, no. 5, pp. 566–76; reprinted in R. G. Burgess (1982) (ed.), *Field Research: a Sourcebook and Field Manual* (London: Allen & Unwin), pp. 168–75.

Zimmerman, D. H. and Wieder, D. L. (1977), 'The diary: diary-interview method', *Urban Life*, vol. 5, no. 4, pp. 479–98.

Znaniecki, F. (1934), *The Method of Sociology* (New York: Farrar & Rinehart).

Zweig, F. (1948), *Labour, Life and Poverty* (London: Gollancz).

Name Index

Subject Index